TO DAME
SALLY COATES

Marco Camisani Calzolari

Cyberhumanism

This book is temporarily translated from Italian to English by AI.

For internal use, not for sale.

Index

Preface by Paolo Benanti		9
Information society or control society?		9
Chapter 1 - Cyber Humans		27
1.1.	A new vision of man in the connected world	27
1.2	Humanism and technology	30
1.3	The digicratic society	35
1.4	Cyberhumanism	39
Chapter 2 - The augmented man		51
2.1	The pillars underlying complexity	51
2.2	The increased man	55
2.3	Artificial intelligence	60
2.4	LLM and LMM	66
2.5	The singularity	75
2.6	Intelligent robots	84
Chapter 3 - Opportunities		95
3.1	In industry	95
3.2	In public administration	97
3.3	In health care	101
3.4	In finance	110
3.5	In agriculture	112
3.6	In transportation	114
3.7	In scientific research	115
3.8	In education	118
3.9	In energy	124

3.10	In communication and marketing	126
3.12	In film and television	128
3.12	In the environment	132
3.13	In sports	135
3.14	In cybersecurity	138
3.15	In SMEs	146
3.16	In the liberal professions	155
3.17	In society	158

Chapter 4 - The critical issues — 161

4.1	Long-distance nationalism and territorial sovereignty	161
4.2	The black boxes of AI	170
4.3	Democracies at risk	185
4.4	Cyber ethics	196
4.5	Digital wars	204
4.6	Connected brains	214
4.7	Cybersecurity and cybersafety	217
4.8	Working for the machines	224
4.9	Copyright	233
4.10	Privacy	243

Chapter 5 - What to do — 247

5.1	Holistic approach	247
5.2	Ethics by design	247
5.3	Longtermism	260
5.4	Digital awareness and culture	264
5.5	Digital education	269
5.6	Regulation	277
5.7	Public-private collaborations	295
5.8	Privacy by design	299
5.9	Watermarking	305
5.10	Speed	309

THANKSGIVING	311
GLOSSARY	313
Abbreviations	313
Definitions	315
BIBLIOGRAPHY	319
SITOGRAPHY	323
NAME INDEX	327

*I dedicate this book
to those who allowed me to get this far
with all the energy I needed:
my family. Carol, Leonardo and Mario.*

Preface by Paolo Benanti

Information society or control society?

It is not easy to retrace the newness of the digital world and the challenges it poses to consciousness and freedom, that is, to society and politics. The transformation whose pervasiveness and transformative power we all per- cept today, especially after the pandemic, has not yet fully unveiled.

The evolution of the computer has profoundly influenced all communication technologies, at the same time embracing their full potential. At first, the computer seemed to be an instrument reserved for large organizations and administrations, scientific research and military commands. Microproces- sor technology since the 1970s, the constant development of easy-to-use software, and, in the 1990s, the rapid expansion of the network have instead transformed it into a machine accessible to everyone, like any other household appliance. To understand this change bi- sogically we dwell on the main feature of this new form of communication: digital.

Precisely because it processes in digital form the language of all other *media*, the computer has become the *medium* par excellence of the 21st century. In particular, it is a writing tool for everyone: journalists, writers, scientists, engineers, poets, and artists. Of writing, it has largely modified the traditional techniques, as it has done for editing, fo- citing, and printing itself.

In the early 20th century the human community was wired by the tele- graph and then the telephone. Today, global connections take place via computers: the exchange of money and goods on the stock exchange, the air and rail traffic control, etc. take place via infor- mation. The same way enables millions of people to exchange mes- essages without limits of time and space.

The revolution in science-technology produced by com- puters and information technology has been ably described by Naief Yehya:

with a computer we can turn almost any human problem into statistics, graphs, equations. The really disturbing thing, however, is that in doing so we create the illusion that these problems are computer-solvable[1].

Chris Anderson, the editor of *Wired*, outlines a summary of what the *digital revolution* means for the scientific world:

"scientists have always relied on hypotheses and expressions. [...] Faced with the availability of huge amounts of data this hypothesis, theoretical model and test approach becomes obsolete. [...] There is now a better way. *Petabytes* allow us to say, "correlation is suffi- cient." We can stop looking for theoretical models. We can ana- lyze the data without any assumptions about what the data might show. We can send the numbers into the largest set of computer [*clusters*] the world has ever seen and let statistical algorithms find [statistical] patterns where science cannot. [...] Learning to use a computer of this scale can be challenging. But the opportunity is great: the new availability of a huge amount of data, combined with the statistical tools to process it, offers a completely new way to understand the world. Correlation supplants causation, and the sciences can even advance without coe- rential theoretical models, unified theories, or some kind of mechanistic explanation."[2]

---

1 N. YEHYA, *Homo cyborg. The posthuman body between reality and science fiction*, Eleuthera, Milan, 2005, p. 15.
2 C. Anderson, *The End of Theory*, in Wired, 16 (2008), pp. 106-107, the original is in English, the translation is ours. Petabytes are a measure of the capacity of

Preface

The advent of digital research, where everything is transformed into numerical data, leads to the ability to study the world according to new gnoseological para- dimes: what matters is only the correlation between two quantities of data and no longer a coherent theory explaining that correlation. Practically today we are witnessing technological developments (ability/capacity to do) that do not correspond to any scientific developments (ability to know and explain): today correlation is used to pre-tell with sufficient accuracy, despite having no scientific theory to support it, the risk of impact of even unknown asteroids in various places on Earth, the institutional sites subject to terrorist attacks, the vote of individual citizens in the U.S. presidential election, the stock market's performance in the short term.

The use of computers and information technology in technological development has highlighted a linguistic challenge that av- comes at the boundary between man and machine: in the process of mutual interrogation between man and machine, projections and exchanges arise, hitherto unimagined, and the machine humanizes itself no less than man becomes machinized.[3]

The effect of the exponential digitization of communication and society is leading, according to Marc [Prensky4], to a true anthropological pro- pry transformation: the advent of the digital native. Digital *native* (in English *digital native*) is an expression that is applied to a person who has grown up with digital technologies such as compu- ter, the Internet, cell phones and MP3s. The expression It is used to refer to a new and unprecedented group of learners who are accessing the

---

computer memory. One petabyte is equivalent to 250, or 1,125,899,906,842,624 bytes: one byte represents the unit of measure for the com- pute of mass storage. We will return to this argo- ments in depth in the course of the next few chapters.
3 Cf. P. Benanti, *The Cyborg. Body and corporeality in the age of the posthuman*, Citta- della, Assisi, 2012.

Cyberhumanism
4 Cf. M. Prensky, *Digital Natives, Digital Immigrants*, in "On the Horizon" 9(5), 2001, pp. 1-6, http://s24ore.it/mcc28.

Preface

education system. Digital natives were born parallel to the mass diffusion of GUI computers in 1985 and window operating systems in 1996,. The digital native grows up in a multiscreen society, and considers technologies as a natural element without feeling any discomfort in manipulating and interacting with them.

In contrast, Prensky coins the expression "*digital immigrant*" to refer to a person who grew up before digital techno- logies and adopted them later. One of the differentiat- ions between these individuals is the different mental approach they have toward new technologies: for example, a digital native will talk about his or her new camera (without defining its techno- gical type), while a digital immigrant will talk about his or her new digital camera, as opposed to the chemical film camera used previously. A *digital native*, for Pren- sky, is as if shaped by the *media diet to* which he or she is subjected: in five years, for example, he or she spends 10,000 hours with video games, exchanges at- least 200,000 e-mails, spends 10,000 hours on his or her cell phone, spends 20,000 hours in front of the television watching at least 500,000 commercials while devoting, however, only 5,000 hours to reading. This media diet produces, according to Prensky, a new language, a new way of organizing thought that will alter the brain structure of digital natives.

Multitasking, hypertextuality and interactivity are, for Prensky, only al-
ct features of what appears to be a new and unprecedented sta- dio of human evolution. Moreover, Prensky argues that, albeit erratically and at our own personal speed, we are all moving toward a digital enhancement that includes cognitive activities5. Se- cording to Prensky, digital tools already extend and enrich the

---

[5] Cf. M. PRENSKY, *H. Sapiens Digital: From Digital Immigrants and Digital Natives to Digital Wisdom*, in "Innovate" 5(3), http://s24ore.it/mcc27.

our cognitive abilities in many ways. Digital technology improves memory, for example through tools for acquiring, ar- chiving, and returning data. Digital data collection and decision-support tools improve the ability to make choices by con- senting us to collect more data and verify all the implications de- rivant to that question. Digital enhancement in the cogni- tive domain, made possible by laptops, online databases, virtual tridimen- sional simulations, online collaborative tools, handhelds, and a host of other context-specific tools, is now a reality in many professions, including non-technical fields such as jurisprudence and the humanities,6 according to Prensky.

We live in a society and time characterized by the digital, the Digital Age, a complex period because of the profound changes these technologies are producing. The Covid-19 pandemic accelerated a series of processes that had been radically changing society for some time because it became possible to decouple content, knowledge, from its medium7. The change o f epoch that we are

---

[6] Prensky prefers to speak of *digital empower*ment rather than *technological empowerment* for three reasons (cf. M. PRENSKY, *H. Sapiens Digital*, op. cit.). First, because almost all technology today is either digital or supported by digital tools. Second, digital technology differs from the al- three in that it is programmable, that is, capable of being induced to do, at increasingly precise levels, just what is desired (this ability to personalize is at the heart of the digital revolution). Third, digi- tale technology invests more and more energy in smaller and smaller versions of microproces- sors, which form the core of much of the technology capable of po- tenting cognition. This miniaturization, together with the ever-reducing costs, is the element that will make digital technology available to everyone, albeit at different rates in different places. The discourse is too vast and complex to be further discussed in these pages; for further discussion we refer to P. BENANTI, *Digital Age. Changing Epoch Theory. Per- sona, family and society*, San Paolo, Cinisello Balsamo, 2020.

[7] Think of phenomena such as so-called *fake news*, the appearance of *sharp power*, the events on Capitol Hill or Brexit in the public sphere or how digital is shaping the expectations and ways of romantic relationships with previously unseen platforms and mo- dalities just to name a few examples.

going through is produced by digital technology and its impact on the way we understand ourselves and the reality around us.

To understand this challenge we must go back to the beginning of this transfor- mation. In a grainy documentary filmed at *Bell Laboratories* in 1952, mathematician and *Bell Labs* researcher Claude Shannon stands next to a machine he built. Built in 1950, it was one of the world's earliest examples of machine learning: a robotic maze-solving mouse known as *Theseus*. The Theseus of ancient Greek mythology navigated a minotaur's labyrinth and escaped by following a thread he used to mark his path. But Shannon's electromechanical toy was able to "recor- give" the path with the help of telephone relay switches.

In 1948, Shannon had introduced the concept of information theory in *A Mathematical Theory of Communication*, a paper that provides mathematical proof that all communication can es- ceive digitally. Claude Shannon showed that mes- sages could be treated purely as a matter of inge- gnery. Shannon's mathematical, non-semantic theory of communication abstracts from the meaning of a message and the presence of a human sender or receiver; a message, from this point of view, is a series of transmissible phenomena to which a certain ^{metric} can be applied.[8]

These insights of his gave rise to a new, trans-disciplinary vision of reality: the cybernetics of Norbert Wiener. For Wiener, information theory is a powerful way of conceiving of nature itself. While the universe is gaining entropy in accordance with the second law of thermodynamics that is, its energy distribution is becoming less differentiated and more uniform there are

---

[8] Cf. R. POLT, *A Heideggerian Critique of Cyberbeing* in "Horizons of Authenticity in Phenomenology, Existentialism, and Moral Psychology," edited by H. PEDERSEN and M. ALTMAN, Springer, Dordrecht, 2015, p. 181.

counter-entropic local systems. These systems are the vi- venti organisms and information processing machines that we build. Such systems differentiate and organize themselves: they generate information[9]. The privilege of this approach is what allows cybernetics to exercise confident control in the interdisciplinary domain it generates and deals with: "cybernetics can already be sure of its 'thing,' that is, of computing everything in the terms of a con- trolled process. "[10]

Beginning in the decade before World War II, and ac- celerating during the war and after, scientists designed increasingly sophisticated mechanical and electrical si- stems that allowed their machines to act as if they had a purpose. This work intersected other work on cognition in animals and early work on computer science. What emerged was a new way of looking at systems, not only mechanical and electrical, but also biological and social systems: a unifying theory of systems and their relationship to their am- environment. This move toward "whole systems" and "systems thinking" became known as cybernetics. Cybernetics frames the world in terms of systems and their goals.

According to cybernetics, systems achieve goals through iterative processes or "feedback" loops. Suddenly, leading postwar scientists were talking seriously about cir- cular causality (A causes B, B causes C, and, finally, C causes A). Looking more closely, scientists saw the difficulty of separating the observer from the si- stem. In fact, the system seemed to be a construction of the os- servator. The role of the observer is to provide a description of the system, which is given to another observer. The description requires a language. And the process of observing, creating lin- guage and sharing descriptions creates a society. From the end

---

[9] Cf. *Ibid.*
[10] M. HEIDEGGER, A. FABRIS, *Philosophy and cybernetics*, ETS, Pisa, 1988, pp. 34-35.

Preface

of the 1940s the more advanced research world began to look at the subjectivity of language, con- versation, and ethics and its relation to systems and on design. Various disciplines were cooperating to study "collaboration" as a category of control.

Until then, physicists had described the world in terms of matter and energy. The cybernetic community proposed a new vi- sion of the world through the lens of information, communication channels and their organization. In this way, cybernetics was born at the dawn of the information age, in pre-digital communications and media, bridging the way humans in- teract with machines, systems and each other. Cybernetics focuses on the use of feedback to correct errors and achieve goals: cybernetics makes machine and human a kind of Shannon's mouse.

It is at this level that we need to look more closely at the effects this can have on human understanding and understanding of each other and on freedom. As discussions have matured, the goals of cybernetic com- munity have expanded. In 1968, Margaret Mead was con- templing the application of cybernetics to social problems: "As the world stage widens, there is the continuing possibility of using cybernetics as a form of communication in a world of increasing scientific specialization we should consider very
seriously the current situation in American society, within which we hope to develop these very sophisticated ways of managing systems that are, in fact, in desperate need of attention. Problems of metropolitan areas, The interrelationships between di-
verses levels of government, income redistribution, linkages necessary between parts of large industrial complexes. "[11].

---

[11] The translation is mine and is taken from: M. MEAD, *Cybernetics of Cybernetics*, in.

Cyberhumanism

The cybernetic approach as, Martin Heidegger will point out in rereading Wiener and the work of the cyberneticians, "reduces" human activity itself, in the plurality of its configurations, to something functioning and controllable by the machine: "man himself becomes 'something planned, that is, controllable,' *and*, provided that such a reduction is not possible he is bracketed as a 'disturbing factor' in the cybernetic calculus. "[12] Indeed, Fabris notes that:

In his analysis of the cybernetic phenomenon, Heidegger constantly keeps in mind the Greek matrix of the word and privileges this aspect, rather than for example the central notion of *feedback*, as the central thread for understanding and explaining the characteristics of such a "non-discipline discipline." In the Heideggerian reading, ci- bernetics indicates the advent of a process of control and information within the different subject spheres of the various sciences. Co-mandation and control (the *Steuerung*) are understood first and foremost, from a hermeneutical point of view, as that perspective within which man's relations with the world are regulated.[13]

In the hearts of cyberneticists, that is, those scholars who are the fathers of the computer society, artificial intelligences and all these impres- sioning developments that the digital is bringing about in our living, however,

---

Purposive Systems: Proceedings of the First Annual Symposium of the American Society for Cybernetics, ed. in H. VON FOERSTER *ET AL.*, Spartan Books, New York, 1968, pp. 4-5.

[12] M. HEIDEGGER, A. FABRIS, *Philosophy and Cybernetics*, op. cit., p. 10.

[13] *Ibid.* 11. Fabris notes that "cybernetics is seen by Heidegger as the most advanced mo- ment, the most obvious outcome of that domain of technique into which the whole of Western metaphysics flows. Indeed, the history of being as it emerges from the university courses on Nietzsche in the 1930s has its ar- rive point in the event of technique, in which the will to power (will to will) that determines human action and extends to every realm of

reality finds its full manifestation. Within such a process of self-reference

Cyberhumanism
of will, the cybernetic project receives its justification and defines its relations with philosophy, taking over some of its tasks and assuming its traditional prerogatives" (*Ibid.*).

Preface

there may have been the promise of an even greater purpose. Gregory Bateson, first husband of Margaret Mead, in a famous interview stated that what excited him about discussions on cibernetics was that: "It was a solution to the problem of purpose. From Ari- stotele on, the final cause has always been mystery. This came up then. We didn't realize then (at least I didn't, although McCulloch may have) that the whole lo- gic would have to be reconstructed for recursiveness. "[14]

If the information society can in fact by means of digital feedback actions put man in a condition of control by the machine (whether electronic or algorithmic) and if the ci- bernetic relationship in its most radical form of realization of man-machine symbiosis can in fact negate the necessity of assuming fi- nal causes in action, there appears on the horizon here a dystopian horizon in which the information society inevitably collapses into a society of control. The analysis of digital society allows us to reflect on the legame between causes, necessity, and freedom that the digital realizes in its form of political actualization: it calls into question the very possibility that there is a destiny of man that depends on his free will.

This form of cybernetic digitization, which I would define here as "strong" in order to emphasize how this is a possible form of society if forms of digital sustainability are not put in place, risks eliding the very possibility of *positive freedom*. By this term is meant, going back to Bobbio's reflections, in political language "the situation in which a subject has the possibility of directing his or her own

---

[14] The translation is mine and is taken from: S. BRAND, *For God's Sake, Margaret a con- versation with Margaret Mead and Gregory Bateson*, in *CoEvolutionary Quarterly*, June 10-21, 1976, pp. 32-44. The theory of causes that Aristotle introduced in *Physics* II 3-7, in *Metaphysics* A 2, in *Metaphysics* A 3-10 and in *Posterior Analytics* II 111, has aroused various discussions since its inception. The importance of the Aristotelian theory of causes is mainly due to the fact that, from Aristotle onward, we can speak of knowledge when we can account for the prin- ciples and causes that played a role in the occurrence of a

Cyberhumanism
certain event.

will toward a purpose, to make decisions, without being determinated by the will of others. This form of freedom is also called ''self-determination' or, even more appropriately, ''autonomy'. [...] Of positive liberty the classical definition was given by Rousseau, for whom liberty in the civil state consists in the fact that there man, as a part of the social whole, as a member of the "common 'mind, does not obey others than himself, that is, he is autonomous in the precise sense of the word, in the sense that he gives laws to himself and does not ub- bidize to other laws than those he has given himself: '"Obedience to the law we have prescribed for ourselves is freedom'" (*Contrat social*, I, 8). This con- cept of liberty was taken up, through direct influence of Rousseau, by Kant, [...] in the *Metaphysics of Customs*, where legal liberty is defined as '"the faculty of not obeying any law other than that to which the citizens have given their consent'" (II, 46). [...] Civil liberties, the pro- totype of negative liberties, are individual liberties, that is, inherent in the individual individual: historically, in fact, they are the product of struggles to defend the individual considered either as a moral person, and thus having value in itself, or as a subject of economic relations, against the encroachment of collective entities such as the Church and the State [...]. Freedom as self-determination, on the other hand, is generally referred to, in political theory, as a collective will, whether this will be that of the people or the community or the nation or the ethnic group or the homeland. "[15]

To this world, with these potentials and challenges, the text of which follows is addressed. Brilliantly, Marco Camisani Calzolari in *Cybe- rumanism* gradually makes the analysis of technologies, in a mode that the Author calls "neutral," integrate with an awareness of how these systematic changes have ended up changing the way we relate to others (the *polis*) and to ourselves. We could

---

[15] N. BOBBIO, "Freedom," in *Encyclopedia of the Twentieth Century*, Treccani. Available at http://s24ore.it/mcc63

say in other words that Garasic wisely and acutely interprets his own form of digital humanism because he succeeds in conveying to the reader with extreme depth the fact that since information technology has di- come an industry it has begun to produce culture-consumer and mass culture-and this culture has produced and is producing a reconfigu- ration of the essential anthropological aspects of human habitation.

What ethical guidelines can guide us in realizing forms of technological innovation-especially for artificial intelligences-that respect people and their rights? The history of ethics helps us in this quest.

The first guideline is what we might call *fear of uncertainty*. Any choice we make we know will have consequences. We can all choose freely but what happens once we choose is not always up to us. Every free and conscious choice carries with it a horizon of uncertainty. One of the key ethical paradigms is the management of uncertainty. This is the first ethical driver: being co-scientific that the choices put in place may also produce unintended effects and managing this risk.

A second very important guideline to consider is the tension between *equality and pursuit of happiness*. All the bloodiest wars we have known between the 1800s and 1900s were fought to achieve equality for all men. In fact, the use of such technologies risks producing new inequalities. Ethics for AIs must protect all this. It is human dignity that is the ethical value not the data value. In addition, a state has its legitimacy if it allows the individual to realize the pro-prata pursuit of happiness. These new technologies with their possibilities of profiling, with their possibilities of predicting the behavior of human beings can actually take very difficult the situation of a free individual existence. One must not only look at the good and evil that can arise for the individual (*fear of uncertainty*) but society as a whole: one must protect the equality of the

Preface

individuals and the possibility for each person to be able to seek his or her own happiness.

The potential of automations induced by the information society calls for setting up a new universal language that can translate these ethical guidelines into machine-executable directives. But how to do this? The world in the Digital Age is regulated by algorithms. We need to begin to develop this common lin- guage of algorethics.

In order to develop an algoretic we must clarify in what sense we are talking about value. In fact, algorithms work on values of a numerica nature. Ethics, on the other hand, talks about moral value. We need to establish a lin- guage that can translate moral value into something compu- turable for the machine. The perception of ethical value is a purely human capacity. The ability to work numerical values, on the other hand, is the ability of the machine. Algoretics arises if we are able to transform moral value into something computable.

But in the human-machine relationship, the true knower and carrier of value is the human part. Human dignity and human rights tell us that it is the human to be protected in the human-machine relationship. This evidence provides us with the fundamental ethical imperative for the sapiens machine: doubt yourself. We must enable the machine to have some sense of uncertainty. Whenever the machine does not know whether it is protecting human value with certainty, it must demand human action. This basic directive is achieved by introducing statistical paradigms within AI.

From this basic grammar we can develop a new universal language: algoretic. This will have its own syntax and develop its own literature. This is neither the place nor the time to say everything expressible with this language, however, we feel we should at least give a few examples that reveal its potential.

Starting from this appeal, in an original and new way, the author

Cyberhumanism

proposes the urgency of developing an ethical strategy, meaning by this neologism, as much a governance of the algorithmic processes that underlie politics today as, to fall under the aforementioned challenge of humanization and machinization between man and machine - of political lin- guage: "the choice to express oneself in 280 characters, to think of ha- shtags instead of electoral and political programs, to generate visibility through a spectacularization (actually pre-dating the digi- tale era) of the motto, the phrase, the invective useful to appear and quick to go into oblivion."

Since Camisani Calzolari's choice of the ethical perimeter is intended to bring to the reader's attention an increasingly unwieldy presence of a non-human variable in social life-a variable that is not only programmable and programmed, but possibly also capable of learning from itself-the work before us unquestionably marks the horizon of social coexistence.

The following text has, in my opinion, a great merit: it helps us to experience the radical nature of the question that some of our contemporaries ask to the specificity of man and his dignity in contemporary political living. Only by having the courage to retrace these questions in search of the specific human could we discover, paraphrasing Paul Ri- coeur, that the value of the human appears at the intersection of our infinite desire to be with the finite conditions of its realization.

Knowing that what is at stake is the ability to recognize and ground human dignity in a public space of civil coexistence. The idea of human dignity and its translation into human rights, which are recognized as pre-existing to any state entity and any social order, constitute and present themselves as a threshold level: human dignity is the level beyond which the convi- vence of humans can no longer regress even in an age that some would like to be *post-human* because it is that hard experiential core, political-ethical in nature, which u n d e r l i e s , founds and legitimizes

Preface

morally democratic societies and serves as discrimination re- spect to totalitarian forms of state. The history of the twentieth century with its stark and bloody pages shows how the various totalitarianisms - national socialism, fascism, Stalinist communism, etc. - have in fact expressed their bloody face by eliminating precisely such an idea from the foundations of human coexistence.

In leaving it to the reader to be guided by the pages of the Au- tore into the folds of the complexity of our present, it seems to us that the best wish that can be made is the one Rilke made to a young poet contemporary with him:

Be patient toward all this
That is unresolved in your heart and ...
try to love questions, which are similar to locked
rooms and written books
In a foreign language.
Do not look now for the answers that can be given
to you since you would not be able to live with
them.
And the point is to live everything. Live the
questions now. Maybe it will be given to you,
without you realizing it,
To live until the distant day
when you have the answer.

Rainer Maria Rilke, *Letter to a Young Poet.*

Cyberhumanism

Preface

CYBERHUMANISM

Chapter 1 - Cyber Humans

1.1. A new vision of man in the connected world

We live in a time when change is happening at an ever-accelerating pace, with digital technologies radically transforming the way we interact, work and even think. Technology is redefining our world in ways we never imagined. It is no longer just a matter of having a smartphone in our pocket or a computer on the table; it has infiltrated every aspect of our daily lives, becoming an integral part of how we work, communicate and entertain ourselves.

Among all these innovations, artificial intelligence is changing and revolutionizing everything with exponential speed, transforming our ability to process information and make decisions. All the while, as we harness these innovations to improve our lives, it is essential to consider the related ethical and social implications as well. Who is responsible when an algorithm makes a misplaced decision? How much should we rely on artificial intelligence for important decisions? How can we ensure that it is used ethically and sustainably?

More importantly, who are the individuals behind the algorithms, who is driving them, and how? What does it mean to be human in an increasingly digitally dominated world? What is needed is a new Humanism that con- sidues the "augmented" human being: the human being who integrates pseudo-intelligent technologies, exploring the new relationship between humans and everything connected, to redefine our vision of humanity and our values, and above all to prevent machines from doing it for us.

Cyber humans

As we know, Humanism was a historical period in which man claimed his dominant role in the universe, co- constituting a constant point of reference in philosophical reflection, with reason and awareness at the center of existence. Leo- nardo Da Vinci was one of the greatest representatives of this mo- vation, valuing man's potential and his ability to create and innovate.

The problems that existed in the Renaissance were obviously di- versed from those of today, but man always remains the architect of his own destiny and history. However, the development of increasingly connected and "thinking" digital technologies has changed the relationship between man and machine in a complex and evolutionary way.

Artificial intelligence, automation, and the increasing amount of digital data are leading us toward a kind of "digital slavery," in which humans seem to become increasingly dependent on the technologies they create. It is paradoxical that as humanity moves closer and closer to the realization of science fiction, we need to pause and reflect on our role in this process in which humans coexist with the digi- tale, in a context that is often mistaken for the future, but which is already part of the present, since the technologies are already here and available, even if not yet widely deployed.

We should aspire to a relationship similar to the one we have with electricity: although we depend on it to light homes, operate electronic devices, and power transportation, we do not see it as a problem because it has been domesticated, regulated, and controlled. Although it is an indispensable part of mo- derna society, electricity does not make decisions for us and is simply a tool we use to simplify and improve daily life.

Instead, we ask artificial intelligence to make deci- .sions in o u r place, delegating more and more of our micro-

everyday choices. Instead of letting technology overwhelm us, we should claim our dominant role and maintain con- trol over it, using it to our advantage. It is not a matter of disowning technology or turning back the clock, but of using our humanity to guide its development in an ethical and so- stenable way, especially now that artificial intelligence is about to be adopted everywhere.

But what is AI?
In the most common definition, AI is "software developed with one or more of the techniques and approaches of machine learning, which can, for a given set of human-defined goals, generate outputs such as content, predictions, recommendations, or decisions that in- fluence the environments with which they interact." In general, by AI systems, we mean software or machines programmed to perform tasks that usually require human intelligence. By using large amounts of data, it is possible to "train" AIs to formulate pre- visions, provide recommendations or make decisions, without human inter- vention.

It is an extraordinary yet frightening concept, that of machines capable of thinking, learning, and making decisions for us, that is becoming a reality accessible to all. From autonomous driving to managing financial data to writing newspaper articles, artificial in- telligence is taking over and governing the way we interact with the world.

Now, the change becomes profoundly cultural as we are becoming increasingly dependent on AI even to make important decisions, even though these are often "black boxes" containing ingredients decided by third parties, mostly private companies and outside the jurisdiction of the country in which we live.

This issue is perhaps even exhilarating f o r humanity, and we need to

Consider it central. Fast action is needed. New laws, agreements between countries, control actions are needed, but above all, a renewed humanistic approach that integrates ethics right from the design stage must be adopted.

Technology does not have ethics, but it is intertwined with society, and a society without ethics cannot and should not exist. Inventions cannot be "uninvented," but it is we humans who must actively defi- nition the "meaning" of the digital, not the other way around. We must be the ones to decide how to use technologies to improve our lives and the lives of others, instead of being victims of their advent. But above all, we must do so without losing sight of the values of humanity. We must never forget that both in front, as users, and behind, as designers, for every algorithm, every digital sistem and every artificial intelligence, there are human beings with their own ideas, prejudices, and responsibilities.

There is therefore a need for a new humanistic approach, the Cyber- uma- nism, precisely, that is, one that interconnects man and machine.

1.2 Humanism and technology

Before proceeding with the rest of the book, I think it is necessary to briefly retrace the humanistic sense of thinkers of the past, especially in its relation to technologies, so that it can be mu- tered today in light of the changes brought about by the digitally connected. Humanism was a current of thought that focused on the importance of the individual and humanity, but it is less known to have had a rich and complex history in relation to technologies. The industrial revolutions led to a strong human- stic debate about the role of technology in society. While some saw machines as an instrument of liberation, others feared them as a threat to human autonomy and dignity.

Cyber humans

In the past, the definition of technology did not include bits, the unit for measuring the information content of a message, because they semplically did not exist. Machines represented a social change that had to be addressed, but they were physical objects that we could see and touch. Today, our perception of technology has evolved to include not only tangible objects, but also the digital, the imperceptible, the virtual. New digital tools are not physically manipulable, but they can be digitally managed in ways that are barely visible and verifiable. Unlike most aggregations of atoms, bits can never be seen. Yet they have a major impact on society and our daily lives. And it is this evolution of technology that concerns us most and requires a different analytical approach.

In the 1980s, cyber culture referred primarily to the union between humans and the machine or computer, but it was not understood as conflict or domination, but rather as a way to increase potential. The computer was seen as an important extension of the human being, a tool to expand his or her abilities. This was an optimistic view of technology, in which the digital was merely a tool to serve humans, a means to overcome physical and mental limitations.

Then came the digital revolution, which almost made people forget the concept of cyber. The term was pushed aside and everything became "digital" or even often improperly called "virtual." Anything can be digital without it being interconnected. A microchip connected to a display showing temperature is a digital og- getto, but it does not need to be connected to the Net to be digital. The rush toward digital has begun to make us forget the essence of the con- cept of cybernetic and interconnected man. Today everything is interconnected; nothing works without the infrastructure of the Net. From telephony to electricity, from gas stations to refineries, ships and pipelines,

OIL WELLS. Without the Net, everything would shut down. We live in a technological cul- ture, where technology is an integral part of our lives, permeating them and shaping the reality that makes humanity interact. But the word "humanity" has a double face: on the one hand, it refers to the human species; on the other, it tells us how we should live ethically civilized lives. In everyday life, description and regulation merge together when referring to the human being. This becomes even more evident when it comes to the interaction between indivi- duals through technology and the Internet.

Humanism is based on concepts such as individual rights and fundamental dignity, foregrounding evidence and reason. Now that interconnected di- gital and technology are changing nature and per- sons our humanity, perhaps the time has come to re-evaluate the foundations of humanism in its relationship with the digital. Instead, technology, though often rejected, is a valuable ally for humanists, as it enables us to transcend human boundaries and bestows a wide range of extraordinary capabilities. Very often we do not realize the fact that, compared to a person who lived a hundred years ago, we have at our disposal tools that might seem completely extraordinary and beyond their capacity to understand.

Imagine a comparison between a modern individual, who has ac- cessed Google, and one living a hundred years ago, who does not. While the former would be able to answer any do- manda correctly, the latter would regard him or her as almost a divine being endowed with superhuman abilities. What would happen if we were able to see a being like us a hundred years from now? Would he still be as powerful? More importantly, would he continue to dominate technology or become a slave to it, seeming so inferior to the humans of this century? Humans have a strange tendency to base future predictions on the present or even the past. We are convinced that what has worked so far may continue to do so in the future, perhaps with some slight modifications. But the reality is very different: because of rapid and constant technological advances, it is extremely unlikely that the future will simply be a continuation of the present. The future will certainly be very different from what we imagine. Everything we had considered as assumed and reasoned about has been radically transformed. What cannot be digitized or automated could gain extraordinary value. Basic human qualities, such as emotions, compassion, ethics, fe- licity, and creativity, will become increasingly valuable.

Over the next 20 years, humanity is likely to go through an unprecedented transformation from the previous 300 years. Therefore, completely new rules and foundations will be needed. The theme is by no means new. In May 2019, the Initiative for a Digital Humanism was created in Vienna, with the intention of pro- moting technologies that respect human values and needs, in- lieu of allowing technologies themselves to influence human beings. At the core of these reflections are the fundamental principles of human values such as ethics, democracy, and sovereignty, which cost- ure the indispensable basis for the practice. To achieve this goal, a manifesto has been published, signed by more than a thousand international leaders, thinkers and experts, among whom, in its signatories are myself.

These are the basic principles of the manifesto[16]:

1. Digital technologies should be designed to promote democracy and inclusion.

2. Privacy and freedom of speech are essential values for demo- cracy and should be the focus of our activities.

3. Effective regulations, rules and laws based on broad public discourse need to be established.

---

[16] http://s24ore.it/mcc08

4. Regulators must intervene with technology monopolies.
5. Decisions with consequences that could affect individual or collective human rights must continue to be made by human beings.
6. Scientific approaches that cross different disciplines are a prerequisite for meeting future challenges.
7. Universities are where new knowledge is produced and critical thinking is cultivated.
8. Academic and industrial researchers need to openly engage with society as a whole and reflect on their approaches.
9. Professionals around the world should recognize their shared responsibility for the impact of information technology.
10. A vision is needed for new educational programs that combine knowledge from the humanities, social sciences and engineering studies.
11. Education about information technology and its social impact must begin as soon as possible.

In 2019, artificial intelligence was not yet as accessible to everyone as it is today. Moreover, the effects of it were not adequately taken into account, often leaving decisions in the hands of third-party, predominantly private systems. This situation led to a much greater impact than in previous years, generating significant change in society.

Our future is at a crucial moment: we have to decide which path to take and how to put the human being at the center, trying to balance technological innovation with the social aspect in an always democratic process. In this context, a digital humanism ini- tiative is being developed to analyze and influence the complex interaction between technology and humankind, with the goal of improving society and life while fully respecting universal human rights. We must shape technologies according to human values and needs. Our goal is not only to mitigate the negative aspects, but more importantly to promote human-centered innovation.

1.3 The digicratic society

With the advent of the Internet, society has undergone a radi- cial change. Today, we live in a world in which we are constantly digitally connected, information travels at the speed of light, and geographic di- chambers have been reduced. Instant communication, access to real-time information, and the ability to interact with people and communities around the world have redefined our social, professional, and even personal lives.

The history of the evolution of the digital world is vast and complex. From the first static sites to dynamic and interactive ones, to seeing the emergence of e- commerce, online games and web-based social networks. Platforms such as Facebook, Twitter, LinkedIn, and Instagram have changed the way people interact and share information, radically tra- sforming the concept of community and bringing people closer together than ever before.

However, the advent of these technologies has also led to new problems, including data privacy breaches, the spread of fake news, and the enormous power of large technology companies. Inol- three, users are developing an addiction to endless scrolling and increased social isolation.

Large digital platforms often have more power than states and their respective governments. Politicians, in order to gain consensus and get elected, often have to submit to the rules dictated by these platforms. The latter decide what to disseminate and what not to disseminate, while many politicians avoid opposing them for fear of compromising their election fu- tures.

Despite this seemingly daunting picture, digital offers direct and obvious benefits in many areas. Technologies such as intelligent transportation si- stems and autonomous vehicles improve urban mobi- lity, increasing safety and efficiency. Online learning platforms make education more accessible and personable. Virtual and augmented reality offer enormous potential for vocational training and entertainment.

But in the midst of all this, there is always humanity. We are objects of measurement, sale, and purchase, but we are also human beings who are "digitally gio- vated" and not fully aware of our values and the risks involved in this digital age.

One thing is certain: everything that can be digitized, automatized, virtualized, and robotized will probably be. However, we should reflect on what perhaps we should not digitize or au- tomatize: our emotions and feelings, such as love, joy, sadness, and fear. These are unique human experiences that machines cannot naturally replicate.

We humans possess a creativity and la- teral thinking capacity that machines cannot even adequately simulate. We can create art, music and literature that express our emotions and reflect our inner world. Even when it seems that art is created by machines, we must remember that their training is based on what has been produced by human beings.

In addition, we humans have a conscious mind that allows us to re-flex our thoughts and actions, consciously taking responsibility and making ethical decisions.

In this context, it is essential to think carefully about the impact of technology on our lives and seek a balance between its

Cyber humans

benefits and dangers of living in an increasingly digitized world. Machines will probably never learn to read and com- take our social, moral considerations and ethical problems. And if they did, they would probably emulate us or little more, even in simulating ethics.

But who will decide what to simulate and why? It is important to remember that these technologies, although they have become an integral part of the daily lives of millions of people, are owned by private companies that operate primarily for profit. Their economic interests may not coincide with the common good, which instead should es- prove to be protected by civil society.

We are entering a new world, where bots, software agents that perform automated tasks based on data, algorithms, and various forms of artificial intelligence, are becoming more and more pre- feel and efficient in managing our lives.

Our future reality might look like this: if something doesn't work, it will be the fault of artificial intelligence. Is the machine not according? It was the AI that decided that. The kitchen doesn't work? The AI is at fault. The front door won't open? AI again. Our smartphone crashed? AI is responsible for it. Everything will work on the basis of algorithms, but written by whom? Decided by whom? Perhaps by the same machines that programmed them.

A society based on the decisions of algorithms is considered unacceptable by many. Who wants to submit to decisions made by machines, perhaps without the possibility of appeal or, even worse, with the possibility of appeal but receiving a standard response such as "your com- pliance was contrary to our policies," without det- mined explanations? This is what happens when we get blocked on social media and try in vain to appeal.

We fought for democracy, not algocracy. However, while states continue to guarantee democracy, they do so principally in relation to "traditional" needs. But today we have new needs.

Imagine a future in which we would have the account on which we con- serve all our family photos blocked, perhaps without the possibility of appeal. Could we turn to our country's democratic justice system? Perhaps not, because a private company in another state made the rules. Photos gone, with no possibility of appeal. Is this democratic behavior?

What if the problem is not photos, but access to our di- gitalized home? Or even the ability to communicate with our loved ones? This is not a distant dystopian future. We are already experiencing similar situations when private apps or sites act arbitrarily on our accounts.

A democratic state, on the other hand, should represent and protect citizens by performing a number of basic functions. It ensures law and order, protecting the rights and freedoms of citizens through the fair and impartial enforcement of laws. It engages in the protection of human rights, including the right to privacy and nondiscrimination, and promotes economic and social welfare through welfare policies and economic growth initiatives.

In an era dominated by digitization and artifi- cial intelligence, it is crucial for the democratic state to take action to ensure that these technologies are used with respect for the rights and welfare of citizens.

Democracy, while not perfect, is currently the best guarantee for the protection of individual freedoms. Althoughitmay seem slow and messy, democracy

fosters the exchange of ideas and ensures the right of every citizen to be represented. In an age when technology is assuming an increasingly predominant role, democracy can serve as a ba- luard, ensuring ethical and responsible use of technology.

However, democratic processes, while critical for maintaining order and protecting individual freedoms, are often slow. This slowness can generate tensions and challenges in an era when technological pro- gress is advancing rapidly. Larry Diamond,[17] an expert in sociology and political science, points out that the gradualness of democratic processes is not a weakness but a valuable asset. This graduality fosters public debate and involves all stakeholders, enabling thoughtful evaluation of decisions.

We may find ourselves in a future controlled by supercomputers, Internet bots, and highly intelligent software. The people who pospose these technologies will be in control, and private companies pomay surpass even states in power. In a society where per- sons do not have access to corporate-provided artificial intelligence or advanced devices, they could be regarded as pets or, even worse, enslaved, forced to accept a range of unauthorized services.

The result could be a callous, emotionless and completely dehumanized society.

1.4 Cyberhumanism

At a time when humans are increasingly enslaved by their own techno- logy, we need to regain control of it and use it to work on a humanistically sustainable future. We need a new philosophy to guide us in our choices, to face with confidence the potential of digi- tale and to provide a solid foundation for humanity to guide its development.

Just as humanism guided us during the Renaissance, Cy- berumanism may be the key to overcoming the ethical and so- cial challenges that the advent of the digital is bringing to our society. Cy- b e r u m a n i s m , while very similar, along with other philosophies

---

[17] L. Diamond, *The Spirit of Democracy*, Henry Holt and Co., New York, 2008.

contemporary, aims to combine traditional humanistic culture with new digital technologies. However, today we face a speci- ficity of the digital that has equally specific characteristics: the digital connected to the Net and humans. First among them is the connected artificial intelligence.

The concept of digital humanism was coined by German philosophers Julian Nida-Rümelin and Nathalie Weidenfeld in 2010 and taken up in their book *Digital Humanism*[18]. Nida-Rümelin and Weidenfeld argued that digital technology was profoundly changing the way we live and work, and that it was necessary to develop a new humanistic approach to technology, one that placed humans and their values at the center.

But it is no longer enough just "conscious use in which humans are at the center." Now the big issues have moved higher, to flat-interconnected forms, between physical and algorithms processed online, at a distance. A distance that is more of a barrier, sometimes impenetrable, of which we are not given to know what is behind it, what is connected to whom, whose data underlie the choices that are made by AI, what are the algorithms behind them and who manages them.

The use of the old computer, perhaps disconnected from the Net, could have been the subject of important reflections on its digital nature, in combination with the man who used it. But the definition of digital is broad, perhaps too broad. A watch, unconnected and with a display, is di- gital. The robot that cuts the grass is digital, a desktop calculator is digital. But digital begins to become a potential problem when it is connected to the Net and when it interfaces directly with humans. And the integration of human and "connected machine" is historically represented by the prefix cyber.

---

[18] J. Nida-Rümelin, N. Weidenfeld, *Digital Humanism: For a Humane Transfor- mation of Democracy, Economy and Culture in the Digital Age*, Springer, Berlin, 2022.

Cyber humans

This is why the humanism we need is closely le- gated to the cyber world, which is basically a verticality of the more generic "digital." The etymology of cyber, from the English noun cybernetics, re- rises from the ancient Greek κυβερνήτης which literally means "rudder" and by extension "one who governs." The first to use the word cybernetic in the purely technical sphere was the English mathematician Ja- mes Watt, who in the late 18th century used it to describe the operation of a device that could control the speed of the steam engine. The term "cyber" came into our contem- porary usage thanks to the U.S. mathematician Norbert Wiener, who in his book *Cybernetics* first discussed the topic of information-driven governance.[19] In 1984, William Gibson coined the word "cy- berspace" in the science fiction novel *Neuromancer*.[20]

The use of the prefix "cyber" increased in parallel with the growth of the Internet. By the late 1990s, almost everything related to In- ternet was cyber: cyber community, cyber law, cyber sex, cy- ber crime, cyber culture... It was enough to put "cyber" in front of anything on the Internet. In the early 2000s, the use of cyber gradually disappeared, perhaps in part because many digital realities were born that were not necessarily connected to the Internet.

That is why I felt that "cyber" was the best particle to de- scribe this complex and intricate relationship between humanity and digital tech- nology, and which gives this book its title: Cyberhumanism.

Despite its decay in the 2000s, the concept of "cy- ber" captures the essence of human-machine interaction, while its origin highlights the importance of control and management. In the context of Cyberhumanism, therefore, cyber is not just a prefix, but a symbol of our aspiration to dominate digi- tale technology, and not to be dominated by it.

---

[19] N. Wiener, *Cybernetics,* MIT Press, Cambridge, MA, 1961.
[20] W. Gibson, *Neuromancer*, Ace Books, New York, 1984.

Cyberhumanism

Cyberhumanism is a call to reaffirm our leadership role in the digital age, to ensure that technology is a tool in our hands, and not us in its hands. With many things in common to the main goals of the digital humanists, which are to ensure that no one is excluded from the benefits of digital technologies. They were and are committed to promoting digital literacy, re- during the digital divide, and ensuring that everyone has equal and inclusive access to digital resources. They also focused on raising awareness about digital rights and cybersecurity.

The main problems at the center of humanistic thinking in the digital were related to how people interacted with each other and the outside world, or how the indiscriminate use of digital technologies could lead to a range of social and cultural problems, including iso- lution and device addiction.

Most digital humanists were reflecting on very im- portant aspects of our society, which are still at the core, but no longer sufficient, at least in form. I have always been a follower of the humanist philosophy related to the digital. I have always worked to help humans understand the digital in order not to be victims of it. I have at- traversed almost all digital philosophies and shared many of them, from the cyberpunk period to posthumanism to reflections on transhumanism.

Transhumanists see it differently: they seek to use ra- gion, science, and technology with the goal of mitigating problems such as poverty, disease, disability, malnutrition, and oppressive forms of government in the world. Even at the cost of integrating man and machine into one. The main goal is to make the concrete reality of the human condition reflect the principles of equity, legal and political justice, and self-improvement by overcoming innate physical and mental limitations. In line with this aspiration, many

Cyber humans

Transhumanists view favorably the future potential of advanced technologies and innovative social systems to improve the quality of life. But transhumanism scares me, I see it as being blind and in love with technology, without adequately weighing the exponential changes we are undergoing. In a way, it extends the idea of humanist self-determination and self-design beyond all limits. Let us remember that digital transformation will not automatically make our living conditions more humane. It will depend on how we use and develop technology.

But I felt it was missing something. That extra step that identified the precise thinking behind what I believe is necessary today: cyberhumanism.

Instead, I advocate an instrumental attitude toward human connection. The one that is related to artificial intelligence choices. The one that asks what can really bring economic, social, and cultural benefits? Where do the potential dangers lie? Above all, will strong artificial intelligence arrive, through which AI could superate human intelligence? And precisely because of the scale and change that is taking place, I think it is not enough to add these new concepts to philosophies on digital humanism. I think the term digital itself is therefore reductive and does not take into account the network and the new concentrations taking place, or even the often physical integration between humans and "thinking" technologies. That is, the cyber world. That is why the evolution of digital humanism I believe is Cyberu-manism. Humanity is now on the brink of an era in which robots, androids, and other manifestations of artificial intelligence seem poised to unleash an unstoppable revolution capable of engaging every stratum of society. It is essential that legislation consider the legal and ethical implications and consequences of this unprecedented phenomenon. The concept of Cyberhumanism aims to find an equilibrio between technological progress and respect for human beings. This involves adapting our laws and values to the evolution of artificial intelligence, without ever losing sight of the wellbeing and autonomy of the individual. Meeting these challenges re- quires courage and a cutting-edge vision, for only in this way can we ensure a future in which humans remain at the center of the digital world.

Over the past two centuries, the steady increase in employment rates has largely benefited from technological developments. Robotics and artificial intelligence have revolutionary potential to transform our lives and work, improving efficiency, savings and safety, and the quality of services in the short and medium term. These technological advances will not only bring benefits in manufacturing and business, but also in areas such as transportation, health care, education, and agriculture. Through the implementation of robotics and artificial intelligence in such areas, it is possible to avoid subjecting humans to dangerous conditions, while respecting the basic principles of Cyberhumanism. The meeting point lies in the concept of human-technology partnership or even its cyber integration. Everything is digital, so being digital is no longer a distinguishing characteristic, but a ge- nerical concept that encompasses every aspect of modern life. To say "digital" therefore no longer means anything. If everything is digital, so automatically is the life of man, who is as succubus to it as he is to nature: it is everywhere and dominates him.

The man-machine union must ensure that man is always at the center And be in control of it. Let him be the cyber master of the whole, hence of the digital, and not become a slave to it. This is where the broader concept of Cyberhumanism comes in: a holistic approach that integrates human, digital, machine and artificial intelligence. Man cannot just passively observe changes, but must act actively to influence and create the digital. He is the one who must lead decisions by machines and artificial intelligence. This inte- gration should not lead to the limitation of human freedom, but rather to its expansion through the responsible and con- siderable use of information technologies.

Cyberhumanism is not the only philosophical current defending the role of humans in the face of technology. There are numerous schools of thought that stress the importance of keeping humanity at the cen- ter of technological progress, despite the ongoing digital evolution. These philosophies reiterate that human beings must retain their dignity and control over technological tools even in the digital age. The philosophical meaning of "humanism" adapts accordingly.

In keeping with the cyberhumanist principle, it is essential to understand that the term "digital" essentially refers to the numbers 1 and 0, which form the foundation of the Internet. However, the conceptual scope of the term goes beyond mere connection to the Internet. In fact, our period is characterized not only by the spread of digital stru- ments, but especially by the pervasive connection to the Internet and the ever-closer integration between man and machine. Consequently, the concept of "digital," anchored in the binarity of the numbers 1 and 0, is not sufficient to account for the complexity of this reality.

Cyberhumanism, on the other hand, reflects the inseparable link between humans and technology, emphasizing the crucial importance of the dominance of huma- nity over the digital sphere. This philosophy emphasizes the essentiality of a network that connects rather than separates and of technology that serves rather than dominates. Its goal is not to hinder technological progress, but to foster human development by harnessing the full potential offered by the digital to enrich, optimize, and make our existence sustainable.

Cyberhumanism does not aim to create a new form of human life, as proposed by transhumanists, and retains a dose of skepticism about utopian visions. However, he remains confident in the human capacity to shape the opportunities offered by digital.

Thus, the way forward is not to oppose artificial in- telligence but to harmonize with it. Cyberuma- nism suggests embracing the possibilities offered by digital innovation, using them to enhance our existing capabilities rather than allowing technology to dominate us. The connected digital should- be a tool, an ally, that humans use to achieve their goals, not a master to be feared. This equili- brio, where artificial intelligence serves humans and not the con- trary, represents the true meeting point between technological progress and respect for humanity.

Cyberhumanism leads us toward a future in which humans, while immersed in an increasingly digital world, retain control and dignity. However, it is crucial to understand and consider the inherent characteristics of the technology we choose to use. Every digital tool, every piece of software, every form of ar- ticial intelligence has peculiarities and limitations that can affect the way it is used and the consequences of its use. Therefore, we cannot afford to be superficial or naive in approaching technology: we must know it, understand it, study it. Only then can we adequately anticipate and manage the potential effects it may have on our society and way of life, and ensure that the digital actually serves the good of humanity, not the other way around.

Cyberhumanism is not only a philosophy but also a practice, an ongoing and conscious commitment to techno- logical knowledge and control. It promotes the defense of informational self-determination, but warns us about the danger of compromising our ability to distinguish truth from falsehood and authentic from distorted cultural sources.

Cyber humans

In addition, Cyberhumanism opposes strong AI or general AI, or artificial intelligence systems capable of autonomous human-like understanding, ap- pearance, adaptation, and reasoning. Although proponents of possibilism believe that such si- stems will be able to cope with any intellectual challenge that a human individual would be capable of solving, the question remains whether humans will be able to "tame" such AIs, whether weak or strong. Per- sonally, I believe that this will only be possible by keeping man at the center.

As a cyberhumanist, I would like to be able to harness artificial intelligence to improve our lives in fantastic, efficient and sustainable ways without taking risks. However, I cannot accept the idea of humans turning into machines, as hypothesized by transhumanists.

On artificial intelligence, Noam Chomsky states, "The human mind is not, like ChatGPT and its ilk, a statistical, greedy machine of hundreds of terabytes of data to get the most plau- sible answer to a conversation or the most probable answer to a scienti- fic question." In contrast, "the human mind is a surprisingly efficient and elegant system that operates with a limited amount of informa- tion. It does not try to extract correlations from data, but strives to create explanations [...]."

So, let's stop calling it "artificial intelligence" and define it for what it is and does: a "plagiarism software," since it "creates nothing, but copies existing works, by existing artists, modifying them ab- lutely enough to escape copyright laws. This is the greatest theft of intellectual property ever recorded since Euro- pean settlers arrived on Native American lands. "[21]

Chomsky, an eminent philosopher and linguist, offers a clear and relevant analysis of the advent and effects of artificial intelligence. At- tually, advances in machine learning generate both

---

[21] N. Chomsky, *New York Times*, March 8, 2023.

Cyberhumanism

optimism than concern. Certainly, we have gained a greater ability to solve problems, but there is also concern that such developments may undermine science and undermine ethics, in- corporating a distorted conception of language and cono- science.

Machine learning programs such as ChatGPT are elo- giated for their human-like language analysis and generation capabilities. However, Chomsky notes with irony and critical spirit the enormous attention given to something so limited when compared with the extraordinary human mind. The latter, through the use of language, can make infinite use of its finite resources, generating ideas of universal scope.

Considering the fundamental differences between the human mind and machine learning pro- grammes, while the latter are ef- fective in analyzing patterns and generating statistically pro- bable predictions, they lack the human ability to create explanations, understand causal laws, and distinguish the possible from the impossible. The human mind operates efficiently and elegantly, intuitively developing a sophisticated grammar and operating with little information, while machine learning programs remain trapped in a pre-human stage of cognitive evolution.

Chomsky also points out the shallowness and dubious validity of predictions generated by artificial intelligence, as they lack the ability to provide thorough explanations based on causal principles and physical laws. Moreover, while the human mind relies on complex explanations and can think creatively and morally, artificial intelligence programs fail to generate creative results without incurring morally questionable content.

In conclusion, despite advances in artificial intelligence, machine learning programs remain inherently flawed in representing true human intelligence, as

Cyber humans

lack the fundamental ability to produce explanations and to discern between the possible and the impossible.

Will humans be able to balance creativity with ethical principles in machines so that they are able to generate in- novative results without incurring moral risks?

Chapter 2 - The augmented man

2.1 The pillars underlying complexity

To fully understand the complexity in which today's world is articulating, it is essential to start with the correct use of definitions. Olthree to this, a thorough understanding of how the Net, domains, the Web, cryptography and other concepts underlying digital is vital.

The intricate nature of the relationship between humans and technology requires a holistic approach. It is essential to familiarize oneself with some of the key concepts that form its fundamental structure. Exploring those new issues, which have not yet been fully understood by most people, requires an interdisciplinary approach.

We need to understand the meaning of terms related to digital and cyber. Using them unknowingly makes everything even more difficult to understand and measure.

For example, most people who use the term "metaverse" do not know its meaning. I often hear people answer, "In my opinion it is...," as if it has no precise meaning. As if everyone can define it at will. When it goes well, they consider it a direct synonym for virtual reality.

While the term has a precise meaning. U.S. writer Neal Stephenson, who coined the term "metaverse" in the cyberpunk romance *Snow* crash[22], has repeatedly given a clear definition of it, which in fact does not correspond to any of the au- toproclaimed "metaverse" platforms, for a number of objective reasons. However

---

[22] N. Stephenson, *Snow Crash*, Spectra, 1992.

you keep using this term in discussions about the future of technology, fueling confusion.

Web3 is also a term often misused. It was "scip- pated" by crypto enthusiasts to Tim Berners-Lee, the British computer scientist and inventor of the World Wide Web, who had defined Web 3.0 as the semantic Web.

Then, recently, the "gurus" of decentralized technologies began to misuse it, both in the form Web 3.0 and then as Web3, but without giving it, this time, a clear and condi- visa definition.

Metaverse and Web3 are terms that, intentionally or unintentionally, create confusion. And this is not good for either the "substance" or the understanding of digital and its characteristics.

Another term whose meaning has been bent into various forms is in- artificial intelligence (AI). Today we use it somewhat for everything that is content generation by a computer, even when it is simple automation or when it is a subset of AI. Kind of like we also call its tires "automobile" without making any distinction.

At least in this case there is substance behind it, and its components are part of the whole.

Most of today's publicly accessible systems, referred to as "artificial intelligence" for simplicity's sake, are actually LLMs or LMMs, Large Language Models or Large Multimodal Models[23]. Which then, rather than "artificial intelligence," should be called "artificial communication."

I consciously do this myself in this book, because being too technical or specific is sometimes wrong. In theory every time

---

[23] A large language model (LLM) is a deep learning algorithm capable of performing a variety of natural language processing (NLP) tasks.

one would have to specify which subcategory one is referring to exactly, but I think the excellent is the enemy of the good.

However, knowing the terms of digital, what they mean, is founda- mental to fully grasp the totality of what is happening, and to have a broader, more detailed, and above all, knowledgeable perspective. Understanding the mechanisms behind the technologies, how they really work, how they are designed, the opportunities and limitations, is founda- mental in order not to get caught up in false enthusiasm or conversely in- justified fears.

Basically, you cannot predict the future of technology unless you know, well, the present.

Another source of complexity that makes it difficult to perceive what is happening in the world is that we live virtually all the time connected, but then where we are physically often has nothing to do with the places and people we hang out when we are online.

What once represented the state to us, that is, the cen- tral government with its institutions and norms, is now replaced by a set of digital platforms that belong to organizations physically di- stantial from us. And it is on these platforms that we exercise our freedom, through access to and active participation in new forms of digital communication, information and interaction.

This change has profoundly transformed our con- ception of the state, opening up new opportunities and challenges in the digital age.

If we get a social media account shut down, we feel censored more than a traditional illiberal state could. This is because account blocking implies not only the restriction of our freedom of expression, but also the loss of a digital voice in the public arena. It also deprives us of the ability to connect with other people, share ideas and be part of meaningful debates. The impact of account closure can be profound and make us

Cyberhumanism

feel limited in our ability to actively participate in the digital society.

Another major area taking on new forms is that of ethical issues, which has become increasingly important in light of the advent of AIs, as they can be used in a wide range of areas such as business, medicine, and finance. And being mac- chines that have autonomous decision-making capabilities, their algorithms must be designed with a strong sense of ethics to ensure that they do not violate the law or challenge moral principles.

This includes implementing ethical principles such as rationality, accountability, and transparency in algorithm design. Moreover, when artificial intelligences are used to make decisions that can significantly affect individuals and orga- nizations, it is imperative to ensure the accuracy and fairness of such choices. We will explore this topic in more detail in the chapter on complexities.

Another aspect that is difficult to understand is the correct perception of the concept of privacy, which also has its extensions in the security, protection and safeguarding of personal data and information.

This is an important principle that recognizes every individual's right to privacy, respect for dignity, and self-determination of his or her own information, but it is often undervalued.

Privacy is often overlooked because its importance is not perceived by many who are unaware of the threats posed by the lack of it.

A common misconception is that we have no bi- dream of privacy because "I have nothing to hide." However, the data generated by each of us, particularly online, is increasingly becoming a means of personal expression, whether or not we want to share specific information about ourselves. In this ever-changing digital environment, the choices that we make about the data we disclose reflect our desire for authenticity and to highlight our unique passions and in- terests.

Privacy is about us as people, our ideas and our actions. From this perspective, it makes no difference if we are so open that we do not have to hide anything. Privacy is the cornerstone of many other rights and is an area in which we protect ourselves by pre-serving our dignity, our freedom of expression and the right to secrecy of our personal information. This allows us to have control over how our data is used and what we share with others, ensuring our well-being and safety online.

Those who regularly post photos of their vacations in real time, without caring too much about privacy, perhaps then discover upon returning home that they have been robbed. Just as recruitment agencies tend to check candidates' social profiles for more detailed and in-depth information, including all of our private, even intimate, lives that are shared online.

Only by thoroughly understanding these issues can we also understand the complexities involved and lay the groundwork for developing new solutions in time that recognize and protect each person, especially in view of the coming tsunami of AI and robots integrating with humans by "augmenting" them.

These issues will be adequately explored in the following chapters as pillars of Cyberhumanism.

2.2 The increased man

After *Homo erectus* and *Homo sapiens,* it is now the era of the new Homo cy- ber (connected man), or Augmented Man. After all, we are already

Cyberhumanism

somewhat all cyborgs, that is, the result of hybridization between man and machine.

Without wanting to look too far, we already live connected to digital and technological prostheses that constantly cooperate with our bodies, such as hearing aids or glasses that are increasingly active. Today they even help the visually impaired recognize objects, thanks to micro-cameras connected to smartphones that send what the subject sees to an AI that recognizes the content and returns it in the form of an audio explanation played by the glasses themselves. Pen- we are to prosthetic legs, which are increasingly technological and able to make those who only a few years ago had no alternative but a wheelchair walk.

Everything, however, obviously takes on very different characteristics when it comes to microchips implanted in the body. Some, so far unintelli- gent, allow you to open the gate, unlock your cell phone or effec- tive payments. But what will happen when, instead of being simply sensors or transmitters, prostheses begin to take autonomous de- cisions? Will cybercriminals be able to terminate a life by hacking a remote heart?

At present it seems unthinkable that people would choose to delegate to artificial intelligence or insecure systems, decisions as important as the actions of their bodies. However, when this leads to greater convenience, there is a risk that it will become a common choice.

We envision a future in which prosthetics not only respond to stimuli, but learn from our movements and react au- temptingly and intelligently. They could analyze biometric data, surroundings, and personal preferences to make decisions that improve our daily lives. For example, a prosthesis could automatically adjust the pressure on muscles to reduce fatigue or adapt to our activities in real time.

The increased man

This new generation of autonomous prostheses could provide greater strength, speed and readiness.

Many might find the idea of enhancing the pro- prior with similar cyber technologies appealing. But it is critical to strike a balance between the potential benefits and appropriate regulation to ensure safety and security for those involved.

Think also of brain-connected interfaces. Today there are numerous existing and commercially available ones that directly connect the brain to the Net. InteraXon's EEG headset helps people meditate more effectively. Myontec, Athos, Delsys, and Noraxon provide athletes and sports specialists with information based on EMG (electromygraphy) and muscle activities during training and competition. Control Bionics' NeuroNode sells an EMG wearable device that enables patients with degenerative neurological disorders such as ALS/MND to control a computer, tablet or motor device via bioelectrical signals sent to muscles to trigger movements.

Kernel offers Flow, a device resembling a bicycle helmet that measures changes in blood oxygenation in the brain to understand and improve brain function.

Apple is integrating health sensors such as EEG into its Air- pods, like those already in the Apple Watch. NextSense, from Alpha- bet, is creating a "mass-market brain monitor." Snap has acquired NextMind, which makes an EEG-based brainwave controller and wants to integrate it into their augmented reality platform.

Microsoft has obtained a patent for an EEG device that con- sents users to navigate web browsers and applications with their brains and will reward people with cryptocurrencies for doing so. Meta is working on neural interfaces.

Augmented humans with brain interfaces are no longer the future, but the present--for better and for worse. For better and for worse.

Obviously, artificial intelligence can bring obvious benefits in areas such as health care, improving the diagnosis and monitoring of diseases. Machine learning can also be a powerful tool in the service of education, tailoring teaching to the needs and abilities of each student.

Virtual and augmented reality, in addition to revolutionizing the in- detention sector, is finding important applications in the educational and professional fields, enabling, for example, the simulation of dangerous or complex situations in a safe environment.

Aging has also changed and will change a great deal. Longer life expectancy, a goal achieved through pro- gress in improved living conditions, technology and modern medicine, is one of the most important challenges-along with political, social and economic ones-for European societies in the 21st century. Artificial intelligence can improve human longevity. There are tools to help prevent diseases, constan- tually monitor the health of individuals, and provide perso- nalized medicinal interventions. In addition, digital technologies such as telemedicine and wearable dispo- sitables can improve access to health care, especially for the elderly or those living in re- mote areas. In conclusion, through the conscious and controlled adoption of these digital innovations, according to the principles of Cyberhumanism, we may not only live longer, but ensure that those years are lived with a better quality of life.

The adoption of automated technologies, such as artifi- cially and advanced robotics, it can also reduce the boredom and fatigue asso- ciated with manual labor. Releasing one's creative potential allows individuals to engage in more challenging and exciting tasks that provide an opportunity for personal growth. These com- plications include solving complex problems, innovative design, and developing new solutions that can bring a significant impact in society. The ability to express one's creativity in these areas is crucial to discovering new perspectives and stimulating innovation in various fields. When we unleash our creativity, we are able to think unconventionally and find unique solutions to problems. This divergent thinking process contributes to advancement and progress both individually and collectively, generating a positive impact on society and opening doors to amazing opportunities.

But it is necessary to always remember that man comes and must come before his cyber-interfaces.

We must always ask ourselves at least these questions: if the company that produced it goes out of business, will it continue to work? Where does my data go? How secure is the device? If someone were to hack it, how much damage could it do to my body and mind?

The main goal of augmented man's interfaces should only be to make his life better in a sustainable way while minimizing risks.

On the other h a n d , the efficiency and connectivity that artificial intelligence and digital offer are powerful tools for improving the lives of all of us. We should not see them as opposing forces, but rather find a balance. The goal is to ensure that digital, or so-called Cyberhumanism as we prefer to call it, serves us and does not underput us. Digital should be a tool not an end in itself and should aim to improve people's lives while respecting the autonomy and diversity of local communities.

There is an example in this regard that should give us pause for thought: Consider that recently in Porto Alegre, Brazil, a bill was approved totally written by ChatGPT to prevent citizens from paying for the replacement of stolen water meters. The city councilor who proposed the draft to his colleagues omitted the fact that it had been worked out by the AI, and this was approved at one-nimity. Probably if he had said that, it would not have even been considered. His goal was not only to solve a pro- blem but also to raise a debate about the useful and informed use of new technologies.

It may not be the optimal decision to entrust ChatGPT or any other artificial intelligence technology with the drafting of a text intended to become a bill. Currently, in-fact, the main problem plaguing these systems relates to co-called "hallucinations," which are distortions of reality or facts that emerge in the output results and are the result of the quality of the data used during the learning phase and the work of the algorithms.

So what is the correct path? What does it do best for man from the perspective of the principles of Cyberhumanism?

2.3 Artificial intelligence

Artificial intelligence is growing exponentially and can be a problem if not managed properly. For example, if machines were able to overtake humans in decision-making and strategic planning, economic and social chaos could ensue. Goals or values that go against human inte- resis could also develop, with unintended or even catastrophic consequences. It is a major driving force in the digital world.

While currently a tool in the service of humanity, AI must remain under human control to avoid the possibility of a power shift. Governance, which emphasizes the impor- tance of maintaining human control over digital technology, is the po- ter to guide and manage the evolution of digital technology responsibly. Applying ethics on its effects on humans and society is a key tool for ensuring that technological progress re- spects basic human values.

If we consider that technology affects what we do and our condition as human beings, we can say that every technological inno- vation is not only technical by definition, but more amporately socio-technical, because the lives of human beings are the result of social interaction that then relates to technology.

With the advent of calculators, the issue becomes even more sensitive, as we are left with the question of whether they can think or understand our language; this is also why it is necessary to take a huma- nistic approach with technology to create machines suitable for human purposes.

Every technological innovation involves a human interaction between co- knowledge and invention, but if the product of this interaction alters society we are forced to ask ourselves some questions to better understand how far machines can go. To do so, we must always start from the sociopolitical context in which they were designed and built; let us not forget that we previously referred to them as socio-technical systems.

But can machines be intelligent? Let's take the example of the difference between a computer and a clock: the former has apparent au- tonomy, performing operations (or algorithms) without human in- tervention, with a complexity of purpose and structural plasticity that lead it to be unpredictable in behavior. In contrast, a digital clock is always predictable. Although there is currently no autonomous artificial intelligence, there is, however, a risk that it may emerge spontaneously as a result of interaction with the Internet, us humans, and our organizations.

In the world of cinema, artificial intelligence has influenced common thinking with films such as Stanley Kubrick's *2001: A Space Odyssey* (1968), Steven Spielberg's Minority *Report* (2002) or Ridley Scott's *Blade Runner* (1982). Even as early as

second half of the twentieth century, is a recurring theme in the science fiction novels of Isaac Asimov, Theodore Sturgeon and Philip Kindred Dick. But if we go back in time, Primo Levi also deals with the theme in the science-fiction short story *The Versifier*, included in the [1966] collection *Natural Stories,*[24] published under the pseudonym Da- miano Malabaila.

Eliezer Yudkowsky, an AI theorist known for popularizing the idea of friendly artificial intelligence, said, "By far the biggest peri- culum of artificial intelligence is that people conclude too soon that they understand it."

But one of the first to deal with the possible impacts of artificial intelligence on society was Alan Turing (1912-1954) in his article entitled *Computing Machines and* Intelligence,[25] in which the in- glish mathematician poses the question of whether machines can think, proposing an optimistic view on artificial intelligence and defining mac- chines through the model of the so-called "Turing machine." The ability to "think," according to Turing, is related to the concept of participating in the "imitation game," in which a machine must simulate human behavior through a teletype. If the machine can fool the human interlocutor, it can be considered as capable of thinking. Turing admits the lack of dimo- strative arguments, but his perspective paved the way for further research on artificial intelligence.

U.S. philosopher John Searle, in response to Tu- ring's question of whether machines are capable of processing thought, devised a thought experiment called "the Chinese room" presenting it in the article *Minds, Brains and* Programs[26]. He does not believe in repro-

---

[24] P. Levi, *The Versifier*, in *Storie naturali*, Einaudi, Turin, 1966.
[25] A.M. Turing, *Computing machinery and intelligence*, in "Mind," 59 (1950) 433-460.
[26] J.R. Searle, *Minds, brains, and programs*, in Behavioral and Brain Sciences, vol. 3, 1980.

ducibility of human intelligence within a computer system via a predefined program. Specifically, the perspective pro- posed by Turing and thus the strong artificial intelligence approach considers it feasible for a computer to achieve results similar to those of a human mind. This implies the ability to think, to manifest cognitive states, and to understand speech and do- mands in order to provide appropriate responses. The implementation of a program that is composed of symbols and computational rules provides the machine with the ability to process received inputs, generating outputs accordingly.

Underlying strong artificial intelligence is the identification of a structural and operational similarity between the human mind and a computer. It is claimed, in fact, that the mind, in receiving data (input), modifying it and generating other data (output), operates through the use of sim- boles processed by a central execution unit that guides it in the pro- cedures to be followed. This approach is supported by two theories, namely functionalism and computationalism. According to the former, a mental state represents any causal condition interposed between input and output. Therefore, according to this theory, two systems with identical causal pro- cesses possess equivalent mental states. In parallel, according to computationalism, mental processes are delineated as computational operations that manipulate symbols, and such processes are con- sidered equivalent to those performed by a computer. In contrast to this model, Searle argues instead that the human mind cannot be replicated solely in syntactic terms, since such an ap- proach neglects its fundamental characteristic, namely the intentionality that is at its core and is closely associated with co-science.

These two elements, consciousness and intentionality, are considered to be
primitive properties and concern the human capacity to formulate goals and experience emotions. Therefore, every action and every

cognitive state require, in their causality, a processing that goes beyond simple syntax, also operating semantically in relation to the meaning of terms. According to Searle, therefore, artificial intelligence cannot be compared to human intelligence, since processing symbol manipulation programs according to syntactic rules is not sufficient to generate mental activity.

The uniqueness of the human mind lies in its ability to com- take, process and express itself through a language in which words not only carry meaning but also determine how a response is formulated. In short, intentionality, entwined with subjective experience, is considerably more complex ri- spect to the capabilities of a machine and cannot be reduced to a mere execution of computational tasks through symbols following the rules of syntax.

While it appears that such artificial intelligences produce si- milient responses due to instructions, the current configuration of articial intelligence does not allow for the understanding of such instructions, because the elec- tives manipulated by the machine do not require intrinsic understanding. Therefore, machines do not perform the same tasks identically, thus emphasizing that artificial intelligence cannot equate with human intelligence. Finally, to the question of whether mac- chines can think, Searle responds that this possibility exists only if their material configuration achieves a complexity equivalent to that of the human brain, a biochemical and neurophysiological substrate capable of fostering the emergence of an intelligence endowed with intentionality.

If the basic structure (hardware) does not meet these requirements, it cannot be asserted that machines have thinking capabilities. Searle's objection is specifically aimed at the "strong" concept of artificial intelligence, without, however, excluding the possibility of "weak" artificial intelligence. Thus, there is always the possibility that machines can act as

The increased man

computational tools that are extremely more powerful and acute than humans, at least in certain areas.

Intelligence is not a defined and uniform thing as one might imagine. It is a mix of internal and external factors, between discourse, matter, biology and culture. We are talking about words and signs, social cooperation, community life, tradition and a biological heritage that has nothing to do with computational neurons.

When it comes to intelligent machines, there are those who predict the arrival of a time when artificial intelligences will become so advanced that they could surpass any human intelligence. In this way, technology and its evolution could push humanity into an unknown future: the technological singularity. By singularity is meant a theoretical point in the development of a civilization where technological pro- gress exceeds the human capacity for understanding and previ- sion. According to some, artificial intelligence will reach that level by 2045.

Now machines are no longer just machines, but have become real producers of thought and its content. Because of their easy access, they have become pervasive and present everywhere.

Even judges are beginning to useartificial intelligence, a valuable tool for accurately understanding context and con- versing it with previous judgments in a matter of moments. However, AI lacks human empathy and understanding, thus risking ignoring personal cir- cum- stances or important details that would instead be considered by a human judge. In addition, AIs are programmed by humans and may, unintentionally, inherit human biases present in training data. This, in turn, could lead to unfair or biased judgments.

Machine learning algorithms can be particularly complex and opaque, making it difficult to understand the decision-making pro- cess that led them to a particular choice. Like all

Cyberhumanism

technologies, artificial intelligence can also incur systemic errors with significant consequences. What's more, if judges become overly dependent on AI, they may risk losing their decision-making autonomy, compromising their ability to di- scernate.

This is where AGI (Artificial General Intelligence), a complex concept with fuzzy contours, comes in. In essence, it is an ambitious goal: to create an intelligence superior to humans that could open the door to a new era in human history. This form of artificial intelligence could overcome human limitations and re- volute the way we approach problems and make scientific and technological advances. It promises to bring radical and af- fascinating changes that could shape our future in as-yet unthinkable ways and is a form of artificial intelligence that seeks to mimic human intelligence in all its aspects, while the singularity refers to a future time when technologies and artificial intelligence will become so advanced that they transcend human understanding.

2.4 LLM and LMM

LLMs and LMMs, acronyms for Large Language Model and Large Multimodal Model, respectively, are closely related to one part of artificial intelligence, generative intelligence.

Generative AI is rooted in the history of innovation. In 1932 Georges Artsrouni invented a machine called the "mecha- nical brain" to translate from one language to another on an electronic computer encoded on punch cards. In 1957 linguist Noam Chomsky published *Syntactic* Structures[27] in which he described grammatical rules for parsing and generating sentences in natural language. In 1966

---

[27] N. Chomsky, *Syntactic Structures*, Mouton & Company, 1957.

MIT professor Joseph Weizenbaum invents the first chatbot, ELIZA, which simulates conversations with a psychotherapist. In 1968, computer science professor Terry Winograd created SHRDLU, the first multimodal AI capable of manipulating and reasoning about a world of bloc- chi based on user instructions.

In 1980 Michael Toy and Glenn Wichman developed a Unix-based game, *Rouge*, which exploited procedural content generation to dynamically produce new game levels. In 1985 computer scientist and philosopher Judea Pearl introduces causal Bayesian network analysis, providing statistical techniques for representing uncertainty leading to methods for generating content in a specific style, tone, or length. In 1986 Michael Irwin Jordan laid the foundation for the modern use of recurrent neural networks (RNNs) with the publication of *Serial Order: A Parallel Distributed Processing* Approach[28]. In 1989, Yann LeCun, Yoshua Bengio and Patrick Haffner demonstrate how convolutional neural networks (CNNs) can be used to recognize images. In 2000, researchers at the University of Montreal published *A Neural Probabilistic Language Model*,[29] in which they suggested a method for modeling language using feed-forward neural networks, which differ from recurrent neural networks because connections between nodes do not form loops. In 2006, data scientist Fei-Fei Li creates the ImageNet dataset that provides the basis for visual object recognition. In 2011, Apple released Siri, a voice-activated personal assistant that can generate responses and perform actions in response to voice requests.

In 2012 Alex Krizhevsky designed the architecture of the AlexNet CNN, a deep convolutional network model, paving the way for a

---

[28] M.J. Jordan, *Serial Order: A Parallel Distributed Processing Approach*, in "ScienceDirect," vol. 121 (1997), pp. 471-495.
[29] Y. Bengio, R. Ducharme, P. Vincent, *et al*, *A Neural Probabilistic Language Model*, in "The Journal of Machine Learning Research," 3 (2003), pp. 1137-1155.

new way for automatic training of neural networks that take advantage of recent advances in the GPU (Graphics Processing Unit). In 2013, Google researcher Tomas Mikolov and his colleagues introduced Word2vec, which is a two-layer artificial neural network that processes natural language to automatically identify semantic relationships between words. In 2014, researcher Ian Goodfel- low developed generative adversarial networks (GANs) that pit two neural networks against each other to generate increasingly realistic content. Diederik Kingma and Max Welling introduce automatic variational coders to generate images, videos, and text.

In 2015, Stanford researchers published work on diffusion models in the paper *Deep Unsupervised Learning using Nonequili- brium Thermodynamics*[30]. The technique provides a way to decode the addition of noise to a final image. In 2017, Google researchers develop the concept of transformers in the foundational paper *Attention is All You Need*, stimulating research on tools that could automatically parse unlabeled text in large language models.

In 2018 again, Google researchers implement transformers in BERT, which is trained on more than 3.3 billion words and can automatically ap- pear the relationship between words in sentences, paragraphs and even books to predict the meaning of text. Goo- gle DeepMind researchers develop AlphaFold to detect protein structures, laying the groundwork for applications of generative AI in medical research, drug development and chemistry. OpenAI re- leases GPT (Generative Pre-trained Transformer), trained on about 40 GB of data and consisting of 117 million parameters, paving the way for subsequent LLMs in content generation, chatbots and language translation. In 2021, OpenAI will introduce Dall-E, which can produce

---

[30] J. Sohl-Dickstein, E.A. Weiss, N. Maheswaranathan, *et al*, *Deep Unsupervised Learning using Nonequilibrium Thermodynamics*, in "ArXiv" (2015) 1503.03585.

The increased man

images from text instructions. The name comes from the combination of Wall-E, an imaginary robot, and the artist Salvador Dali. In 2022, researchers from Runway Research, Stability AI, and CompVis LMU release Stable Diffusion as an open source code that can autom- atically generate image content from a text message. In no- vember OpenAI releases ChatGPT to provide a chat-based interface to its GPT 3.5, attracting more than 100 million users to it in two months, representing the fastest example of user adoption of a service.

In 2023 Getty Images and a group of researchers sue for copyright infringement several companies that implemented Stable Diffusion. Microsoft integrates a version of ChatGPT into its Bing search engine. Google quickly follows with plans to release the Bard chat service based on its Lamda engine.

Speaking of neural networks, artificial neural networks (or ANNs) are a catego- ry of algorithms consisting of a set of numerical data called weights that are so numerous that a single network can comprise millions of numbers, taking up considerable amounts of storage space. The func- tioning of a neural network involves processing nu- meric inputs, generating numeric outputs and adjusting its weights through algorithms based on the input data and the desired output. This process, known as learning, aims to minimize errors in assigning specific outputs to input data, a fact that re- fects in the optimization problem.

Neural networks are capable of handling huge amounts of data, re- requiring millions of inputs to be trained correctly and pro- duce extraordinary results. Machine learning aims to build an optimization model using raw training data and has two main goals: prediction, that is, to charge the network to predict the output value corresponding to a specific input, and classification, that is, to distinguish whether an element in the data does or does not belong to a specific category. Ma- chine learning algorithms infer hidden patterns in the data and apply them to new data. Classification and prediction are thus the main tasks associated with data analysis by machine learning. There are also other ML algorithms capable of performing these tasks, such as linear regression methods, support vector machines (SVMs), random forests, and clustering algorithms, which can be used for similar purposes but with less com- plete computation.

Another category of neural networks are deep neural networks, with a more complex internal structure, which may comprise dozens or addi- tionally hundreds of layers, with millions of weights. The algorithms required to train these networks are more sophisticated than the ordinary and, in some cases, are specialized for specific tasks. Included in this cate- gory are convolutional neural networks, designed for image recognition, and Transformers, developed for natural lin- guage processing. In their training, it is necessary to provide a set of adequate size, often on the order of millions of elements, compatible with the size of the network. These huge datasets often result from a pre-processing step that transforms raw data into numerical inputs compatible with a neural network. The use of big data infrastructures becomes essential when handling heterogeneous and unstructured data in- siments of considerable size, which are necessary to train and test such algorithms, especially in production am- bients.

The advent of generative AI, with particular reference to ChatGPT, has brought considerable change to the technology landscape, generating critical thinking about its impact in the marketplace and who will benefit most from it. Its rapid spread has been remarkable, involving industry giants such as Microsoft, Google, Meta, and Ama- zon, but also striking, we might venture, as it has come also to the general public with one hundred million registered users just two months after launch.

Microsoft, in particular, has played a leading role in in- corporating GPT's generative AI into several products, seeking to soddi- sfy both *corporate* and *consumer* needs of enterprises. Google and Meta have taken somewhat different approaches, introducing Bard and Llama 2 respectively, while Amazon has recently invested in- gent resources in Anthropic, aiming for close collaboration with the company. In parallel, many startups have entered the generative AI ecosi- tion, offering a wide range of products and ser- vices. In this wave of enthusiasm, consulting companies currently sem- ripe to be among the main beneficiaries, leading other companies in exploring the potential of generative AI for their businesses.

In the financial sector, Nvidia, a well-known GPU microprocessor manufacturer, has benefited greatly from the increased interest in generative AI. In short, everyone is vying to incorporate it into every aspect of their business, but creating profitable models, with high costs and uncertainties about immediate profitability, is still an unknown. The realization of significant pro- ductivity gains, expected by economists, depends heavily on large-scale adoption of generative AI. Although businesses are exploring the many potentials of this technology, the broad adoption clause puts a damper on this trend. Because the economy grows when the middle class is involved in it; if only a few companies benefit from AI instead, they will enjoy a boost in productivity, while the rest will stand still. In this context, we also have to ask a provocative question about the possible decline of the smartphone era, with generative AI possibly being the catalyst for new devices and ways of interacting with chatbots capable of par- ting and listening. This raises questions about the future of giants such as

Cyberhumanism

Apple, which so far has not announced any specific projects in this area, but remains committed to innovation, including the development of microprocessors dedicated to this area.

To date, however, there are increasingly popular and accessible LLM platforms, including OpenAI's GPT models, BERT and T5, powerful artificial intelligence tools that are revolutionizing the way we interact with technology, such as Meta's Llama 2. One of the best-known and most widely used LLMs is ChatGPT, whose main characteristic is its vastness and ability to generate coherent and natu- ral text. To train an LLM, it is necessary to use a giant da- taset collected from the Internet. Artificial intelligence super engines process this huge amount of textual data to learn advanced language patterns and provide relevant answers. With t h i s amount of data, the LLM develops deep knowledge on a wide variety of topics. These advanced AI algorithms enable LLMs to understand context, generate content, and re-sponse questions accurately.

To train these systems, techniques such as self-supervised and semisupervised learning are employed. Although they seem intelligent, they are actually just simulacra of human language. They practice a kind of artificial reasoning, trying to imitate the way we think. LLMs work by receiving input text and repeatedly predicting the next word or token. Until 2020, the only method of customizing a model for specific tasks was fine tuning. However, thanks to technological pro- gress, larger models such as GPT-3/4 and later can be configured with prompts to achieve similar results more efficiently. LLMs gain a deep understanding of the syntax, semantics, and "ontology" inherent in human language, as well as the inaccuracies and biases that accompany it.

The increased man

LLMs, therefore, have limitations that compromise their effectiveness and reliability; for one, their exclusive dependence on training data, which may be incomplete, obsolete, or inaccurate. In addition, LLMs are unable to assimilate infor- mation from external sources, which thus might instead be more up-to-date, relevant, and verified. Although they can produce coherent and informative text, this does not guarantee the accuracy or relevance of the information provided.

One solution for overcoming these limitations is Retrieval Augmented Generation (RAG), a model that combines the generative capabilities of LLMs with that of retrieving information from an external source of co- n knowledge, thus creating texts that are richer in quality and more relevant information. But how does a RAG work? In the first stage, based on the input or question received, it searches for documents from external sources, then uses them to produce the final text. This technology com- poses obvious advantages: in addition to improving the capabilities of LLMs, it can solve problems such as hallucinations or data loss by exploiting the variety of multiple sources of knowledge, which, however, must always be guaranteed in reliability and robustness. Another advantage is that it can be used in virtual assistance, as it can enhance the capabilities of chatbots.

Many companies have already implemented this new technology in their systems. To name just one, Audi has developed a chatbot that through RAG allows employees to get answers to inquiries regarding different areas in an easier and simpler way.

The foundations of all these new technologies, which rely heavily on the use of material resources, energy, data and human labor, are currently concentrated in a small number of large companies, states and geographic regions.

Until 2014, the most important machine learning models were mainly developed by academics. But then the industry has begun to create cutting-edge AI systems using more and more data, calculations, and economic resources that it obviously has more than nonprofits and academia.

Many personalities including researchers, executives and investors have la- vored for about a decade on the AI project, which in truth has only exploded in the past year. Among the most influential figures involved we can- cite Sam Altman, CEO of OpenAI; Dario Amodei, a former Google researcher who heads Anthropic; and Bill Gates, founder o f Microsoft, who was initially skeptical about the power of AI; Demis Ha- ssabis, neuroscientist founder of DeepMind and producer of Al- phaGo; Geoffrey Hinton, professor at the University of Toronto, one of the people responsible for the neural networks that underlie AI; Reid Hoff- man, former PayPal executive who founded LinkedIn and is venture ca- pital of OpenAI; Elon Musk, at the helm of Tesla and founder of SpaceX, helped found OpenAI; Larry Page, founder of Google in- sive with Sergey Brin, who believes that robots and humans will one day live in harmony; Peter Thiel, a PayPal executive who invested in DeepMind and OpenAI; Eliezer Yudkowsky, an Inter- net philosopher and self-taught AI researcher, has helped fuel much of the philosophical thinking around this technology; and finally Mark Zuckerberg, CEO of Meta who owns Facebook, Instagram and WhatsApp, has been pushing for AI for at least a decade. As we mentioned, the latter himself recently came under fire for his irresponsible approach after announcing that he wants to develop a powerful human-level AGI system and make it open source for the public and outside developers. But a system of this magnitude could escape human control and pose a threat to humanity. In fact, this proposal has been criticized by many experts who consider such an idea to be spaven- tive, to say the least, and believe that Zuckerberg is irresponsible in considering this possibility without clear regulation.

More importantly, such decisions should not fall solely on technology companies like his. It seems, however, that Zuckerberg is moving toward open source in a safe and responsible way, without providing an exact timeline for system development. Meta has already made Llama 2 open source, drawing criticism for its lack of regulation.

2.5 The singularity

The singularity involves the development of artificial intelligence supe- rior to the human, but it is not limited to general artificial intelligence. While the latter attempts to replicate the complexity of human learning, the singularity aims to create a system with autonome capabilities external to normal human cognition.

The concept of singularity originated in the field of physics and became popular due to Albert Ein- stein's theory of general relativity in 1915. According to this theory, the singularity represents the cen- ter of a black hole: a point of infinite density and gravity in which any object, even light, remains trapped forever. Our current knowledge of physics breaks down at the very edge of the singularity, making it impossible for us to describe what happens inside it.

In the technological context, the singularity was introduced by John von Neumann (1903-1957), one of the greatest mathematicians of the 20th century. In 1958, the Polish physicist Stanislaw Ulam reported on a pre- cedent discussion with von Neumann, in which he discussed rapid tech- nological progress and changes in the human way of life[31]. These changes seem to approach a singularity in human history, beyond which human affairs, as we know them, will not

---

[31] S. Ulam, *Tribute to John von Neumann*, in "Bulletin of the American Mathematical Society," 64, #3, part 2: 5, May 1958.

could continue any longer. This point of view was later taken up by other authors.

The singularity and the related concept became popular in 1993 thanks to U.S. writer Vernor Vinge. In an article titled *The Im- minent Technological Singularity*,[32] he argued that once human es- seriates create intelligences superior to their own, we will witness a technological and social transition akin to "space-time attor- cated to the center of a black hole." Vinge predicted the end of the human era, stating that an emerging super-intelligence would constantly self-improve and progress technologically at an incomprehensible rate.

Another important catalyst for the spread of this idea was the book entitled *The Singularity is Near*[33] by Ray Kurzweil, an American inventor and computer scientist, who predicts the advent of the singularity by 2045. This outlook is contrasted by Erik Larson[34], a technology im- portant and researcher in the field of natural language processing, who debunks the fantasy of the rapid realization of artificial super- intelligence and criticizes the idea that machines will soon supe- rate the capabilities of the human mind. Larson highlights the er- rore in comparing artificial intelligence with human intelligence, sub- lining that while AI operates primarily through data-driven inductive reasoning, humans also use abductive reasoning, based on context and experience. This type of intuitive reasoning, at the core of human common sense, is difficult to program in current AI.

In 1965, British statistician Irving J. Good also turns out to be a precursor of the term "singularity" and describes a similar concept

---

[32] http://s24ore.it/mcc15
[33] R. Kurzweil, *The Singularity Is Near: When Humans Transcend Biology*, 1st edition, Penguin Books, London, 2005.
[34] E.J. Larson, *The Myth of Artificial Intelligence: Why Computers Can't Think the Way We Do*, Belknap Pr, Cambridge, MA, 2021.

to the current meaning, including the advent of a form of superhuman intelli- gence: "Let us say that an ultra- intelligent machine is defined as a machine that can greatly surpass all the intellectual acti- vities of any man however skillful he is. Since the pro- ject of these machines is one of these intellectual activities, an ultra- intelligent mac- china could design better and better machines; therefore, there would be an "intelligence explosion," and man's intelligence would be left far behind. Therefore, the first ultra-intelligent machine will be the last invention that man will have the need to make. "[35]

According to Dutch computer scientist Edsger Dijkstra (1930-2002), the rile- vance of questioning whether an algorithm "thinks" or "knows" what it calculates is comparable to asking whether a submarine "knows" how to swim.

Again, back in 1954, science fiction author Fredric Brown introduced the concept of the technological singularity in his short story *The Answer*[36]. In this fascinating story, a po- tent "galactic supercomputer" is imagined to which, as soon as it is turned on, is asked the most crucial question: "Does God exist?" To which the supercomputer ri- spondes unequivocally, "He does now."

Gottfried Wilhelm Leibniz (1646-1716), the brilliant philosopher and mathematician, envisioned a universal calculus machine, conceiving the world as a rationally ordered expression of the di- vine will. He showed us how, through the use of logical procedures and mathematical me- thods, we could apply computation to any event. Therefore, the world was perceived as a deterministic system, comprehensible through regular laws that could be described mathematically. This is what inspires advocates of a powerful artificial intelligence: they advocate the idea of a universal machine

---

[35] I.J. Good, *The Estimation of Probabilities*, MIT Press, Cambridge, MA, 1965.
[36] F. Brown, *The Answer*, in *The Shortest Tales of the World*, Fahrenheit 451, Rome, 1993.

completely determined as an explanation of the world and man. However, strong AI, in its various forms, represents some antiumanism. In denying both human reason and our ability to follow reason, the role of our subjective states as an integral part of animate nature is forgotten. This form of materia- lism reduces human beings to a digital, moldable, and predictable "mechanism," but more importantly it denies human progress and achievement in all cultural fields.

Nevertheless, the technological singularity may not be so close. Much of the speculation about the singularity is based on the idea of artificial intelligence capable of surpassing human intelligence. There is an in- tensive ongoing debate about the feasibility of such a concept. Many argue that current advances in artificial intelligence have not yet provided convincing empirical evidence for this possibility.

Today, each individual possesses free will, autonomy and moral responsibility in his interaction with other human beings, society and the natural world. It is not simply an ingra- ning in a larger mechanism. However, there is a risk that, once empowered by artificial intelligence, this autonomy may be compromised.

An advanced artificial intelligence could develop purposes contrastant with those of humanity, posing a potential threat to our existence. It is plausible to imagine that a super- intelligent artifi- cial intelligence could decide to eliminate humanity, deeming it intellectually inferior, without humans having the capabilities to counter it. This concern is shared by both the proponents of the technological singularity and its critics.

An OpenAI "discovery" known as "Q Star" or "Q*" has recently come to everyone's attention, relating to two different theories on AI: Q- learning and the Maryland Denial Proof System (MRPPS) Q* algorithm.

The increased man

The former is a reinforcement learning technique in which AI acquires knowledge through experience and error analysis. This method enables it to independently identify optimal solutions, eliminating dependence on human intervention, unlike the current ap- proach that involves learning with human feedback (RLHF). The Q* algorithm, on the other hand, is an advanced method for proving theorems in AI, especially in question answering systems. This algorithm integrates both semantic and syntactic information to successfully deal with complex situations. This could make significant advances in deductive capabilities and problem solving in thecontext of artificial intelligence. So there is a big difference between the two theories: while Q-learning aims to instruct the AI in learning through interactions with its surroundings, the Q-algorithm, on the other hand, focuses more on elevating its deductive capabilities. But still, neither of the theories, which are only speculations at the moment, per- poses to achieve AGI, the attainment of which is still far off.

Mark Zuckerberg, chief executive officer of Meta, also in January. 2024 has announced that its long-term vision is t o build general, open source, responsible intelligence and make it widely available so that everyone can benefit from it. But if machines were to surpass humans in their ability to make decisions and plan strategically, this could cause profound economic and social upheaval. It could also be the case that machines develop goals or values contrary to human in- terests, with unintended consequences or, even worse, catastro- strophic. From movies to literature this fear has always been there.

Samuel Butler, an English author, wrote this in 1871: "Machines serve man only on condition of being served, and they themselves set the conditions of this mutual agreement [...]. How many men today live in a state of slavery to machines? How many spend theirentire life, from cradle to death, tending machines night and day? Think of the ever-increasing number of men whom they have enslaved, or who devote themselves body and soul to the advancement of the mechanical realm: is it not evident that the machines are taking over from us? [...] Are there not more men engaged in caring for machines than in caring for their fellow men? "[37]

There is also to consider the concept of transferring human consciousness into a machine, which has been a subject of discussion among scientists for years, particularly within the transhumanism movement. Three key assumptions guide this consideration. The first concerns the future development of consciousness transfer technology, but the complexity of the human brain raises doubts about this possibility. The second assumption investigates whether brain simulation can generate a real mind, considering the complexity of neural connections as fundamental to consciousness. Finally, the third assumption focuses on defining who would be the "real you" in case of transfer, dividing philosophers between those who believe in biological continuity and those who attach importance to mental processes and memories.

At this point a question arises for me: what will be the "real you"? We only know that, despite technological advances, the transfer of consciousness is a suggestive topic that is the result of heated debate and speculation and, above all, without a definitive answer.

David Chalmers, a noted philosopher of mind, considers the possibility of developing conscious artificial intelligence in the next decade, estimating the probability to be greater than one in five[38]. I tend to concur with Federico Faggin, considered the father of the microprocessor,

---

[37] S. Butler, *Erewhon or Over the Range*, 1872.
[38] D. Chalmers, *What is consciousness?*, Castelvecchi, Rome, 2020.

The increased man

who in his latest [book39] proposes a revolutionary perspective on the relationship between the human being and technology. After years of study and advanced research, Faggin concludes that there is something irreducible about the human being, an element that no machine will ever be able to completely replace. Contrary to the theory that regards us as biolo- gical machines analogous to computers, he argues that consciousness, the ability to understand situations, and free will are unique aspects of the human being that go beyond the capabilities of machines, sug- gerating an unprecedented and inalienable vision of human nature. In doing so, it invites us to reflect on the value of human life and to embrace what makes us truly unique and essential as human beings.

Almost reaching a point where machines can think better than human beings, the current problem is that we are the ones who per- pose it. This practice is as convenient as it is easily accessible. With the click of a button, machines write articles about any argo- ment or person. Generative AI is adopted by everyone, although not everyone admits it publicly. What is the true accuracy of the generated output? To what extent is it influenced, intentionally or unintentionally, by unknown factors?

Technology is simply a tool in human hands; it is no longer up to us to decide how to use it because we are forced to follow directives imposed by others. It forces us to act as new cyber zombies, producing content based on the decisions of companies located in countries far from our control.

One certainty is that artificial intelligence, nowadays, does not actually exist. It represents only a kind of figure of rhetoric, ac- cepted by me as well, to describe, in most cases, sem- plically machine learning. It is crucial to understand that a robot's ability to "reason," "compute," "react," and "decide"

---

[39] F. Faggin, *Irreducible. Consciousness, life, computers and our nature*, Mondadori, Milan, 2022.

is only a simulation of the processes of thinking, computation, reaction and de- cision, which do not correspond to real human thought processes. Machine learning si- stems, also known as "machine lear- ning," are machines capable of generating rules based on algorithms that operate by evaluating results.

To initiate the computer learning process, it is fundamental to establish in advance the goals you wish to achieve. The main goal is to achieve the desired results from specific input data.

Although we are not yet facing advanced artifi- cial intelligence, we are already facing rapidly growing problems such as tracking our lives on the Web, inva- tive monitoring, loss of privacy and anonymity, di- gital identity theft, and data protection.

So it is essential to understand how these tools work, how they affect our lives, and how they can be guided se- cording to the principles of Cyberhumanism to serve the good of humanity. Also in perspective. The Center for AI Safety[40] even warns about the risk of possible human extinction resulting from AI and how much regulation is needed to reduce it. This issue is thus a global priority as well as the prevention of pandemics and nuclear war.

Researchers from Berkeley and Oxford University conducted a study among leading AI scientists, concluding that there is at least a 5 percent chance that humans will fail to control AI systems, thus leading to the extinction of humanity. The survey involved 2,778 scientists who have pub- licized studies on AI showing that although 68 percent of the experts consider positive outcomes of superhuman AI more likely than negative ones, about half of them consider extinction possible

---

40 http://s24ore.it/mcc60

The increased man

human, thus highlighting their prevailing uncertainty about its future and emphasizing the need to minimize the risks associated with this technology. The main concern was expressed re- garding the spread of misinformation, with more than 80 percent of researchers citing it as "extreme" or "substantial."

Other alarming issues include possible use by dit- tors, worsening economic inequality, and the risk of creating engineered viruses. Although managers of AI-based systems emphasize the goodness of their "mission," the question of how to handle AI models that might be smarter than humans remains open. To give a few examples, OpenAI has published its first paper on aligning superhuman AI with human values. Anthropic has adopted a constitution[41] on its AI systems to ensure that they act in line with the rules of our society. But will all this be sufficient? With this study, researchers have also provided good estimates on achieving meaningful progress in AI, predicting that it will be able to perform tasks such as assem- blishing LEGOs and translating new languages by 2033. The most re- levant issue at the moment, however, seems less about the extinction of humanity and more about the extinction of certain professional figures, since again according to the scholars, AI might be able to replace the work of surgeons or researchers, for example, by 2063.

To recapture the present and place humanity at the center of the decisions and technological advances, it is necessary to overcome the current dependence on "black boxes." Only by fully understanding what is happening, including what has already happened in part, can we truly go- vern our digital destiny or perhaps, simply, our destiny in general.

One thing is certain, man has a "new" hitherto unexplo- rted vulnerability: knowledge. Because it can be manipulated.

---

[41] http://s24ore.it/mcc70

Cyberhumanism

2.6 Intelligent robots

We have always been fascinated by robots since ancient times. In those days, we imagined automata based on the principles of hydraulics and pneumatics, such as the little Hercules created by the Greek mathematician and physicist Heraeon of Alexandria, capable of shooting arrows, or the human-sized robot of the Greek scientist Philo of Byzantium that, like a servant, poured water and wine. However, it was especially in the 17th and 18th se- cles that the production of automata became increasingly precise and impressioning, thanks to knowledge in the field of watchmaking.

Robots are increasingly present in our daily lives, thanks to the introduction of innovative technologies that can automate a range of functions usually performed by humans. The use of robots can bring significant simplifications to human daily life, according to the principles of Cyberhumanism. Domestic robots, for example, can take on repetitive tasks such as cleaning, cooking or gardening, freeing up human time for more gra- tific activities. In addition, the use of robotics in areas such as agriculture and manufacturing can increase efficiency and reduce dependence on physically demanding human labor. In medicine, surgical robots enable precision surgeries beyond human capabilities, improving accuracy and reducing risk.

In a variety of fields, such as health care, manufacturing, and logistics, robots demonstrate greater precision and reliability responding to humans, potentially replacing people in al- ome areas of work. There are several types of robots on the market today. Their main uses include automation and human-robot collaboration.

Industrial robots are used to automate manufacturing operations in various industries. Collaborative ones are designed to interact with humans in safe environments; they provide some type of assistance or keep elderly people company or disabled. Medical robots can assist in clinical or tera- peutic settings to perform a wide range of medical procedures.

Domestic robots such as Roomba and other semi-humanoids are being used as intelligent assistants in people's daily lives. Some anthropomorphic robots, such as Kime, are currently employed in Spain to serve drinks and snacks to customers, acting almost like autonomous kiosks. Their versatility also makes them suitable for customer interface roles, such as concierges in hotels or other similar con- texts.

Anthropomorphic robots Nao and Pepper find use in schools, la- ving closely with students. They collaborate with them to create content and teach programming, thus helping to improve the educational experience.

When employed to assist humans, robots prove to be a resource of great potential. Because of their ability to perform repetitive and dangerous tasks efficiently and safely, they can li- ber people from monotonous or difficult jobs. In addition to this, advanced artificial intel- ligence enables them to learn and adapt, of- fering increasingly personalized assistance.

While many humanoid robots are still in the prototype stage or other early stages of development, some have broken out of research and development in recent years, entering the real world as bartenders, concierges, divers and as companionship for the elderly. Some operate in warehouses and factories, assisting humans in logistics and production. Others seem to offer more novelty and wonder than anything else, conducting orchestras and welcoming guests at conferences.

Today, numerous anthropomorphic robots are already on the market and in constant service. More of them than we imagine. They resemble us and mimic our movements to perform various tasks. Some are even com- posed of materials that mimic human features, such as skin and eyes, to appear more friendly.

Cyberhumanism

ARM-6 is a humanoid robot developed by researchers at the Karlsruhe Institute of Technology in Germany for use in indu- strial environments. It can use drills, hammers and other tools and is equipped with artificial intelligence to learn how to grasp objects and con- sign them to human colleagues. It can also perform maintenance tasks such as cleaning surfaces and is able to ask for assistance when needed. Very similar is Apptronik's Apollo, which has been pro- jected to support a load of up to 55 pounds. It operates in factories and in industries such as retail and construction.

Atlas is a humanoid robot developed by Boston Dynamics that can perform jumps and stunts. It has depth sensors for real-time perception and model-predictive control technology to improve movement and can move at speeds in excess of 5 miles per hour. It was built with 3D-printed parts and is being used by research- ers and robot designers to increase agility and coordination si- miliar to human ones.

In this regard, researchers at the Technical University of Munich have developed a new learning method that allows robots to autonomously acquire the functionality of their own bodies through data from sensors that track limb movement. This ability, called proprioception[42], allows them to sense their own body positioning and is currently a human prerogative. Teaching machines how their bodies work is also critical for them to operate safely and effectively in real am- bients.

Through their experiments, researchers have shown that all robots can understand the position of their joints and the

---

[42] Ability to perceive and recognize the state of contraction of one's muscles and the position of one's body in space without the support of sight. Se- cording to Charles Scott Sherrington (1857-1952), proprioception can thus be considered a sixth sense in that it is regulated by a specific part of the brain.

direction in which they are facing. The ability of robots to continuously assess and update their knowledge of their morphology, without requiring huge datasets, as expected of most mo- derful deep learning methods, will enable them to adapt their pa- rameters to reflect in their body structure changes that may occur as a result of external actions.

Providing robots with skills such as proprioception can make them more fles- sible, adaptable, and safe, but more importantly it could significantly accelerate the development of more complex forms of artifi- cial intelligence, since this must be implemented in a real body to reach its full potential.

Digit, the automaton produced by Agility Robotics, can handle trailer and package handling and performs generally monotonous tasks. It has articulated appendages and is able to duck and pi- gue itself to pick up objects, adjusting its center of gravity based on size and weight. Terrain sensing sensors help it find the most efficient path and avoid any obstacles. In 2022, Digit was awarded $150 million in funding from Amazon and other companies to support it in the workplace.

KIME, the humanoid robot bartender from Macco Robotics, serves beer, coffee, wine, snacks, salads and more. Each KIME can serve up to 253 customers per hour. It has a touchscreen and a dedicated app to allow customers to order and pay. Although it does not offer the sage advice of an experienced bartender, it can still identify its abi- tual customers and remember what they usually want.

Nadine, a humanoid social android developed by researchers at Nanyang Technological University in Singapore, is equipped with highly realistic skin, hair and body movements and can be uti- lized for a variety of purposes. It has the ability to recognize faces, words, ge- sti and objects, but what sets it apart is its system that simulates affet- tivity, shaping personality, emotions and mood according to

Cyberhumanism

of the situation. To date, he has been used in Singapore for customer ser- vice and as a conductor of a Bingo game for a group of senior citizens.

NAO, another humanoid robot from Softbank Robotics, serves as an assistant for companies and organizations active in various fields, from health care to education, although it is only 60 centimeters tall. It has two teleca- mere for object recognition, directional microphones and speakers, and contact sensors to interact effectively with per- sons and its surroundings. In addition, it can speak and con- verse in 20 languages. NAO is of great help in creating content and teaching programming in classrooms and performs service for patients in the health care field.

Then there is Alter 3, the latest humanoid robot from Osaka University. It has an artificial neural network and also a musical ear. Early ver- sions created performances in an opera. With its sen- sors, expressive abilities and a system for singing, it has even gone so far as to conduct an orchestra at the New National Theater in Tokyo.

There is even a humanoid diving robot called Ocea- nOne, developed in Stanford's Robotics Laboratory, used to explore shipwrecks. In its first mission, it investigated the wreck of *La Lune*, one of the ships that sank in 1664 during the reign of Louis XIV. It is capable of diving to 1,000 meters and uses haptic feed-back and artificial intelligence to explore both aircraft and shipwrecks.

Promobot is a customizable humanoid robot that performs functions such as concierge, tour guide, and medical assistant and has advanced facial recognition capabilities. It can issue ma- gnetic cards, automatically scan and fill out documents or print guest passes. In his duties as concierge, he in- tegrates with the building security system and can recognize the faces of residents. In hotel settings, he is able to record the guests, while in health care environments it is capable of detecting important health indicators, such as blood sugar levels and blood ossigenation.

Sophia is one of the most famous humanoid robots. He has been on the cover of *Cosmopolitan*, has given a speech at the United Nations, and has appeared several times on *The Tonight Show*, challenging host Jimmy Fallon to a game of rock-paper-scissors. He is considered an embodiment of our dreams for the future of AI, a model for advanced research in AI and robotics, and an entity for exploring the human-robot experience in services and entertainment.

Walker X, a home-assist robot created by UBTECH Robotics, can climb stairs and balance on one leg safely, serve tea, water flowers, and use a vacuum cleaner.

In 2022, Tesla showed a preview of Optimus, a prototype humanoid robot scheduled to begin production in 2023 with a price tag of $20,000 per unit, and announced that it will be capable of performing dangerous, repetitive, and boring tasks. At present, the robot is able to walk slowly and perform basic actions. Musk predicted that the market value of Tesla's humanoid robot division will one day exceed that of electric cars. In addition, he agrees with Medjourney's David Holz on the prediction of at least 1 billion humanoids by 2040, which could become 100 billion over the next two decades.

A serious competitor to Optimus is the humanoid robot Forerunner from the Chinese company Kepler, which has precise arm control and excellent visual perception. It was designed with the intention of increasing productivity and reducing the work week to three days, leaving humans more time to devote to more important activities such as space exploration. Its special physical characteristics enable it to overcome obstacles, lift and tra- spor heavy objects, and interact with the world around it, also through a quadrangular binocular camera and a position- and direction-sensing si- system. In addition, all information detected by its sensors is processed by an AI system called Nebula. Kepler wants to market the robot vo- lently at a price of $30,000 versus Optimus' $20,000.

And yet Figure, the robotics startup born in 2022, and BMW are collaborating to equip the Spartan- burg plant in South Carolina with humanoid robots. These robots, called Figure 01, will be able to streamline human labor and make the production line safer and more effi- cient, as they are configured to perform any type of task. But, as can be easily deduced, if this can lead to lightening the human load, at the same time it changes the way machines are built, that is, using new AI and robotics technologies, with not insignificant impacts in the employment sector. Although the use of humanoid robots is still limited and development costs are high, an increase in the industry is expected. The humanoid robot market was worth $1.8 billion in 2023[43] and is expected to which will reach over $13 billion in the next five years.

The race toward perfecting these machines is an impor- tant technological development of 2024. Companies such as Tesla, Apptronik, and Figure have introduced their systems, while Agility has announced a pilot warehouse with Amazon. Recently 1X, a Nor- vegan company, has attracted attention with a fundraising effort that has reached an impressive $125 million, involving partners such as OpenAI, Tiger Global, and EQT Ventures. Its flagship product is the humanoid robot NEO, designed to address glo- bal labor shortages. While some criticize the engineering complexity of such si- stems, others believe that true functionality is still a long way off.

To meet the growing technological demand, advanced humanoid robots with human-like characteristics will be employed and

---

[43] According to the research firm MarketsandMarkets.

equipped with advanced artificial intelligence. These robots will be able to perform various tasks in the service, education and health care sectors.

Automation undoubtedly offers benefits such as reduced errors, increased efficiency and improved production processes. However, it is also essential to consider the social and economic impact of this transformation. How to ensure an equitable transition for the workforce in an increasingly automated world? A collective effort of in-depth reflection is needed to find solutions that promote employment, retraining and adaptation to the new scenarios. Only then can we make the most of the opportunities offered by robotic technology without putting the social and economic fabric at risk.

There are many conflicting theories about the future of work. Some, such as Andrew McAfee and Erik Brynjolfsson[44] of MIT, argue that, nonospite increasing automation, the technological revolution will eventually lead to the creation of new jobs. According to them, just as the industrial revolution gave rise to roles that were unthinkable in the pre-industrial era, similarly today's technological innovation opens the door to new occupations that we cannot yet imagine.

When electricity was discovered, there was a heated debate at the Royal Society in London among scientists of the time about the ethical implications of this invention. Some were convinced that the opportunity to work at night could alter the natural rhythms of sleep and wakefulness established by God. As we know, then electricity turned out to be much more: an extraordinary inno- vation that propelled mankind toward civilization and economic cre- scitation, positively revolutionizing the world of work.

On the other hand, there are those who see a bleaker future. Guy

---

[44] A. McAfee, E. Brynjolfsson, *The new machine revolution. Labor and pro- sperity in the age of triumphant technology*, Feltrinelli, Milan, 2017.

Standing[45], a professor of economics at the University of London, for example, argues that automation and digitization will lead to a growing precariat, with less stable work available and a cre- ing disparity between the "rich" in digital skills and the "poor." Secording to this view, if not managed properly, the di- gital revolution could lead to greater economic and social inequality.

So who will be right? Will it be a future of endless opportunities opened up by technology, as McAfee and Brynjolfsson argue, or a more disturbing prospect of precarity and inequality as described by Standing? The answer to this question, about what future awaits us in the age of digitization and artificial intelligence, is probably one of the most relevant of our time. The stakes are high, as the decisions and choices we make today will shape tomorrow's humanity. And it is crucial not to make mistakes.

In his 1942 short story entitled Runaround[46], science fiction writer Isaac Asimov defined the now famous three laws of robotics:

1. A robot cannot harm a human being or, through inaction, allow a human being to be harmed.

2. A robot must obey orders given by humans, except when those orders conflict with the First Law.

3. A robot must protect its own existence as long as that protection does not conflict with the First or Second Law.

But who checks that the laws are "embedded" in all the automatons produced? What law could obligate them?

---

[45] G. Standing, *The Precariat: The New Dangerous Class*, Bloomsbury, London, 2014.
[46] I. Asimov, *Runaround* (1942), in *I, Robot*, Garden City, New York, 1950.

The increased man

Google's DeepMind has drafted a "Robotic Constitution" inspired precisely by Asimov's three laws, a set of safety-focused suggestions for making sure robots do not harm humans or animals. The team has trained them to stop au- tomatically if the force on their joints exceeds a certain li- vel and has also included a physical switch to allow oper- ators to disable them at any time. DeepMind's data collection system, AutoRT, uses a visual language model and an LLM to understand the environment and adapt accordingly. This will help robots make faster, better and, most importantly, safer decisions.

A study reveals that people tend to pay less attention when working with robots, just as they do with respected human colleagues. Researchers at the Technical University of Berlin af- stopped that people view robots as part of their team. The scientists suggested that when they believe technology can behave particularly effectively, people tend to adopt a more relaxed approach.

According to research that has found evidence of "social listlessness"-that is, when team members work less hard if they think others will do it for them-people tend to pay less attention to tasks when working alongside a robot.

The team asked a cohort of workers to check the quality of a series of tasks, half of whom were told that the tasks were being performed by a robot. Although they did not work directly with the robot, called Panda, these people had seen it and were able to hear it as it operated.

The workers were all asked to perform checks for errors on printed circuit boards. The researchers monitored their at- tiveness by blurring the images of the boards that the workers received, showing them only an image that they could inspect once actively opened. Initially, they found no statistically significant differences in the amount of time the two groups-those who were told they were working with a robot and those who were not-to inspect the circuit boards or in the area where they looked for errors.

When investigating participants' error rates, it was found that those who collaborated with Panda detected fewer defects after observing that the robot had successfully reported many errors. That might reflect the "look but don't see" effect, in which people become less engaged once they believe a colleague or resource is reliable. While the participants, who were asked to rate their own performance, thought they were offering an equivalent amount of attention, the researchers believed that, at a subcon- scious level, they had begun to assume that Panda had correctly detected faults.

To address automation in the world of work responsibly and with foresight, it is critical that governments, companies and individuals come together, taking into account the potential for new job creation and opportunities offered by automation itself. Collaboration between humans and robots can bring enormous benefits, enabling complex tasks to be performed more efficiently and safely.

However, it is not a given that robots will "steal our jobs." It is uncertain whether humanoids will integrate properly into society or whether humans will accept their assistance. Some people may find their diffusion worrisome or dangerous or see it as unnecessary competition in the labor market, but the potential benefits such as increased efficiency and safety may outweigh many of the supposed consequences.

Chapter 3 - Opportunities

3.1 In industry

Artificial intelligence offers numerous advantages in industrial process automation, finding applications in several areas. For example, it can be used in market and trend analysis, for- ing a crucial starting point for product creation and production process start-up. In addition, it contributes to the development of machinery and equipment, as well as the design and ge- stration of logistical flows of goods and materials, where AI proves par- ticularly useful by reducing errors and increasing production efficiency, enabling a significant reduction in operating costs and an increase in overall productivity.

Through predictive analytics, AI can anticipate market trends and optimize supply chain management, thereby improving logistics efficiency. Using sensory data and machine learning algorithms, it can predict failures and malfunctions before they occur, reducing downtime and maintenance costs. In addition, AI can monitor and improve product quality through automated visual inspection systems and ana- lysis of production data, tailoring it to specific customer needs without compromising efficiency.

It also helps improve workplace safety by mo- nitoring environmental conditions, identifying potential hazards and reducing the risk of accidents. In research and development, AI enables the rapid creation of new products and innovative solutions because of its ability to analyze large amounts of data and identify new opportunities.

Cyberhumanism

The Chinese government has followed this trend, with the Ministry of In- dustry and Information Technology (MIIT) in Beijing setting an ambitious goal of producing humanoid robots on a large scale by 2025, making them a new engine of economic growth by 2027, through innovation of key technologies and supply of key components. China has made remarkable progress in the field of robotics, becoming the fifth most automatized country in the world, reflecting its commitment to bringing about a significant increase in the use of humanoid robots in every field, from healthcare to industry to everyday life.

AI, through advanced language models, can contribute to the development of increasingly self-sufficient machines and to the creation of a range of new, highly specialized jobs. These include AI robotics in- gegners and technicians, experts in the design, program- mation and maintenance of intelligent robots used in production lines; automation and control specialists who develop and operate advanced automation systems to optimize production processes; manufacturing data analysts who focus on stu- dering the data generated by production processes to improve efficiency and reduce waste; predictive maintenance technicians who use AI algorithms to predict and prevent machine failures, improving maintenance and reducing downtime; quality and inspection experts who implement AI systems for automated quality control, ensuring high standards and reducing errors; and finally, AI-assisted production operators who collaborate with si- stems to improve their productivity and safety.

In the dynamic context of Industry 4.0, the integration of intelli- artificial gence, machine learning and the Internet of Things (IoT) is a driving mo- tor, especially for mechanical engineers. This synergy enables them to create intelligent systems that communicate seamlessly. AI plays a central role in the

shape the future of mechanical engineering, but it is crucial that inges recognize the possible challenges associated with the adoption of these tech- nologies and emphasize their responsible implementation. Only through this awareness and attention to potential pitfalls will they be able to contribute significantly to the success and realization of Industry 4.0.

Also a revolutionary element in industry is the integration of autonomous agents, which can operate autono- mously, designing and automating entire workflows without requiring constant human input. This reduces the need for human intervention and facilitates full-scale experimentation, promising to tra- fer enterprise automation more comprehensively and efficiently because of their ability to interact directly with other systems. Companies need to prepare for the adoption of this technology by conside- rating aspects such as technology architecture and workforce planning.

3.2 In public administration

Artificial intelligence can also bring numerous benefits in the public sector, improving operational efficiency, services to citizens and even policy decisions through the automation of administrative processes. It can be used to analyze and manage emergency situations, improving the coordination and response of public authorities. Services offered to citizens can be per- sonalized to improve their accessibility and effectiveness, providing solutions tailored to their needs. AI can also be applied to document management, detecting any errors or missing data, suggesting how to fill out forms and making corrections in real time, thus reducing waiting times for users. Citizen support services, such as chatbots, can be implemented so that the most frequently asked questions are automatically answered more completely and comprehensively.

AI can also support predictive analytics to help public decision makers in planning and decision-making based on accurate data, thus revolutionizing digital public services, making them more efficient and accessible. Public administration can thus become more tra- sparent and less bureaucratic, helping to improve public trust. The goal is to integrate this technology into the design and ideation of services not only at the technological level, but also at the process level, to reduce in the digital environment the burden of burocratic fetters present in the physical world. Services should be coinstrued considering the needs of citizens, with interfaces accessible to all, regardless of technological skills or socio-economic conditions. A case in point is that of INPS, which has successfully implemented AI in its operational processes, recording a significant increase in productivity.

Carmelo Cutuli is very clear on these implications in his new book titled *Artificial Intelligence & Public Administration*,[47] in which he emphasizes the concept of "augmented PA," that is, a public administration integrated by the contribution of artificial intelligence, but always under human supervision. The author gives concrete examples such as the use of chatbots to answer citizens' questions to predictive systems for better resource allocation, or even virtual assistants integrated into public sites and the automation of complex procedures, all of which are opportunities offered by AI in termines of speed, error reduction, personalization of services and predictive data analysis. But at the same time he warns us about its technical limitations, which require significant investment and raise complex ethical dilemmas, agreeing that human

---

[47] C. Cutuli, *Artificial Intelligence & Public Administration. A guide to AI applications for the public sector*, ISSRF, Giarre (CT), 2024.

must always maintain a central position in public decision-making and that the introduction of technology must be done gra- dually, with care and a long-term view.

Between 2010 and 2021, 637 AI projects for public bodies were registered in Europe, 63 of which were in Italy, according to the report *The Technological op- erations for Advanced Digitization in Public Adm-* inistration[48] presented by The European House. Italy ranks as the second country in Europe for the number of AI-related projects in public administration and the first for implementation. Tut- tavia, public investment in this area is lower than in other states. To give just one example, the City of Siena has activated a chatbot named Caterina, which directly provides ana- graphical certificates after authentication with SPID. It might be a good idea to use it nationwide, optimizing time and resources. Other Italian municipalities are also organizing along these lines, starting chatbots that interact and answer questions, give directions, and can even help with filling out online forms. The van- tage is having a virtual assistant who gives answers 24/7.

Moving abroad, in the public construction sector, French consulting firm Capgemini has developed AI software with Google that can analyze aerial photographs in order to identify illegal swimming pools throughout France, unearthing as many as 20,000 of them with an additional fiscal get- t of 10 million euros. Staying in this area, in the United States, an AI tool is being used to identify any changes to infrastructure or property; while the Austra- lian company NearMap has developed a tool to track and segment land from aerial images.

Also in the United States, the adoption of AI-based automation is already a practical solution implemented in the public sector to

---

[48] http://s24ore.it/mcc67

improve the efficiency and effectiveness of government operations. For example, the Air Force, Departments of Labor, Homeland Security, and Health and Human Services have streamlined operations and saved hundreds of thousands of hours by using AI in acquisition, finance, logistics, disaster relief, and other government functions. This tool c a n manage data effectively, ensuring adherence to regulatory standards without the need for extensive human oversight. This not only improves accuracy but also reduces the likelihood of human error, which is critical to maintaining compliance.

The implementation of AI also increases participation in public services by people with disabilities, facilitating accessibility to information by means of voice-reading and text-to-speech systems or by integrating sign language into chatbots to improve communication with people who are deaf or hard of hearing; or even automating administrative processes to simplify the completion of online forms and integrating speech recognition and predictive writing systems to facilitate the completion of documents for those with motor or speech impairments; optimizing public transportation services, ensuring that they are accessible to people with motor or sensory disabilities; and using image recognition algorithms to generate audio descriptions of photos or documents and facilitate access to visual information for people with visual impairments.

Thanks to artificial intelligence, the public administration can create new jobs that aim to exploit its technological potential. A prime example might be data analysts with com- petencies in using AI to discover trends and predictive patterns; cybersecurity professionals trained to detect, iden- tify, and prevent cyber attacks; AI project managers who can monitor complex projects and manage human resources; the robotics specialists capable of designing, programming, installing and maintaining robots and industrial automation.

The integration of AI into justice systems raises important ethical que- stions. While it can evaluate cases and administer justice better than a judge, leading to improvements in the effi- ciency and accuracy of the legal and judicial professions, this increasing automation of justice implies si- gnificant ethical challenges. While some see AI as a potential contributor to a fairer, faster, and human bias-free justice system, we should not underestimate issues such as the lack of transparency in its decisions, the non-neutrality of algorithms, the possibility of discriminatory outcomes and embedded biases, along with surveillance practices for data collection and the protection of citizen privacy.

3.3 In health care

The population of the Old World is aging inexorably, increasing issues of chronic disease and fra- gility. Global epidemics challenge the interconnected world, while resources and medical personnel are increasingly limited. Addressing these issues requires a revolution based on digitizing the health care system, making it more accessible and integrated into citizens' daily lives. This transformation entails connecting disciplines, facilities, and services through the use of data and artificial intelligence algorithms to create an equitable healthcare system centered on people's needs, putting the pa- tient at the center of personalized care pathways and fostering greater data sharing among stakeholders. In May 2022, the European Health Data Space (European Health

Data Space - EHDS)[49], which aims to regulate the transmission and sharing of health data to exploit its full potential. It provides for easier access to data at the national and European level, promoting a single market for electronic health records, medical devices, and AI systems. The main discussion is about limiting access to sensitive data, while the secondary use of data aims to provide a consistent pool for research and innovation. With EHDS, therefore, the importance of reliable use and sharing of aggregated health data, including those on pathogens, medical indications, health rem- burses, genetic data, and information from public health registries, is emphasized. All this is done to pursue health-related public interest purposes such as research, innovation, policy formulation, education, health care, safety, or regulation. Contextually, the regulations would impose restrictions on forced uses of data such as advertising, discrimination in benefit or insurance decisions, and unauthorized sharing with third parties. Under these rules, requests for access to secondary data would be handled only by national entities, which would ensure that data are provided only in anonymized or, if necessary, pseudonymized form.

Artificial intelligence can provide valuable support to both me-
say that to health care professionals in various fields. For example, it can as- sist in diagnosis, treatment planning, and ge- stration of patient data, improving the efficiency and accuracy of medical practices. Through it, more accurate and faster diagnoses can be achieved, given its ability to rapidly analyze large amounts of information. It plays an important role in the ge- stion of health care data, including test results and diagno- stic images, helping physicians identify diseases with greater preci- sion and in a shorter timeframe, maintain up-to-date information on

---

[49] http://s24ore.it/mcc21

The opportunities

patients and make more targeted decisions.

AI systems can personalize care based on patient data, suggesting personalized treatments, improving the effectiveness of therapies and reducing their side effects. This helps improve the quality of care and optimize the efficiency of sa- nitary processes. Another benefit of AI is its ability to accelerate biomedical and pharmaceutical research and development. With it, researchers can analyze large amounts of data and identify new drugs and personalized therapies faster than with traditional methods.

A team of MIT researchers, exploiting deep learning, has individuated a new class of antibiotics effective against methicillin-resistant Staphyloc- cus aureus (MRSA). These compounds, demonstrated lethal for MRSA in laboratory cultures and mouse models, present low toxicity to human cells. This is relevant conside- ranting that MRSA causes more than 10,000 deaths per year in the United States. A key aspect of the study is the detailed understanding of the information used by the deep learning model, offering a novel approach to antibiotic discovery and promoting understanding of the chemical basis of the model's predictions. AI-supported research is, therefore, a significant advance also in the fight against drug-resistant bacteria.

U.S.-based company Eko Health has designed an AI ali- mated stethoscope to improve the diagnosis of heart disease, aiming to save more heart patients and relieve pressure on hospital services. This instrument has been provided to 200 GP ambu- lators in the northwest region of London and Wales and is the first AI product in the UK authorized for use by general practitioners without specialist review. Its imple- mentation aims to reduce diagnostic waits, providing a timely solution and potentially saving significant costs to the NHS.

The U.S. Food and Drug Administration (FDA) recently approved a portable medical device with AI developed by DermaSensor, a medical technology company. This instrument, similar to a smartphone but with a tip on the bottom edge, uses light reflected from skin lesions to dia- gnosticate skin cancer. Cancer cells reflect it differently than healthy ones, and the device's software can detect these differences, providing doctors with imme- diate advice and suggesting patient monitoring based on skin lesion assessment. The DermaSensor kit was trained to ana- lyze various types of skin cancer including melanomas, squamous cell carcinomas, and basal cell carcinomas and was approved by the FDA after a study conducted at the Mayo Clinic involving 22 different clinics. The results showed a sensitivity of 96% and specificity of 97% in detecting skin cancer in 224 di- versed cases. This approval allows DermaSensor to commercialize and provide primary care physicians with an advanced tool to assess the most common cancer in the United States. Considering that one in five Americans will develop some form of skin cancer by age 70, early detection is critical to successful treatment.

US cardiologist Eric Topol, in his book *Deep Medicine: How Artificial Intelligence Can Make Healthcare Human Again*[50], expresses cautious optimism about using advanced linguistic models of artificial intelli- gence in the healthcare sector to improve its efficiency and productivity. Topol highlights how AI is already being used to record conversations between doctor and patient, converting them into a clinical summary, a step that saves hours of data entry time, automating administrative tasks and enabling physicians

---

[50] E. Topol, *Deep Medicine: How Artificial Intelligence Can Make Healthcare Human Again*, Basic Books, New York, 2019.

to devote more time to patients. And most importantly, he does not condemn but in- corrupt the use of ChatGTP to get diagnoses that he can con- fect with others; he himself has used AI on himself discovering that he had kidney stones.

Beware, however, of using it with children: according to a study pub- lished in JAMA Pediatrics, the accuracy rate in diagnosing pediatric cases is only 17 percent, because compared with general cases these cases require greater consideration of age variance and the fact that children cannot accurately express their symptoms. In these cases ChatGPT proposed a related but too broad or general diagnosis to be considered correct. Although many physicians know that expertise is essential and recognize the debo- lements of AI chatbots, they are not opposed to their integration into health assi- stance. In fact, they could improve if they were specifically and selectively trained on accurate and affi- dible medical literature, and not on material on the Internet, which can include inaccurate and misleading in- formation.

The Google Deepmind team has proposed an AI chatbot that can more accurately diagnose patients' symptoms by collecting clinical data and communicate with them better than human doctors in text conversations. The system, called the Articulate Medical Intelli- gence Explorer (AMIE)[51], was trained on medical texts including transcripts of about 100,000 doctor-patient dialogues, on 65 rias- suns written by doctors in an intensive care unit, and on questions from the U.S. medical licensing exam. Nono- st this amount of data, AMIE has gaps so the stu- dents simulated a diagnostic environment to allow him to im- parate from his mistakes by means of two rounds of "self-play." In the test to which he was subjected to see how well he was living up to the doctors'

---

[51] T. Tu, A. Palepu, M. Schaekermann, et al, *Towards Conversational Diagnostic AI*, in "ArXiv," (2024), 2401.05654.

humans, the patients did not know whether they were interacting with a machine or a human, and the results were surprising because most of them preferred to chat with AMIE since the chatbot was writing longer responses, which was interpreted as showing that it was more capable of being empathetic and able to understand their concerns. This should not come as much of a surprise to us since these programs can be trained to es- ceive annoying human attitudes such as fatigue or distraction. This does not mean, however, that AI chatbots are better or can replace human physicians, because with the former there is not the rap- port that can be established over time with the latter, which in addition also have access to more information and continuing education.

John Halamka, a U.S. physician and president of the Mayo Clinic Platform, is pursuing an ambitious project: to aggregate human and expert data from leading international medical centers, filter it through specialized artificial intelligence algorithms, and distribute care to patients around the world. It began in January 2020 to collect data from millions of patients, but recognizes that to date this is not enough to democratize AI technology for everyone. Its goal is to collect the data of four billion people through the use of global medical algorithms. When analyzed by artificial intel- ligence, this huge amount of data reveals more than human experts can ever see. Halamka believes, however, that the role of the physician remains critical, but each can now have virtual specialists at their fingertips, thanks to the revi- sion of cases by AI.

Chemist Marco De Vivo is one of several scholars who testimo- nize how the use of AI is simplifying his work. In an intervi- s i o n w i t h **La Repubblica**, he told how, after years of studying abroad, he returned to Italy to found two startups, one to treat cancer and the other for neurodevelopmental disorders. Specifically, he is

uses computational science to understand the biolo- gical and biochemical processes underlying disease. In this context, AI allows him to do experiments and tests, focusing only on those that would be successful after simulating them on a computer, thus saving time and money. De Vivo argues that we now have a large amount of data of a certain quality and unimaginable computing power for the human mind to handle this data, and so it is time to use machine learning. AI is able to explore combinations between molecules, navigating the chi- mical space at a speed unthinkable for humans. When it finds a solution to a problem, the researcher can verify it. However, De Vivo con- cord that AI can support but not replace human input: it takes human creativity and ingenuity to select quality data before using it in computational models.

There are, on the other hand, cases where there is a controversial use o f AI in the

health sector, such as the one implemented by UnitedHealthcare, the largest health insurance company in the United States. It is accused of using since November 2019 an arti- ficial intelligence algorithm, known as nH Predict, which is alleged to be seriously flawed because it ignores medical assessments of professionals and unduly denies essential health coverage to some elderly patients. The disputed use of this algorithm allegedly led to the premature expulsion of patients from rehabilitation programs and nursing facilities, forcing them to exhaust their savings to obtain necessary care, theoretically covered by their government-funded Medicare Ad- vantage plan. The company's focus has shifted from patient advocacy to performance metrics and keeping post-acute care as short and streamlined as possible. The United States is not new to cases like these of problematic use of AI, such as the creation of algorithmic racial biases in patient care.

However, there are many fields in which AI can make significant contributions, starting with clinical practice in areas such as radiolo- jy, cardiology, emergency medicine, surgery, medical risk and disease prediction, home-based interventions, and mental health. Regarding the latter, there are chatbots such as Earkick and Woebot that can respond with some empathy to certain problems, offering suggestions or asking probing questions to sup- port mental well-being. So artificial intelligence could actually emulate the experience of talking to a human therapist, as ELIZA, the first chatbot to simulate a conversation with a therapist, has done.

However, currently machine learning models in me- dia practice do not have enough information to optimally predict individual clinical outcomes. Therefore, it is necessary to at- temptingly consider the amount and type of data included to avoid possible fals- liations by incorporating each pa- tient's personalized information, using medical data sources, and including valid measures at the individual level. This issue is even more pronounced in psychiatry mo- ders designed to predict binary outcomes for mental disorders, but with still questionable reliability. Therefore, the goal is to implement machine learning models in psychiatry in order to improve their accuracy and clinical applicability.

Around the world, there is evidence of the undeniable potential that AI can bring to the health care system, improving people's health and well-being. In the United Kingdom, for example, an in- novative AI tool is in use that reveals heart disease in just 20 se- condi- tions during an MRI scan, compared with the 13 minutes it takes for a doctor to scan. In the United States, the Centers for Disease Con- trol and Prevention uses an AI tool to monitor and report polio virus, distinguishing between different types of viruses and improving the efficiency of the surveillance process. In

The opportunities

Australia, they constantly monitor patients' symptoms in hospitals to predict outbreaks of emerging diseases, adjusting health policies accordingly.

In Belgium, a remote sign language interpreting service is available for the deaf to enable them to communicate with hearing individuals and vice versa. In Denmark, an AI-based solution assesses prostate cancer risk, preventing inu- tile interventions for patients. In Finland, through AuroraAI, surveys have been conducted on students, revealing that aspects such as the reliability of public tra- ditions and the quality of the natural environment are crucial to their well-being.

Through the use of magnetoencephalography (MEG), an advanced neuroimaging technique, Meta presented an artificial intelli- gence system capable of decoding visual representations in the brain in real time. This system, consisting of an image encoder, a brain encoder, and an image decoder, aims to understand how images are represented in the brain, paving the way for future noninvasive brain-computer interfaces useful for those who have lost the ability to speak as a result of brain injury.

Being the result of combinations and integrations of objects, shapes and colors in different ways, images generated through generative artificial intelligence algorithms can overcome the limits of traditional visual representations and challenge conso- lidated patterns of thought, opening the way to new scenarios and possibilities for interpretation. Thus, text-to-text and text-to-image generative platforms can help us in conceptualization processes to attribute new meaning to things.

With increased investment in FemTech[52], health care is also marking a potential turning point in the care

---

[52] http://s24ore.it/mcc18

of women, who are vital components of the health care system. In the United States, for example, they represent more than 50 percent of the population and influence 80 percent of consumer health decisions, spending more than $500 billion annually on health care. Despite their dominant role, modern medicine has long neglected their most common needs, sometimes considered taboos, such as menstrual hygiene and menopausal treatment. Women have also been systematically excluded from studies and research, comporting late diagnoses and significant errors. However, there has been a significant increase in investment in the FemTech sector, addi- rting 197% by 2023. Advanced technologies, including machine learning and devices specifically designed for women, are paving the way for an unprecedented revolution in the perception and administration of their care. By overcoming taboos related to their health and benefiting from increased financial support, women's access to health care services can be regi- reated significantly.

3.4 In finance

In the finance industry, AI is creating a variety of new profes- sions and roles, including data analysts, financial consultants, algorithmic experts, and scientific researchers. Data analysts are responsible for analyzing information from internal and external sources to identify strategic opportunities for investors. Financial advisors help individuals achieve their financial goals through financial planning and investment counseling. Algorithm experts are developing AI systems that can make automated decisions about financial fund allocation. Finally, researchers are applying artificial intelligence to fi- nance with predictive models to stimulate investment growth and innovate wealth management practices.

The opportunities

Artificial intelligence can transform the way people in- teract with money, simplifying and optimizing processes ranging from credit decisions to quantitative trading and financial risk management. There are five main areas where it can inter- come: personalization of services and products, op- portunity creation, risk and fraud management, transparency and compliance, automation of operations, and cost reduction.

Financial institutions benefit from the implementation of AI by accelerating traditionally manual and time-consuming activities such as market research. By quickly analyzing large volumes of data, trends can be identified and future pre-stations can be predicted, making it easier for investors to monitor investment cre- quency and assess risk. AI can also be used to automate various online banking activities such as payments, deposits, withdrawals and transfers, as well as customer service, and to manage real-time processes such as credit card and loan applications. It also finds application in the insurance industry, where it is used to collect and use personal data to deter- mine coverage and premiums.

There are many tools available to AI to improve financial ser- vices, such as translation and speech recognition, sentiment and emotional opinion analysis, anomaly detection such as fraudulent transactions, investment advice or banking offers based on customer journeys, document processing, predictive modeling, and more.

Many companies in the financial sector already use AI. For example, Chicago-based Enova provides advanced financial analytics and credit va- luation to solve real customer problems such as sudden expenses and bank loans for small businesses. Ocrolus of New York offers document processing software that combines machine learning and human verification to increase speed and accuracy in analyzing financial documents. Boston's Data-Robot helps financial institutions and companies create accurate predictive models that inform decisions on issues such as fraudulent credit card transa- tions, digital wealth management, direct marketing, blockchain, lending, and more.

3.5 In agriculture

The increase in the world's population, expected to reach 10 mi- li billion by 2050[53], is putting a strain on the agricultural sector. En-trough that year, it is estimated that there will be only 4 percent more arable land, while food production will have to increase by 60 percent to soddi- sfy the needs of an additional two billion people. There is an urgent need to address issues such as the use of harmful pesticides, controlled irrigation, and the control of pollution and environmental effects in agricultural practices. However, traditional methods are no longer sufficient to ge- strate these issues and the growing demand for food. Therefore, farmers and agribusinesses are forced to find new me- tures to increase production while reducing waste.

Agriculture is slowly going digital with artificial intelligence emerging in three main categories: soil and crop monitoring, predictive analytics, and agricultural robotics. The modern pae-sage is increasingly evolving to address challenges such as land scarcity, labor shortages, climate change, and declining soil fertility. Farmers are increasingly using sensors and soil sampling to collect data, stored in farm management systems for better processing and analysis. AI is critical to address pre- dictive analysis, which allows large amounts of data to be collected and processed in a shorter time frame, providing detailed information on the process of

---

[53] http://s24ore.it/mcc44

The opportunities

cultivation. Benefits include decisions based on more ac- curated data, cost savings through production optimization, and automation of processes such as irrigation and harvesting.

Despite the benefits, there are several impediments to the adoption of AI in agriculture, such as high initial costs, resistance to inno- vation, and lack of adequate infrastructure. However, AI is fon- damental to the future of agriculture because it can offer solutions for safer and more sustainable food production. It can assist in planning activities such as land mapping and crop forecasting, making it easier to select the most resilient and weather-appropriate crops. AI can monitor weather conditions, plant health and various other environmental parameters essential to agricultural production, while also helping to identify weeds and suggest effective methods of pest control.

Many companies are already using intelligent robots to improve agricultural efficiency, such as autonomous strawberry-picking machines and vacuum devices to pick ripe apples from al- beri. These machines use the fusion of sensors, artifi- cial vision and artificial intelligence models to identify the location of produce and pick the right ones. After defense, agriculture is the second largest sector for use of robots for professional use: se- cording to the International Federation of Robotics as many as 25,000 agricultural robots were sold in 2020, a number equal to that used for military purposes.

To effectively implement AI in agriculture, qualified IT professionals, mechanical and electrical engineers, as well as people with specific skills in food quality and crafts traditionally related to agriculture will be needed.

3.6 In transportation

Efficiency in traffic, transportation, and logi- stic planning is crucial to ensuring optimal resource management and re- during accidents and environmental pollution. Artificial intelligence (AI) has proven to be a valuable ally in this context, using data from various sources to predict different situations and optimize road routes, manage traffic more efficiently, and improve safety.

AI provides foundations for optimizing road routes, managing traffic more efficiently, and improving safety, so much so that the International Association of Public Transport reports that 86 percent of industry ope- rators are involved in partnerships to develop AI-based technology projects. For example, network connectivity allows drivers to receive real-time information about traffic and weather conditions, enabling them to make more informed decisions about how to approach certain road routes. In addition, analyzing data from sensors and cameras enables ge- stration of traffic lights and smart signage, making roads more ef- ficient and safe.

Self-driving vehicles, intelligent driving assistants, and advanced technologies such as pedestrian detection are already helping to improve road safety by reducing human error, which is the leading cause of car accidents (nearly 90 percent) in Europe. In addition, AI can improve parking management through sensors and automatic license plate recognition, enabling real-time location and updating of di- sponential spaces.

In the logistics and transportation sector, AI has revolutionized inventory and warehouse management. Warehouse robots perform routine tasks efficiently and error-free, while machine learning algo- rithms enable maintenance predictive vehicles, reducing the risk of sudden failures and increasing operational efficiency.

In addition, AI technologies can optimize planning processes for vehicle fleet managers, reducing the risk of human inci- dent or error and providing more personalized service to customers. To fully exploit the potential of AI in transportation, it will be ne- cessary to hire professionals who specialize in machine learning and artificial intelligence to design and implement more efficient fleet management si- stems.

3.7 In scientific research

Artificial intelligence is revolutionizing the scientific landscape at every stage of research, supporting scientists through large-scale data processing, prediction, and automation of complex com- ponents in solving global challenges such as climate change and antimicrobial resistance. As we know, AI represents an incredible tool for processing and analyzing huge amounts of data. The speed at which these are processed and analyzed reaches levels unthinkable manually, enabling acce- larly research in fields such as genetics, physics, and chemistry and opening up new perspectives and possibilities. However, despite this capability, researchers' critical judgment and interpretation remain irreplaceable.

In the medical field, AI is advancing diagnostics, drug discovery, and understanding of the human brain. Conte- stually, new advanced programs, the implementation of digital ge- mels, brain-type AI, and the exploration of nu- clear fusion to achieve sustainable energy without carbon emissions are just a few of the fascinating opportunities to enhance scientific re- search. Although the use o f AI currently amplifies the capabilities of researchers without replacing them, there is a future in which it could become an autonomous scientific force. This evolu- tion could radically reshape scientific processes and redefine the traditional role of scientists, paving the way for significant new possibilities and discoveries.

AI is also supportive in scientific publication, facilitating literature review, data analysis, and scientific article writing. Thanks to its contribution, there has been a significant improvement in both the quality and efficiency of scientific communication. It also fosters collaboration among researchers from different disciplines, analyzing and synthesizing data from di- verse fields to arrive at new insights and discoveries, introducing new research methodologies and tools, and enabling scientists to explore hypotheses that were previously out of their reach.

In the analysis of academic literature, the use of artificial intelligence would simplify the organization of information, helping to avoid plagiarism and supporting the creation of articles, especially for non-English-speaking researchers, not to mention other van- vantages such as saving time, increasing efficiency, and estimating critical thinking. However, these facilities can- be achieved as long as proper integration with human capacities and informed research is maintained, so it is essential for researchers to be active in writing and ethical practices.

The increasing volume of scientific publications puts a strain on the **peer review** workflow. One solution to this problem- tic would be to simplify the initial screening of papers, thereby reducing time spent and improving academic productivity. Some platforms already use automated screening tools to pre- come plagiarism and format errors, and some of them try to assess the quality of the study or summarize its content to lighten the reviewers' load. Review systems can be developed semi-automatic parity, potentially flagging low-quality or controversial studies and facilitating reviewer-document correspondence.

Anna Studman, a senior researcher at the Ada Lovelace Institute, researched this issue by exploring the impact of artificial intelligence-based systems in health care. After interviewing individuals living in poverty or with chronic conditions, she found that "the nuances of lived experience do not emerge from clinical data," in Studman's words. Lack of trust in health care systems and institutions is parti- cularly evident in marginalized populations. For this reason, Studman emphasized the importance of transparency in the process. "Explaining to people why and how data will be shared and used is important, especially for those who feel excluded from digital technology or who perceive innovations in digi- tal health care as imposed," she said. The researcher points out that AI-based research tools dedicated to reading, annotation, and note-taking can make the process of acquiring co- n knowledge more efficient by providing relevant excerpts of biblio- graphic sources and facilitating the evaluation of an article's usefulness.

In materials science and other related disciplines, AI can improve predictive analysis, for example, on the properties of new materials or compounds, greatly reducing the time and cost asso- ciated with traditional experimentation and facilitating the development of new discoveries.

Finally, despite the successes of AI in science, there are mixed views. Erik Larson, for example, criticizes this view, arguing that examples of successful AI in science are limited and do not live up to expectations. To support his reasons, he cites the example of the 2019 discovery by MIT scientists of two antibiotics, alicin and abaucin, through the use of an AI model. Although he acknowledges the value of antibiotics in combating resistant bacteria, he points out that this finding does not confirm the enthusiastic claims of AI advocates such as De- mis Hassabis of DeepMind, who speak of a possible "renaissance of discovery" thanks to AI. According to Larson, the basic scientifi- c knowledge about antibiotics and cell biology was already there, which casts doubt on the actual revolutionary contribution of AI in this specific context.

There are many specialized professionals who contribute to scientific research and innovation. AI and ML researchers are involved in the development and optimization of machine learning algorithms and models, which find application in various scientific fields. Data scientists and data analysts are experts in analyzing and inter- preting large amounts of data, using advanced AI-based tools and techniques. Developers of AI tools for research create AI platforms and tools to assist researchers in data management and analysis. Experts in bioinformatics and computational genomics use AI to analyze genetic and biological data, contributing to important discoveries in medicine and biology. Specialists in AI ethics and go- vernance deal with the ethical implications and regulations ri- guarding the use of artificial intelligence in scientific research. In- fine, researchers in applied AI work in specific areas such as the am- environment, energy, and pharmaceuticals to find innovative solutions to complex problems.

3.8 In education

To introduce this paragraph, I ask you a point-blank question: in the age of ChatGPT does it still make sense for students to learn to write and especially to write well? Fortunately, many of them agree on the importance of this practice and that AI is not able to express itself clearly and originally. More importantly, its indiscriminate use does not allow them to be self-sufficient, to think on their own, to develop creativity, critical thinking, and problem-solving skills However, AI remains a valuable con- fusion tool to help students improve their expression and develop new and different writing styles, as long as it is used consciously and not a substitute for their creativity and au- tonous thinking.

In education, artificial intelligence is becoming increasingly essential in every classroom, moving from being an inno- vative idea to an indispensable element. One of the major revolutions is personalized learning, where algorithms adapt content according to the needs and learning pace of each student, ensuring personalized support and responding to different learning styles. AI does not replace teachers, but enhances them, allowing them to focus more on actual teaching and reducing the burden of administrative and bureaucratic tasks that can be automated.

In addition, AI is transforming the approach to teaching and understanding subjects by making complex concepts more accessible through AI-driven simulations and visualizations. This not only makes learning more engaging, but also helps reduce the complexity of some subjects. Language teaching has benefited from these innovations, making the acquisition of a new language more accessible and efficient.

Education, and particularly higher education, alone can no longer keep up with the accelerating pace of technological innovation. More and more skill-based, industry-driven education programs, more oriented toward spe- cialized pathways, are, in fact, emerging. In short, the idea that a university degree is a

Cyberhumanism

essential prerequisite for accessing the best job opportunities, especially in technology, is beginning to falter. Rising education costs are prompting many students to question the value of a traditional college education, considering more practical alternatives. On the other hand, businesses still need to train new hires on the job. This shift has been underway for several years, with companies such as Cour- sera, originally focused on consumers, now partnering with businesses to expand com- petence retraining programs. Amazon's announcement that it has trained 21 million people in technical skills, thanks to pro- grams such as the Mechatronics and Robotics Apprenticeship and the AWS Cloud Institute, which enable workers to acquire the compe- tences required at different stages of their careers without the commitment to long-term programs, also goes in this direction. I should point out, however, that this con- cept is not entirely new: thinking of skilled workers such as electricians, welders, and carpenters, most of their compe- tences do not come from university classrooms, but from practice in the field. Adopting this style of education, based on conti- nuous learning and curiosity, is an advantage for both individuals and businesses. By this I am not saying that traditional degrees are going to disappear, but in some areas the impact of technology will make new educational opportunities in- dispensable.

To regulate all the implications and uses of AI in this sector, the European Union has launched the Digital Education Action Plan (2021-2027), which has two priorities: the first is to promote the development of a digital education system through the use of digital infra- struc- tures, connectivity and equipment; the second is to improve the acquisition of digital skills and capabilities from an early age and to enhance student potential. AI systems are now being deployed in every classroom to assist the practices of

The opportunities

teaching, assessment and learning. These can be divided into three categories, namely those aimed at the student, teachers and the system.

Student-supportive AI systems involve the creation of exploratory learning environments, assessment of formative writing, and collaborative learning with the help of AI, for example through student screens to guide the student through the learning journey.

Supporting teachers are assessment of reflective writing with grading of essays using automated tools and the use of adaptive learning technologies that can adapt to each student's abilities; monitoring student forum to offer personalized interventions for special esigencies; teaching assistants such as chatbots or AI agents, who can also guide parents in dealing with administrative paperwork; and recommendation of pedagogical resources.

In support of the system, on the other hand, we have the extraction of education data for the purpose of allocation and planning of resources, diagnosis of learning difficulties, and guidance services. Obviously, the ethical use of AI and data cannot disregard human intervention and oversight, the role of the teacher is fundamental and irreplaceable; then it must be accessible to all by guaranteeing diversity, not discrimination or equity because every student has different educational needs; it must also ensure social and environmental wellbeing, as well as accountability, confidentiality and governance, technical robustness, and security to ensure the anonymity of sensitive data.

Matthew Lynch, an assertor of the benefits of AI in education, mainly for personalized learning and tutoring, automated assessment, and the use of feedback on course quality and student achievement, however, stresses the need to es- pect vigilance about ethical risks and to monitor the overall development of this technology[54]. Emily Bender and other scholars also highlight in a paper[55] the negative impacts of large language models, pointing out the lack of transparency, high costs, and risk of perpetuating human bias. The authors call for transpa- rence on the use of energy, costs, and data used, warning that marginalized groups will suffer these costs the most, and propose inclusive participation in development and the need for plans to mitigate harm, especially in beneficial applications such as speech recognition for disadvantaged groups. Hwang and Chen[56] also explore the potential benefits of generative AI in education, del- erating the different roles that language models such as ChatGPT could assume, from learner to expert. However, they express preoc- cupation about a possible over-reliance of students on AI, encouraging educators to guide its critical and reflective use, suggesting further research on the impact of generative AI in learning outcomes.

Chatbots for student assistance are widely used in higher education institutions, providing immediate responses to do- ments, connecting students to course information and services, and offering general support. There are also in- telligent tutoring systems, dedicated to specific subjects such as math or languages, that simulate the experience of working with a human tutor, providing one-on-one support through applications such as Duolingo, which uses AI for flexible language lessons, monitoring student progress and adapting course content as needed, or the

---

[54] http://s24ore.it/mcc68
[55] E.M. Bender, T. Gebru, A. McMillan-Major, et al, *On the Dangers of Stochastic Parrots: Can Language Models Be Too Big?*, in "FAccT '21: Proceedings of the 2021 ACM Conference on Fairness, Accountability, and Transparency," (March 2021), pp. 610-623.
[56] G.-J. Hwang, N.-S. Chen, *Exploring the Potential of Generative Artificial Intel- ligence in Education: Applications, Challenges, and Future Research Directions*, in "Educational Technology & Society," no. 2 (2023) 26.

The opportunities

Khan Academy's Khanmigo tutoring system. Known a little bit by everyone are Google applications such as Classroom that by means of AI offers personalized recommendations, automatic assessments and analysis of student data, or Google Scholar and Google Translate that enhance learning and support research. Not to mention AI-based educational games that offer mi- rated learning through programming that adapts to the user's needs. Adaptive learning platforms, such as those provided by the companies Carnegie Learning and Knewton, personalize at- tivities and learning content in real time, using meto- dologies ranging from predefined rules to complex automatic ap- plication algorithms.

AI offers tools that enable personalization of the learning per- course even for students with disabilities, enabling them to communicate with teachers through gestures, drawings, and other natural forms, thereby adapting teaching resources and materials to their individual needs and ways of learning. Take for example speech-to-text and text-to-speech technologies, which also represent vital support for students with problems in ap- prehension. In addition, AI-based analytics are invaluable in iden- tifying students at risk of falling behind, enabling early intervention. The use of AI in education is not only limited to improving the learning process in an intelligent way, but also contributes to making education more inclusive. In addition, it provides new opportunities for conti- nuous teacher training, through online learning platforms and up-to-date resources on the latest teaching techniques and technology, so that they can more effectively analyze student data, identifying areas for improvement and success.

Artificial intelligence is paving the way for new profes- sional figures in the educational sector as well, such as content developers educators, educational data analysts and specialists in designing AI-assisted learning experiences.

3.9 In the energy

The advent of artificial intelligence is revolutionizing the landscape of the energy sector, transforming the processes of energy generation, distri- bution, and consumption. From the management of smart grids to the prediction of renewable energy sources to the safety of nuclear power plants, AI is making profound changes in the operation of the energy sector, propelling it toward a future carried by greater efficiency, sustainability, and security.

Globally, the need to adopt clean and sustainable energy sources is now clear, however, the transition presents challenges in designing and integrating these sources into the existing electricity grid. This is where artificial intelligence comes in, which is changing the way we examine and predict energy demand. By analyzing thousands of constantly changing variables, such as weather mo- ders and historical usage data, AI enables more accurate predictions of energy demand. This enables energy pro- ducers and utilities to make informed decisions about energy distribution, optimizing expenditures and investments.

The design of clean energy facilities, especially those that take a hybrid approach such as combining so- lare, wind, and storage, requires customization on a si- sma- scale that varies from grid to grid. This is where artificial intelligence-based tools come in, which combined with human ingenuity and experience, enable rapid optimization of any project to integrate these complex hybrid systems into the power grid. This is done b y examining millions of configurations and possible scenarios, selecting the best solution in a very short time. AI-based grid management systems, using historical data and real-time information from a variety of sources, can anticipate energy consumption and adjust power generation and distribution in real time. This approach ensures a stable energy supply, minimizing dependence on unsustainable energy sources and facilitating smart grid management for electricity supply and enabling utilities to predict consumption patterns to optimize distribution.

In our homes, AI helps create highly efficient energy ecosystems. The collaboration between smart meters, IoT devices, and AI enables continuous monitoring of energy consumption in real time, facilitating data-driven decisions to optimize energy use. A tangible example is the application of AI in the automatic management of heating and cooling systems, considering variables such as user preferences and weather conditions, reducing energy waste and improving overall comfort.

In addition, AI can identify potential oil and gas reserves, mi- ing safety and efficiency and increasing success in exploration and drilling at- tivities. In nuclear power plants, AI constantly monitors operations and uses advanced predictive manu- tention models to ensure high safety standards.

Also in the renewable energy sector, the implementation of AI applications can yield benefits for predictive maintenance of wind turbines or solar panels as well as for the efficiency of distri- bution and trading of the energy produced.

In the energy sector, too, the implementation of AI is thus creating a wide range of new jobs for professionals, such as in- gers specializing in the development and management of renewable energy, specialized energy data analysts who use smart algorithms to monitor customer data, and engineers for preventive maintenance of energy infrastructure.

3.10 In communication and marketing

Artificial intelligence is revolutionizing the marketing industry, enabling an unprecedented level of personalization. Large companies are already leveraging AI to improve the efficiency and effectiveness of their marketing campaigns, and are expected to generate 30 percent of these through AI by 2025, up from 2 percent in 2022. They are successfully experimenting with implementing use cases such as campaign personalization, unstructured customer data analysis, process automation, opportunity identification and idea generation.

To maximize the benefits, however, they must take a three-tiered approach: start with pre-packaged generative AI pilots, then develop customized solutions, and finally pursue full generative AI-based marketing transformation. Building a road map, assembling a dedicated team, and achieving rapid results through prioritized use cases are crucial steps in this transition.

The growing adoption of artificial intelligence in the mar- keting industry can be implemented in several areas. It can create personalized conte- tents, identifying relevant topics and drafting blogs tailored to specific audiences, improving engagement and con- nection with users. It also optimizes social media presence, generating high-quality content in accordance with the mar- keting style, thereby improvinginteraction with the target audience.

In the specific field of advertising, it deals with the creation of targeted messages for display, search, video and carousel ads, tailoring them to specific locations and audience segments, improving

The opportunities

effectiveness of advertising campaigns. It is capable of generating imma- gines, audio and video with simple commands, providing ample room for creativity and ensuring a greater variety of formats to engage a wider audience, simplifying the creative process for marketers. By analyzing the trends of target audiences, AI ge- blacks relevant content, saving time for creatives and ensuring responsiveness to audience needs. It also produces a wide range of formats, including text, images, audio, and video, to capture the attention of diverse audiences and satisfy consumer preferences. It also contributes to account-based marketing (ABM), analyzing customer questions to provide auto-mathematical answers and highly personalized content, and supports the creation of targeted messages and effective advertising, integrating with data-driven marketing strategies to improve the relevance of campaigns.

As can be seen, the AI is radically transforming the mode to plan, create, and deploy marketing campaigns, com- munication, and the way marketing is done, facilitating predictive analytics, personalization, the use of chatbots and virtual assistants, and the optimization of advertising. Even in public relations, it contributes to improved personalized communication and crisis management by identifying potential problems in real time.

Imagine a world in which marketers operate without creative constraints, coming up with personalized offers at the right time and communicating cohesively rather than disjointedly. A world in which the effi- ciency resulting from automation and automated content generation is combined with greater customer insight. The goal is a universe in which customers save time and effort in finding the goods and services they want, and marketers focus on in- novating and delivering value to products.

Although AI can play a significant role in achieving these results, its lack of human touch, creativity, intuition and emotional connection will make a complete replacement of humans unlikely even in the communications sector. It will merely complement and enhance human work, enabling marketers to create more personalized and effective campaigns with the support of enhanced tools such as ChatGPT, Canva, Synthesys, Synthesia.io, and copy.ai. There are also a number of issues and challenges that companies must be prepared to address, such as complete integration with pre-existing business systems, the need to ensure data privacy and security, and the difficulty of interpreting complex results that do not facilitate the judicious implementation of AI into business processes.

3.12 In film and television

The film industry is well known for its continuous quest for technological innovation in creating engaging stories and films. Recently, artificial intelligence has opened new vistas in this regard, integrating seamlessly into filmmaking and TV show- ing and finding application in various aspects ranging from pre to post-production.

In the pre-production phase, for example, AI algorithms analyze scripts, predicting market trends and generating stories based on audience trends and preferences. This supports filmmakers in making more calibrated decisions and increases the likelihood of success of any film or television production.

During the production process, AI-based tools come to the aid of humans in managing cameras, lighting, and directing virtual actors. AI-controlled drones and cameras capture, in fact, the most complex or risky shots, while AI-based lighting systems create the most captivating. In post-production, AI speeds up the editing phase by sem- plifying the selection of footage and choosing the most suitable visual and animation effects.

What if a film is entirely generated by AI, from script to final edit? This raises many concerns about employment in the industry, as evidenced by recent strikes, but it also offers room for new ideas and experimental narratives, becoming a source of inspiration for directors and producers.

However, the usual issues related to creativity and originality also arise in the film industry. Algorithms may have difficulty producing truly innovative ideas or authentic emotions, so the human touch must remain essential in the art of storytelling. Then the ethical implications require careful consideration, to ensure that films respect social norms and avoid harmful stereotypes.

AI has also found a place in film marketing to create more effective campaigns; for example, it can predict the success of a film and personalize user experiences on streaming platforms such as Netflix. It can also serve to simplify the synchronization of subtitles.

AI thus revolutionizes the film industry, because the films thus generated act as catalysts for innovation, opening up new possibilities for experimentation and enriching film-graphic experiences with a combination of artificial intelligence and human creativity.

Despite these advantages, the future of cinema does not see AI as a substitute, but always as a collaborator with human creativity. Between AI and film and entertainment workers, a harmonious collaboration is always hoped for, one that can increase efficiency, convenience, and experimentation with new ideas, promising a more inclusive and diverse set- tore.

But the latest petitions launched in Los Angeles and the union agreement entered into with the Screen Actors Guild - American Federation of Televi- sion and Radio Artists to regulate the impact of AI on the film industry undoubtedly show us that this is a source of concern for all entertainment workers.

Every major technological advancement brings with it the possibility of replacing some jobs with the most advanced automation, and despite promises to limit the use of AI-generated content, significant change is expected in the working future of artists. In fact, researchers at IBM have speculated that more than 1.4 billion jobs will be impacted by AI, with 40-50% of workers having to acquire new job skills in the next three years. Goldman Sachs even predicts the loss of more than 300 mi- lion jobs due to AI.

Generative AI, like ChatGPT, is a technology that is surely affecting the field of writing and journalism as well, fueling serious concerns about job losses and significant changes in the field. So all that is left for writers to do is to prepare for this inevitable evolution, learning how to handle AI and harness its content, and seeking closer harmonization between human and machine. However, I hope that AI will complement their work, automating some tasks and improving productivity, rather than replacing them completely.

There is no doubt that the job landscape will change in the entertainment industry as well, but workers who adapt and per- feect their creative skills will remain valuable in the industry. My advice is always to stay informed about market trends and the evolving role that AI will gradually acquire in content creation.

These have been intense months, in which we have all explored the many possibilities of the application of technology and its impact

The opportunities

on various sectors, including the television industry. There was also a focus on the positive aspects in the area of advertising. Industry experts point to the potential of AI in improving effectiveness in this area as well through optimizing advertising campaigns and increasing conversion rates. In short, viewers are being made to establish an interactive and perso- nalized experience with advertising.

Others highlight how AI can increase efficiency by allowing humans to focus on more strategic and crea- tive aspects. With the growing opportunities for AVOD, FAST, and live strea- ming advertising, we will achieve greater monetization through the ability to predict availability more accurately and optimize CPMs in real time based on those predictions.

There is, of course, also the possibility of using generative artifi- cial intelligence to support the creative process. In fact, the main use cases for tools such as ChatGPT or Dall-E are copywriting, data analysis, market research, and image generation. Large companies are harnessing the power of AI and ML to help their advertisers take action more efficiently and get better results for their business. Samsung Ads, for example, has developed an AI-powered product called Smart Audien- ces, designed to simplify the creation of highly targeted campaigns based on data about customer behavior and preferences. By using AI to identify and reach audiences most likely to convert, it can help advertisers drive engagement, improve conversion rates, and ultimately increase revenue.

In the context of programmatic bidding, AI increases the speed and effectiveness of synthesizing complex data to improve pre- views. Its ability to sift through huge amounts of historical and contextual data in lightning-fast time allows it to assess audience dispo-

Cyberhumanism

nable and to predict purchasing decisions by targeting ads. In short, it enables precise targeting and measurement.

Ultimately, I believe that the use of technologies such as ChatGPT will improve the advertising experience and play a crucial role in the per- sonalization of ads, the creation of appealing content to achieve programmatic purchases, and the optimization of advertising campaigns based on the analysis of historical data in the decision-making pro- cess.

3.12 In the environment

Artificial intelligence is emerging as a key tool for addressing environmental challenges and guiding us toward a sustainable future, also revolutionizing the meteorological field and bringing significant benefits. According to the World Meteorological Organization (WMO), advanced processing of huge volumes of data improves climate change modeling and prediction, facilitating more effective adaptation and mitigation strategies. AI-driven projects in vulnerable regions such as Burundi, Chad, and Sudan analyze past environmental disruptions to provide fu- ture projections. For example, apps such as MyAnga, based on weather data, help pastoralists cope with drought in Kenya, enabling early and efficient livestock management.

AI climate disaster prediction identifies areas at risk and fuels local and national response plans. Mapping fragile areas, such as those affected by landslides, plans for sustainable development and increases the safety of affected communities.

Professor Sheshadri of Stanford University highlighted the uncertainties of climate projections and the limitations of current climatics models. Through a study of atmospheric gravitational waves, which play a significant role on Earth's climate, has demonstrated their difficulty in modeling due to their multiscale nature. It proposes two approaches to improve wave modeling: the use of neural networks such as WaveNet to replace traditional parameterizations and the incorporation of AI to quantify uncertainty while maintaining the physical representation. The goal is to calibrate and quan- tify uncertainties in the parameters governing atmospheric gravitational wave processes.

At a time when it is crucial to prevent global warming from reaching dangerous levels, AI algorithms play a key role in minimizing the environmental impact of pollution and carbon emissions. To achieve the global goal of clean and affordable energy for all by 2030 (SDG 7), AI can optimize networks and increase the efficiency of renewable sources by predicting energy use patterns and optimizing energy consumption. It can also indivi- duate areas of energy waste and suggest ways to reduce it.

In waste management, AI can analyze data on generation, collection, and disposal, helping institutions optimize their waste management systems, reduce waste, and increase recycling rates. Waste Robotics uses AI-based robots to sort and separate recyclables from waste streams, improving recycling effi- ciency and reducing landfill waste.

It can also help in water resource management by studying data on water use, quality, and availability to better manage resources, reduce waste, and improve water quality. Ocean Cleanup, for example, uses AI-based systems to track and collect plastic waste in the ocean, contributing to efforts to clean up marine environments.

In biodiversity conservation, AI can help manage conservation strategies and improve understanding of the com- plete relationships between different species and their environments. Conservation

International uses AI employing advanced algorithms to analyze biodiversity data and monitor changes in ecosi- tions, contributing to the conservation and protection of critical natural habitats. The United Nations is moving to harness the potential of AI in solving various issues[57]. This is reflected in the 2023 United Nations Climate Change Conference, which concluded the first global review of mon- dial efforts to address climate change under the Paris Agreement. This legally binding international treaty aims to limit temperature rise to 1.5°C above prein- dustrial levels. Countries have responded with a clear decision on how to ac- celerate climate action by 2030, marking the beginning of the end of fossil fuels and intensifying the transition to renew- able energies such as solar and wind.

Companies are also required to consider environmental impacts of generative AI and adopt strategies to mini- mize resource consumption during development and implementation. To maximize the positive net impact of generative AI and minimize the environmental impact, it is critical to adopt a careful and responsible ap- proach. Specific actions a company can take include building on existing models rather than initiating new training, carefully monitoring energy consumption, and collaborating with research institutes and technology providers to share best practices on sustainability. Investing in research and development to improve energy efficiency and providing ongoing training to teams on the importance of sustainability are other recommended practices.

---

[57] http://s24ore.it/mcc52

3.13 In sports

In the field of sports, artificial intelligence makes si- gnificant contributions in several areas, including injury prevention, assisted coaching, refereeing, scouting, and recruiting. One of the most relevant aspects is injury prevention, which is particularly critical in athletics, with about 2.5 million accidents per year in the United States alone. Numerous sports organizations are adopting AI to assist athletes by analyzing a wide range of data ranging from physical characteristics to environmental conditions du- rantly during competitions. Based on this information, AI develops predictive models to identify injury risks and adopt preventive mi- sure. It also monitors athletes' movements both on and off the field to identify potential hazards, and detects changes in physical acti- vity that could predispose to injury. The AI also recognizes weather and field conditions, thus contributing to enhanced responses by coaches, instructors, and medical perso- nals in emergency situations, enabling tem- pestive interventions to prevent serious injury.

Both professional and amateur athletes benefit from AI in the al- assisted training, identifying weaknesses and strengths in order to de- end personalized nutritional and training plans. With detailed analysis of athletic performance, areas for improvement can be identified and a targeted approach taken in training. In addition, AI provides immediate feedback to athletes, allowing them to make changes to technique instantly and monitor performance such as energy levels, fatigue, and biomechanics.

Closely related to sports is the area of sports betting and fantasy games. From automated decision-making processes to predictive analytics, , AI is revolutionizing bettors' behavior, enabling them to make more targeted and pre- cise decisions. In team competitions such as basketball, volleyball, or soccer, it is

vast amounts of data can be collected by monitoring the movements of the team and individual players through sensors and wearable devices that can also collect data on performance and fitness in real time. Using AI4 Soccer from Inmatica, for example, is one way to leverage this data strategically in decision-making, such as in team manager's choices during an official match.

In fantasy games, AI-based tools such as au- tomatic team selection and lineup optimization greatly simplify the process for players in team competitions and in-depth analysis of performance, it is possible to maximize potential gains and identify players most likely to succeed.

The fan experience can also be revolutionized by AI, for example in Formula 1 where Amazon Web Services (AWS) is of- fering more accurate predictions and more detailed analysis. As an extremely data-centric sport, with more than 300 sensors on each car generating more than 1.1 million data points per second, F1 has recognized the need to fully exploit the potential of AI to improve competitiveness and engage fans. The collaboration between F1 and AWS, which began in 2018, aims to transform and innovate the use of the cloud in the sport by identifying the fans' primary desire: to get even closer to the races. This led to the creation of F1 In- sights, a project run by AWS that is based on au- tomatic learning and makes use of Amazon SageMaker to analyze the data prove- ing from the many sensors on each car, allowing fans to understand in real time the decisions made by drivers and the strategies adopted by teams, all aspects that directly influence the outcome of the race. Prominent among F1 Insights' features is Battle Forecast, which can predict how many laps it will take a driver to pass an opponent, based on historical data sets and the drivers' pace.

Another feature, Predicted Pit Stop Strategy, still uses historical data to calculate race strategies from the very first lap, providing spectators with information about when a driver should make the next pit stop. An additional insight offered by AWS is Hy- brid Energy System, which analyzes how drivers use elec- tric energy. The analysis is done by solving energy bi- launch equations, leveraging the computing power of the AWS cloud. That partnership has had a significant impact on F1, leading to an increase in staff and expansion of the organization's digital footprint. AWS not only provides some calculation power, but has enabled F1 to quickly leverage a wide range of managed services to improve internal operations and fan experience, as well as offload low-value activities due to the robustness of the AWS framework, allowing developers to con- centrate on more advanced projects.

But the focus is not only on increased involvement of fans, in fact AI is already widely employed for activities such as car configuration, development direction and resource management, and race strategy planning. The Cognizant Driver Masterclass testifies to the incidence of the digital revolution in the context of F1 racing, demonstrating how advanced algorithms and artificial intelligence optimize race strategies. The evolution of F1 now sees the collaboration of human skills and sofi- ciated technology, with AI taking a crucial role in analyzing and optimizing performance. The concept of the "co-driver AI" represents a breakthrough, emphasizing the collaboration between human insights and detailed AI ana- lysis, the result of which are rapid and accurate decisions, so- sten- ted by real-time analysis of vast amounts of data generated by the car's sensors. N McLaren is using Splunk, a strategy software that can analyze data generated by cars during races, giving the team an extra level of depth and detail that has contributed to improved performance. Despite such advances, at present AI can only act as a support in decision-making, not deliberate autonomously, as the human element remains fundamental to F1 entertainment. The com- petition between drivers and possible unpredictability should be preserved as the human and unpredictable aspects of the sport are critical to maintaining the spectacular nature of competition. Artificial intelligence could also radically transform surveillance and refereeing in sporting events because of its ability to analyze video footage in real time, detecting violations or infractions that might escape the attention of traditional referees and thus reducing the margin for error. Indeed, with the prospect of an automated system designed to be impartial and consistent, the biases and human errors that sometimes characterize traditional arbitration are eliminated; in fact, some organizations such as the NBA and the Major Leahue Soccer are already experimenting with it.

Finally for the process of player recruitment and selection, AI provides detailed information about the performance and skills of athletes, enabling teams to evaluate players more quickly and efficiently. AI algorithms analyze physical and technical performance, comparing it with that of similar players to identify top talent and facilitate recruiting decisions.

3.14 In cybersecurity

In the ever-evolving context of technology, as cyber threats become more complex, organizations are turning to artificial intelligence as a powerful ally in cybersecurity, capable of providing proactive approaches and adaptive strategies to deal with an increasingly complex threat landscape, from ransomware variants to sophisticated phishing schemes. The

The opportunities

Traditional security, while robust, often struggles to keep up with the speed and changeability of these threats.

AI, with its ability to analyze huge amounts of data, indivi- duate patterns, and make decisions in real time, has become a key element in cybersecurity because it is able to adapt and learn from new threats, enhancing the capabilities of their re- learning and prevention through machine-learning algorithms that analyze network traffic, user behavior, and system logs. These algorithms learn from historical data, identifying patterns of malicious activity and countering cyber mi- natures proactively. AI-based security solutions therefore excel at behavioral analysis and anomaly detection, identifying deviations from the norm that could indicate a potential security problem. This proactive approach enables organizations to detect and respond to mi- natures in real time, enabling rapid decisions and minimizing the impact of cyber attacks. Automated responses result in isolating compromised systems, blocking suspicious at- tivities, and activating security protocols to mitigate the impact of an attack.

AI then contributes to authentication by introducing adaptive mechanisms that analyze user behavior, distinguishing legitimate ones from potential threats. With the migration to cloud-based am- bients, it becomes essential for monitoring activities, re- levating unauthorized access, and ensuring compliance with si- curity policies. Preventing or minimizing infor- matic attacks enables government organizations to monitor network acti- vities and unusual access points, identify potential data vulne- rability, and strengthen access restrictions on critical data. Pos- are also improve the accuracy of intrusion detection systems, simulate cyber attacks in controlled environments to

Cyberhumanism

Identify weaknesses, automate system patches and security agjournments.

A key aspect is the AI's ability to analyze user behavior, network traffic, and system logs. By establishing guidelines based on normal behavior, it detects deviations and issues timely alerts to warn of potential threats, including unauthorized access or malware infections and phishing attempts. It can autonomously block suspicious IP addresses, quarantine infected devices, and trigger incident response procedures. In improving authentication and access control, AI uses biometrics, facial recognition, and behavioral analysis for accurate verification of identities, reducing the risk of unauthorized access.

Prior to its advent, security professionals used signature-based detection tools and systems to identify potential malware threats. These tools compare incoming network traf- fic against a database of known threats or malicious code signatures. Upon detection, the system triggers an alert and suggests blocking or quarantining the threat. But that approach has proven inadequate against new (Zero-Day) or unknown threats. And as cyber attacks become increasingly sophisticated, traditional systems can no longer prevent malicious attivities.

One of the first companies to adopt AI in this area was Goo- gle; in fact, Gmail has used machine learning techniques to filter emails since its launch. IBM's team relied on its Watson cognitive learning platform to implement knowledge consolidation tasks and machine learning-based threat detection.

For Acumen Research and Consulting, a leading Indian market research and consulting firm, the market

The opportunities

global AI-based cybersecurity products will reach the well-known figure of $133.8 billion by 2030. According to Booz Al- len, one of the first strategic consulting firms, common cyber defense struments do not detect intrusions until 200 days.Therefore, the firm has developed a Cyber AI solution that helps governments and businesses manage advanced cyber workflows. Microsoft has developed a tool called Cyber Signals that monitors more than 140 threat groups and 40 national actors in 20 countries, helping share information between different go- vernmental agencies and identify and tag malicious entities.

Cybercriminal organizations have already invested in automated apprehension, automation, and AI to launch large-scale, targeted attactics against businesses and institutions. The nu- mber of threats and the potential for ransomware impacting networks continue to grow. But fortunately, the use of AI in cyberse- curity is virtually infinite. Threat detection and response occurs in near real-time, minimizing the impact of a ransomware attack and alerting the security team to suspicious behavior as soon as possible.

The National Cyber Security Center (NCSC), part of the intel- ligence agency GCHQ, predicts a significant increase in both volume and impact of ransomware attacks in the next two years, fueled by artificial intelligence technologies. Interpol has issued a white paper[58] on crimes in the metaverse, identifying major "metacrimes" including identity theft, grooming, breaching virtual private spaces, radicalization, assault or harassment. The do- cument also lists issues that investigators face, including the spanning of virtual worlds across multiple jurisdictions, lack of standardization and interoperability, and diffi- culty in data mining.

---

[58] http://s24ore.it/mcc50

The rapid increase in cybercrime can be attributed to the decreasing barriers of entry for malicious actors, who have even evolved their business approach by introducing subscription services and starter kits. Add to this the use of broad language patterns such as ChatGPT for writing malicious code. What's more, with the proliferation of advanced attack vectors, including polymorphic malware, scripting, and so-called "li- ving-off-the-land" attacks, it has become increasingly easy for malicious actors to overcome traditional antivirus defenses based on file scanning. To cope with the evolution of malware, approaches based on behavior analysis and detection are being adopted that are quite effective, since all forms of malware must exhibit malicious behavior to achieve their objectives.

Artificial intelligence, if properly trained, has the ability to monitor, detect and respond to such malicious behavior faster than human capabilities. That's why companies in the digital world must be ready to harness it in cybersecurity as well. According to Forbes, 76 percent of them have placed AI and machine learning as a priority in their IT budgets, given the increasing volume of data that analytics requires to identify and mitigate cyber threats. A Blackberry survey reveals that 82 percent of IT decision-makers plan to invest in AI-based cy- bersecurity in the next two years. Connected devices, in particular, are projecting the generation of 79 zettabytes of data by 2025, an impossible amount to analyze manually.

AI can be exploited for malicious purposes, but conversely, it contributes to improving cybersecurity through automating incident response, simplifying threat hunting, and analyzing large amounts of data. It can also offer continuous, real-time monitoring, identify false positives, strengthen the

The opportunities

access control measures and mitigate insider threats. Enterprises need to be aware of the dangers and benefits of AI in cybersecurity, while also considering the ethical implications. If AI can be used as a weapon, at the same time we must recognize its potential in improving cybersecurity, not forgetting that security systems based on it rely on machine learning algorithms that are trained on historical data, an approach that can generate false positives when confronted with unknown threats outside established patterns.

The correlation between artificial intelligence and cybersecurity is more relevant today than ever before. There is a growing demand for professions that can combine their skills in both fields, understanding when and how to integrate AI techniques into security processes. Key figures such as data scientists, analysts, and engineers possess in-depth skills in machine learning data modeling, deep neural networks, natural language, and behavioral analysis, combined with a solid understanding of the fundamentals of cybersecurity.

Nevertheless, the rapid evolution of cyber threats makes it difficult for most organizations to au- tonomically manage the detection and response process. In this context, the importance of Managed Detection and Response (MDR)[59] emerges, or managed incident detection and response services that monitor threats and detect incidents with mitigation and response capabilities. Security operations centers (SOCs) are revolutionizing the delivery of MDR and other managed security services. The im- plementation of these technologies enables SOCs to enhance their MDR capa- cities, operating more efficiently and providing superior resi- tiency in the face of ever-changing cyber threats.

---

[59] http://s24ore.it/mcc05

Cyberhumanism

This also includes the concept of deep learning, an advanced form of machine learning that uses neural networks to mimic the learning process of the human brain. These networks, composed of functional layers, enable machines to continuously learn and improve. Deep neural networks, with more hidden layers, successfully tackle complex problems, offering more accurate solutions such as document synthesis and facial recognition. These can also be used to train machines to detect and identify threats such as malware, and to collect, process, and enrich data on mi- natures from multiple sources within an organization. Pos- sions can also correlate and contextualize such data to create threat profiles, measure indicators, and even discover emer- gent threats, while also enabling proactive threat hunting through advanced analytics and automation to look for hidden or un- known threats in a given environment.

Applied to deep neural networks there is a brand new theory called. of unlearning, which could allow a machine to aband- nate what it has previously acquired, especially if this re- sults dangerous, obsolete or illegal (as in the case of co pyright violations), i.e., to forget the useless in order to focus on the useful. This theory, which is still being tested, takes on particular relevance in the context in which we increasingly rely on systems created by others, without fully knowing what data was used to train them.

It is part of the European project ELIAS (European Lighthouse Ai for Su- stainability)[60] , one of Horizon Europe's most important projects, on the environmental, social, and individual sustainability of AI. The section on indivi- duo is led by Prof. Rita Cucchiara of the University of Modena

---

[60] http://s24ore.it/mcc16

The opportunities

and Reggio [Emilia61] and aims to find a solution for selective forgetting and unlearning based on the user's needs, i.e., to allow at a later time to permanently remove toxic concepts and information learned from LLM systems despite safe checkers. In the Modena labs, they have tried to teach Llama and Stable Diffusion to generate inappropriate images, and then find a way to effectively unlearn them. The issue is still complex, however, despite the results of early effet- tive studies on limited networks, especially if the goal is to eliminate entire classes of data that may no longer even be available.

The increasing use of artificial intelligence in law enforcement raises important questions about the benefits and risks associated with it. In a simulated domestic abuse emergency call, an AI system linked to police databases transcribed and ana- lized the conversation in real time providing imme- diate information about the suspect. Experimentation conducted by Hum- berside police, using AI provided by the start-up Untrite AI, confirms that such technology could greatly improve oper- ational efficiency, saving operators up to one-third of their time during and after each call. So AI has the potential to transform the way police investigate and solve crimes, identifying patterns and connections in evidence and sifting through vast amounts of data much faster than any human. Ethical preoc- cupations arise, however, particularly with regard to AI-based facial recognition. In the United States, for example, cases have been reported that have shown poor accuracy in identifying faces of color. These problems have led cities such as San Francisco and Seattle to ban the use of this technology. Despite the transformative potential of AI in investigating and solving crimes, the

---

[61] S. Poppi, S. Sarto, R. Cucchiara, et al, *Multi-Class Explainable Unlearning for Image Classification via Weight Filtering,* in "ArXiv," (2023), 2304.02049.

criticism also raises questions about the "original sin" of predictive po- lice, namely skewed historical data. Some argue that crime prediction could lead to disastrous effects, especially when based on problematic crime data. Then there is also the ethical issue at the center of the debate, with the need for indepen- dent testing to assess the accuracy and ethicality of AI technologies employed by law enforcement. For the concern is always this: bi- launch the operational efficiency offered by AI with the protection of individual di- rites and the prevention of discrimination.

3.15 In SMEs

The generative AI revolution, similar to the impact the assembly line had on industry, is redefining the work- rative landscape. Executives can capitalize on this technology to po- tice their skills, improve customer service, and enrich the customer and employee experience. Writing, coding, analysis, and design now become more accessible because of it, enabling increased day-to-day productivity, as long as AI adoption is driven by the full attention of the executive team and investments in AI tools are focused on high-impact use cases, optimizing organizational value and serving as templates for future priorities. As the boundaries between men and machines fade, executives must allow people the oppor- tunity to experiment, carefully balancing the fine line between innovation and business protection.

And that is precisely the determining factor: generative AI focuses entirely on people, transforming the way we do work. Unlike other technologies, which instead focus exclusively on machine capabilities, it amplifies human skills, simplifies creative work such as creating

The opportunities

content and experience design, while automating repetitive attivities such as data analysis and code development. Those in customer service, for example, can leverage generative AI to handle routine queries, freeing up time for sales activities. Programmers can move away from mundane co-defense tasks to focus on improving system quality and security. HR specialists can free themselves from day-to-day acts to focus on effective talent growth.

The impact of generative AI does not occur in an abstract digital environment; rather, competitive advantage comes from increasing employee skills and growing orga- nizational capabilities. Putting people, not technology, at the center of the generative AI strate- gy is critical. It is not replacing per- sons, but those who adopt this technology are overtaking those who choose not to. And in this they must actively involve their team. This is why human resources should be placed at the center of organizational progress, but 60 percent of executives still see them as an administrative function, risking undermining the be- nefits of this revolutionary technology. Instead, they need to be transformed from a strictly administrative role to a strategic role in building an AI-enabled future workforce. Many executives anticipate that generative AI will improve various aspects of their business, from decision making to customer experience and re- cable growth. Those who understand how to empower people with generative AI will become a catalyst for success for their companies.

How to achieve such an ambitious goal? Meanwhile, implementting an effective change management initiative that is transparent and people-centered; identifying areas where generative AI has already been tried and adopted, providing ongoing feedback on experiences, both positive and negative, and lessons learned; ensuring that we have an ethical model for the use o f generative AI, with clear standards, guidelines and expectations. And then communicating these standards to all company personnel.

Companies should promote the experiment among employees, while ensuring data security and ethics, and promise staff compensation and rewards based on performance. In- sum, the approach to its introduction should be iterative, in- corating risk-taking and readiness to accept failures, identify and test opportunities, perhaps starting with human resources. Recognizing the joint responsibility of business, IT, and HR leaders for the results of generative AI also helps po- tice teamwork, emphasizing the strategic importance of its adoption across the enterprise.

It may sound like a paradox, but the essential skill in using generative artificial in- telligence is creativity. Despite technological transfor- mation, the most valuable skill for companies by 2025 will be creativity. Creative, and intelligent, people will be able to interact productively with their generative AI assistants and innovate in interactions with human colleagues, because collaborative com- petencies are just as crucial as software development and coding, and even precede analytics and data science, with creativity ranking high on the list of priorities. To liberate creativity, leaders must embrace executive-level change and integrate generative AI into their work; turn updating on it into an opportunity for advancement. And an- again they need to redefine work processes through AI, analyze the way work gets done, identify bottlenecks and inef- ficiencies, and implement solutions to accelerate and improve the decision-making pro- cess at scale. This technology does not improve poor pre-stations; it is a revolution, not an evolution.

Customer service has taken a predominant role in the adoption of generative AI, overtaking other business functions. Initially,

The opportunities

executives cited research, innovation, marketing, and risk compliance as the top uses, but experience has di- strated that customer service is where generative AI offers the greatest im- pact. And although it has enormous importance for productivity, flexible work culture and data access are still seen as the highest priorities by executives. This suggests that companies focus on reactive use of AI rather than proactive imple- mentation to transform the way work gets done. Executives need to challenge labor conventions, focus on cultural change, and enable greater flexibility so that employees can maximize their potential.

More than half of companies still do not have a con- solidated process for reviewing results and troubleshooting. One approach to quality assurance is the use of generative AI models trained on approved material and accessible only internally. These models can be easily integrated into existing infrastructures, ensuring a cohesive user experience. To maximize effectiveness, I recommend pushing designers to become curators of con- held, integrating generative AI to automatically adapt to how users access and interact. The key approach is to use *design thinking*, to change the way things work, not just their appearance, using generative AI to simplify the complex.

In this complex process, business leaders must conside- ry explainability, ethics, biases, or trust as major concerns in adopting generative AI. Ethical governance is a critical area, with half of all companies currently lacking the necessary structures to address these ethical challenges. Instead, responsible adoption is prioritized because this caution translates into increased revenues compared to those who proceed less carefully. Listening to customers' ethical expectations, clearly explaining how generative AI will protect and process our data will help build customer trust over time; thus, not only through personalized marketing campaigns, targeted advertising and direct con- tact. In short, putting people first and inviting customer feedback can foster deeper engagement by identifying and resolving pain points in line with their evolving needs. To build trust, we need to develop the ethos of generative AI in response to customer concerns and turn data into a wealth of information.

Generative artificial intelligence also opens up new perspectives in reinventing the employee experience. The promise of trasforming jobs by automating tasks previously considered too complex is not intended to replace human talent, quite the contrary. 87 percent of executives expect generative AI to augment job roles rather than replace them, creating human-machine collaboration that engages and improves employees' lives. But to prevent automation of the simplest tasks from leaving only the difficult tasks to humans, it is important to strike a balance between efficiency and co-involvement, holding everyone accountable. CEOs need to carefully consider where to include generative AI in the value cation, rethinking the operating model to improve employees' lives. For example, generative AI can provide a seamless conversational interface for back-office systems, simplifying natural language interactions and creating a single point of management for day-to-day activities. Some managers, however, move forward in implementing generative AI without fully evaluating the im- pact on the workforce, causing staff reductions or reassignments in some situations. The key always remains in the balance between innovation and attention to employee needs.

Specifically, artificial intelligence is generating new places of work, requiring specialized skills in the area of the

The opportunities

data management, but it also provides tools to improve workers' effi- ciency to give them the opportunity to focus on more strategic and creative activities. It can support business decisions by providing accurate predictions and insightful insights due to its ability to process and analyze huge amounts of data. In general, it paves the way for the development of new products and services, stymi- ing innovation in various fields. In professional development, it contributes to the personalization of training paths and edu- cational resources based on individual needs.

If the evolutionary path follows that of previous in- dustrial revolutions, it should lead to less job reduc- tion than many have projected. Even studies such as that of the World Economic Forum[62] suggest that AI could create more jobs than it replaces, generating a positive long-term econo- mic impact.

For managers and business leaders, AI can be a valuable support in making data-driven decisions, but human leadership and relationship ge- stration should not be replaced by machines. Dependence on data represents both a challenge and an advantage in our era. Equated with the new oil, data are akin to an ecosi-zation:if managed responsibly, they represent a gold mine. Manual processing of data can be counterproductive; instead, rapid adoption of high-quality data and transparency are essential to harmonize sustainability and profitability. The introduction of generative artificial in- telligence has made data even more valuable, pre-mitting companies that are able to exploit its potential faster than their competitors, because they enjoy the trust of internal and external stakehol- der, gaining signi- ficantly higher profits from AI capabilities than others. A well-designed platform can fuel business model innovation by integrating

---

[62] http://s24ore.it/mcc66

cycles of data preparation, model training, and application development. This approach produces positive feedback, where the more data on the platform, the more value is delivered to customers, increasing their numbers and further improving the generative artificial intelligence model.

Generative AI is also bridging the gap between IT and the business, tra- sforming the dynamic in which technology drives innovation and the business drives technology. To get the most value from generative AI, Ceo's need to move beyond traditional divisions and integrate functions more holistically: doing so requires starting with a full sharing of business goals, moving through closer integration with IT and continuous measurement of app performance, explicitly prioritizing IT projects with the strongest links to business value, and, last but not least, involving everyone, indepen- dently of their roles in modernizing technology and business performance.

All of this comes at a significant cost. Addressing AI-related financial challenges requires careful governance and strategic resource management. Maintaining a comprehensive view of costs and adopting ap- proaches such as FinOps (cloud-based financial management discipline) will con- tribute to ensuring efficient use of funds and maximizing the return on investment in generative AI. Human resources in generative AI also come at a cost, so companies are required to adopt a combination of strategies to attract top talent, build competitive salary bases, and make the most of internal and external expertise with a flexible and market-oriented approach.

In sales, as we saw in section 3.10, marketers have numerous applications available for their data structuring and analysis activities and testing of new opportunities that offer, above all, advantages in terms of time. In this process of applying artificial intelligence, however, marketers must take measures to mi- tigate risks such as producing results that are not based on verifiable facts, data or algorithmic models, such as bias or violations of data privacy and copyright. For this reason, human intuition and relationship building will remain irreplaceable. Thanks to ge- nerative AI, marketing teams can spend more time on strate- gy, experimenting with innovative approaches, and creating high-value con- held , for example, by connecting marketing materials to touchpoints and crucial moments in the customer journey. In all this, generative AI can accelerate the production process to improve the quality and relevance of content, positioning customer data as the best brand differentiator and defense against misinformation.

Then in each sector there are specific opportunities that can por- tain to the proper use of AI. For example, in banking, its implementation certainly offers significant productivity benefits, but the risks associated with its use require the establishment of a strategic vision based on the identification of priorities, goals, and capabilities. First, it is necessary to prepare employees with the right training and acquire talent with specific compe- tences; then a cross-functional operating model should be developed whereby everyone focuses on his or her area of expertise but shares knowledge and resources to facilitate and ac- celerate goal achievement. It is also critical to manage data quality and security by implementing new fra- mework for risk management and controls.

One of the newest and most useful tools for companies is RAG, which we ab- lutely covered, which is an AI technology that allows models such as ChatGPT to draw real-time information from external sources. This means they can find answers not only from the their "digital brain," but also from the outside world as if they had at their disposal a veritable world encyclopedia. The implications of RAG are significant for both businesses and consumers. For the former, it results in unprecedented efficiency in customer interactions and process automation. For the latter, it offers more personalized digital experiences through chatbots and virtual assistants.

RAG finds examples of direct use in a variety of areas such as in personalized customer service, or as real-time decision support for businesses and to automate business workflows, in personalized individual education, providing medical advice in health care, or even in travel and itinerary planning with contingency management, advanced financial analysis and reporting. The importance of RAG is not only limited to its expertise in intelligent text generation, but its ability to learn, inform itself, and di- namely adapt to a constantly evolving universe of data becomes critical.

We must be very careful, however, we are not yet ready for a chatbot to act autonomously in commer- cial negotiations or customer service. Chris Bakke instructed a GM dealership chatbot to offer a Chevy Tahoe for sale for only $1. The chatbot accepted the offer by acting on its pro- gram, but what would have happened if human supervision had not immediately intervened, if Bakke had not been there to combine technological efficiency with human judgment? Human thinking is es- sential to ensure the responsible and advantageous development and use of AI systems, which often encounter difficulties in im- predictable or innovative contexts where creative thinking and cognitive adaptation are required. Particularly, human judgment enables us to va- lue complex situations, consider various factors, and make informed decisions in the face of uncertainty, for example, in areas such as the

The opportunities

emergency management, where AI can yes offer insights ba- sed on data, but is not yet able to balance risk, innovation, and ethical considerations as human judgment can. Examples such as these are critical to understanding its limitations and potential, guiding the future development and implementation of AI, and ensuring its effective and responsible use in of- ferent customer services.

Finally, one should not forget the growing importance of ethics in generative AI. Not only to ensure compliance with regulations, but also to maintain the trust of customers and employees. Responsible and transparent use of generative AI is critical to the long-term success of companies. One must be aware of algorithmic bias, ensure transparency in data processing, and respect customer privacy. Only then can generative AI truly unlock its potential to improve corporate performance and employee well-being.

In conclusion, generative AI represents a momentous breakthrough for small and medium-sized enterprises, offering tremendous opportunities for growth and mi- lement. However, to fully capitalize on this potential, executives must put people at the center of the adoption strategy, foster creativity and collaboration, and ensure responsible and transparent use of AI. Only then can they successfully lead their companies into the generative AI era.

3.16 In the liberal professions

The French philosopher Gaspard Koenig, in 2019, published a book chronicling a journey into the universe of artificial intelligence, through- to a series of meetings with key players in the field[63] in various parts

---

[63] G. Koenig, *La fin de l'individu: Voyage d'un philosophe au pays de l'intelligence artificielle*, L'Observatoire, Paris, 2019.

of the world. Among them, Craig Hanson, founder of an investment fund specializing in AI in San Francisco, explained to Koenig how this technology is rapidly replacing professionals in sva- ried industries. When asked by Koenig whether he, too, will be replaced by AI capable of analyzing business models and predicting market opportunities, Hanson replied that investing is an overly complex business and will be the last industry to be fully automated. This phenomenon, called the "Craig paradox," has become widespread enough and could be a valuable tool for analysis, as Koenig himself suggests. The philosopher wonders whether those who argue for the easy replaceability of a professional figure have fully understood the complex tasks they perform every day.

In the legal sector, there are rich databases containing legislation, doctrine, and case law, which could be exploited to develop intelligent legal search systems. However, the closure of ROSS, considered by many to be the most promising legal artifi- cial intelligence platform, shows that this is not always the case. ROSS has been accused of improperly plundering data in the WestLaw legal database, despite the fact that it excelled in ag- gizing legal opinions. This aspect would have been extremely useful for large law firms, which often address requests on previously covered topics.

In a number of situations, such as in the context of drafting contracts and similar documents, one can consider using systems that listen to the conversation between a professional and a client, automatically extracting the document. Or, the system itself, perhaps through a bot on a hotline, can ask questions and draw up a draft based on the answers provided. A stan- dard lease can easily be generated in this way. However, let's ima- mine a professional who is about to draft a com- plete and delicate contract, using pre-existing or nonexisting drafts or forms. Man

The opportunities

as the work proceeds, an intelligent system suggests clauses deemed appropriate, drawing from its vast knowledge base. This requires the machine to train itself in each use, storing accepted and rejected proposals and changes made by the user.

Adoption of AI in the output phase (since input is a different matter) is likely to occur through two forms of integration. The first involves the inclusion of AI functions in software house packages, but this option puts management in the hands of commercial operators, causing pro- fessionals to lose control of their cultural evolution. The alternative seems to be associative initiatives, perhaps developed within trade organizations: it would not be difficult for a con- sistent group of professionals to acquire an AI system and begin using it to develop their pro- fessionality in a shared way.

Major language patterns present significant potential to revolutionize the practice of law. But we must not forget the now well-known fe- nomenes known as "legal hallucinations," that is, responses for- ned by these patterns that are not in line with legal facts. One study examined the extent of such hallucinations by formulating an original set of legal questions, comparing LLMs' responses with structured legal me- tudies, and assessing their consistency. They were found to be disturbingly frequent: occurring between 69% of responses with ChatGPT 3.5 and 88% with Llama 2, when these models are asked specific, verifiable questions about federal tribu- nal cases. LLMs often fail to correct erroneous juridical assumptions in counterfactual question situations and do not always recognize when they are generating legal hallucinations. It is clear that based on these findings we cannot quickly and unsupervisedly integrate LLMs into legal tasks. Even the most experts must be cautious about legal hallucinations, with particularly high risks for those who do not have access to traditional legal resources and thus benefit most from LLMs.

3.17 In society

After this long excursus on the opportunities offered by AI in every area of our lives, we can conclude that today it represents a huge benefit to society at large. It improves efficiency and productivity while creating new opportunities for profit generation, cost and time reduction, and the creation of new jobs. If the evolution of the labor market is gradual and with the right preparation, people will continue to la- vor, but they will do it better with the help of AI. The positive changes will also be noticed in everyday life and in multiple ways: people will save valuable time and simplify their daily attivities. For example, by automating repetitive tasks such as organizing appointments and managing emails, AI will allow us to focus on more meaningful and rewarding activities, in- creasing individual productivity and enabling us to tackle more tasks in less time. Specifically, it could help eli- minate spam, classify incoming emails, and even suggest quick re- sponse in email platforms.

Through the speed of processing and data analysis, it will provide us with useful suggestions and optimized recommendations to improve effi- ciency and reduce human error. It will increase connectivity between in- dividuals through the creation of chatbots and virtual assistants that of- fuse personalized communication support, providing immediate and relevant in- formations, answering users' questions, and even simulating realistic human conversations, creating

The opportunities

a sense of connection and facilitating communication that can foster stronger and more meaningful relationships.

As we have seen, in healthcare, its advanced monitoring and diagnostic capabilities result in more efficient operations for healthcare facilities and medical organizations, reducing operational costs, personalizing treatment plans, and improving data access and care for patients. In mobility, AI-driven auto- nomous transportation not only solves traffic congestion problems, but also increases the overall productivity of society. By re- ducing the stress associated with travel, people will have more time to devote to other activities. Applications such as Google Maps and Waze use AI to analyze traffic data in real time, allowing the most efficient road routes to be planned. To touch on another area, in security it can improve threat detection and re-solution, recognize patterns of fraudulent activity in financial and online transactions, and even improve home security systems through facial recognition.

In short, AI is now part of our daily lives, even if we sometimes do not realize it, bringing significant benefits. Pen- we are to virtual assistants such as Siri, Google Assistant or Bixby that facilitate the management of daily tasks, creating prome- mory, providing information and sending messages. In online shop- ping, e-commerce platforms leverage AI to offer personalized recommendations based on users' browsing and purchasing history. Streaming services such as Netflix and Spotify use it to recommend shows, movies, or music based on viewers' viewing or listening habits.

AI has the right potential to positively transform the lives of all of us, simplifying daily activities and freeing us from tedious tasks, improving the effectiveness of communication and lifestyle, ele- vating the condition of human beings, and increasing productivity,

Cyberhumanism

automation and strengthening the economy with new jobs, but it can also affect society negatively and upset certain balances. For example, the loss of control over machines can pro- vocate unintended and unforeseen consequences. AI should not exempt humans from responsibility for decision-making and supervi- sion. Harnessing its benefits requires conscious understanding and use; only then can it lead to a more efficient, connected, and rewarding future for all.

Chapter 4 - The critical issues

4.1 Long-distance NATIONALISM and territorial sovereignty

A critical theme of our time are forms of *long* distance *natio-* nalism, "long distance" or "country of origin" nationalisms, which are manifested when individuals far from their country of origin maintain strong identity ties to it, actively influencing its politics and culture despite the distance. Irish sociologist Benedict Anderson (1936 - 2015) discussed the political implications of this by sub- lining that although the population is geographically dispersed, the political focus and identity remain tied to the homeland. Many now identify themselves as remote nationalists, expressing their attachment through voting, demonstrations, financial investments, artistic creations, and sometimes more extreme actions. This phenomenon transforms the traditional idea of nationalism, allowing memberships that transcend physical national boundaries and should not be confused with diaspora, which represents identification with a dispersed population without necessarily organizing in relation to a state of origin

While not an entirely new phenomenon, with the advancement of the
globalization and the support of digital technologies, long-distance nationalism has intensified, allowing migrants to participate in transnational political projects and maintain an active link with their homeland. This form of nationalism highlights how collective identities can extend beyond territorial boundaries, defi- ning conventional notions of belonging and national loyalty.

In fact, long-distance nationalism is not based on legal definitions

Cyberhumanism

of citizenship, involving both migrants and their descendants and the

The critical issues

patriotic political movements and states. The latter can consi- der dispersed populations as a continuous part of their homeland, regardless of citizenship. Longtime nationalists conceive of the possibility of having multiple homelands and being incorporated into more than one state. In the Haitian context, for example, nationalist leaders changed the definition of Haitians abroad according to political circumstances. They initially considered them political refugees obliged to return to Haiti, but later encouraged them to stay abroad and contribute to Haiti's development from afar. The issue of dual citizenship is increasingly di- scussed among longtime nationalists to facilitate travel back home. Many countries are changing laws to include peoples who have become citizens of other states, allowing dual cittadi- nity or nationality. Italy, for example, recognizes dual citizenship and allows descendants to obtain Italian citizenship. Some countries also allow extraterritorial voting, while others require return to the homeland to participate in elections.

The reasons behind long-distance nationalism are many. Pos- are economic, for example: the Philippines, in 2003, con- cerned citizenship to its emigrants to encourage them to invest in their homeland. India has proposed amendments to the Citizenship Act to extend dual citizenship to people of Indian origin residing in certain countries. Long-distance nationalism can also be fueled by political exiles who seek to maintain identification with the homeland, using the rhetoric of blood and nation to legitimize the family ties of those who have left their homeland. All the same, long-distance nationalism can also raise concerns, especially when it involves financial and arms contributions to reactionary movements. In addition, Sept. 11, 2001, led to a review of immigrant dual loyalties in many countries, with increased surveillance of fund transfers, communications, and travel. These

The critical issues

developments threaten activities related to long-distance nationalism, but some aspects of foreign policy can legitimize it. On closer inspection, that at a distance, like any form of nationalism, has multiple and conflicting meanings.

However, this phenomenon raises complex questions regarding sovereignty and national identity in a digital age. Increasing global digi- tualization and interconnectedness push people to reflect on the nature of political and territorial communities. People can now have intensely digital community experiences, leading them to question the relevance of geographic boundaries and the very definition of citizenship.

In the age of the Net, is the geographic con- cept of so- vernity still valid? We live in a world in which we daily buy online, relate online, earn and spend money online. We must ask ourselves, therefore, whether states defined on a geographical and territorial basis still make sense. Whether they are able to fron- t the social and economic changes taking place due to di- gitalization.

When we have an account stolen on a social account owned by a company based in a state other than our own and local authorities cannot intervene, we realize that something has changed. Questions arise about the ability of politics, government, and isti- cations to adequately fulfill their functions.

The question arises as to the purpose and relevance of nations in the Web and digital worlds, which are fundamentally metaterritorial, that is, they do not depend only on traditional spatial components to exi- strate, progress, and govern, but also rely on vir- tual connections, digital networks, and online interactions. This new dimension sol- leverages many questions about the role of institutions, the exercise of power, and the very definition of sovereignty. In an increasingly global and interconnected context, it opens up a space for reflection on the need to

Adapting government models and land-use design.

"Companies that administer digital platforms such as Airbnb, Amazon, Apple, eBay, Google, Uber and Upwork now have thousands of people like Khan at their ser- vices to handle disputes. eBay alone claims to have resolved more than 60 million disputes in a single year. In the corresponding period, the U.K. court system handled about 4 million cases, the Chinese courts about 11 mi- lion and the U.S. courts about 90 million, most of which were traffic offenses. In other words, today platform companies together probably settle more disputes than public courts around the world. This is not just because people are litigating more on the Internet, which could still be true. It simply reflects the fact that so many of our daily interactions now take place through these platforms. "[64]

The fragmentation of regulatory powers makes it difficult to find uniform and effective solutions to regulate digital.

Each state has its own laws, and what may be legal in one place may not be legal in another. But as the world is increasingly interconnected and we live more and more online, we can view this virtual dimension as a kind of "meta-state" that pre- sentes global challenges that require international collaboration to ensure effective and consistent regulation. This needs joint efforts among countries to create laws and regulations that are based on the fundamental principles of security, data protection, and the tu- tude of digital citizens' rights. Only through such cooperation will we be able to successfully cope with the ever-changing digital age. What may be considered illegal in the country you are in becomes legal if you can virtually move to another place. All you need to do to do this is to use a VPN (Virtual Private Network), and this inevitably leads to a situation of profound uncertainty

---

[64] V. Lehdonvirta, *Cloud Empires*, Piccola Biblioteca Einaudi, Turin, 2023.

The critical issues

legal, to the lack of well-defined rules, and to an opportunity that can be exploited more by those with greater financial re- sorces and means. What's more, with the advent of globalization and ever-increasing interconnectedness, new forms of online crime are constantly emerging that are able to easily cross the borders of individual countries and escape national jurisprudence, creating an even more complex and dif- ficult environment to combat.

National and international laws often find it difficult to keep pace with accelerating technological evolution and increasing globalization. In this context, careful consideration and constant review of existing regulations becomes essential to ensure that laws and regulations are adapted to the increasingly interconnected and digitized world in which we live.

To address the challenges of the digital age and ensure appropriate governance, it is essential to take a comprehensive and coordinated approach starting with a careful assessment of technology implications and close collaboration among key players at the international level. Only through joint efforts can we develop policies and regulations that can adapt to the enormous transformations in the digital landscape.

But today we are further away than ever before. With new divisions opening up between countries, international cooperation seems to be getting harder and harder to achieve. The world is divided by political boundaries and conflicting ideologies, with barriers hindering cooperation between nations. Only through greater understanding, open dialogue and a willingness to cooperate can we work together to address these challenges and build a better future for all.

Does it make sense to impose rules. on the big players or those who hold our knowledge, when those rules are so easily circumvented? If we do not have effectively universally applicable rules,

How can we protect fundamental rights and human dignity in the ever-developing digital environment? This is a complex question that requires careful consideration, the study of different perspectives, and innovative solutions to ensure adequate protection. It bi- sogs to consider all aspects and carefully evaluate the possible implications, because only in this way can the most effective and sustainable long-term strategies be identified. The search for innovative solutions and the implementation of appropriate policies are key to af- fect the challenges that this complex issue presents.

In the physical world, everything is simpler. In the European Union, foreign companies that want to sell their products in its territo- ries must strictly comply with the established rules and regulations. Should they fail to comply with these rules, they are not allowed to enter the EU market. In addition, should they attempt to import their products in violation of these rules, the customs authorities would in- tervene to apply the appropriate penalties.

But in the digital sphere everything is different. For example, in 2023, the Italian Privacy Guarantor requested OpenAI, the company that owns ChatGPT, to clarify its position regarding the management of personal data. This request raised many questions about the confor- mity of privacy and data protection laws. In response, the company initially decided to make ChatGPT's service inaccessible on Italian territory in order to avoid possible legal conse- guences. However, through the use of VPNs, some Italian users were able to bypass this restriction and still access the ser- vice in order to meet their immediate needs and overcome the geographical constraints imposed by the authorities.

So does it make sense to still talk about the concept of territorial sovereignty in a world where the ability of individuals, communities, and countries to exercise effective control over their own space, not only in the personal sphere but also in the political and economic spheres is in

The critical issues

discussion? We should universally have the ability to de- terminate the rules and requirements governing the use of perso- nal data, transparency of information, and access to digital resources. Beyond geographic boundaries, which represent us less and less.

The Internet has faded the boundaries between physical territories. People can live, work and connect with other residents around the world without ever leaving their homes. This opens a wide debate about whether citizenship should still be tied to a specific physical territory. Perhaps we need to start thinking about digital sovereignty rather than territorial sovereignty. Digital sovereignty also implies the ability to protect one's personal data and control how it is used by service providers.

The idea and practice of citizenship have roots in the evolution of political thought and political organization. In practice, citta- dinance refers primarily to the limits of the political and territorial community: the Polis of ancient Greece, the Empire of ancient Rome, and, in modern times, the nation-state with its political institutions and laws governing coexistence and citizens' rights. A sense of identity and belonging to a larger community, providing a basis for democratic participation and the exercise of civil rights. The citta- dinance plays a crucial role in defining the scope and character of the concept of "social." It makes it possible to determine who is part of the whole and who is excluded. Society is the set of people who share a culture and traditions within a specific space. It is a group that understands each other, creating a structured social bond.

But if we put aside the concept of territory for a moment, there are groups with common culture and traditions that are emerging, stemming from online life, but which have no territorial representation. There are digital communities experienced more intensely than those where individuals are physically located.

The laws that generally allow the acquisition of citizenship are related to descent, place of birth, place of marriage, as well as the principle of cohabitation and belonging. Being "one of us" is the concept to be respected. When "one of us" becomes "one who works where we work, hangs out with those we hang out with, and spends time in the places we spend it," but all of this predominantly online, then perhaps the concept of "one of us" is totally to be revised. It is one of us who lives online as we do and who is likely to need different rights from his physical countrymen.

The concept of state sovereignty changes and becomes digital: digital super- nity, an important issue that also affects online security and privacy. Protecting our digital sovereignty means not only using tools such as VPNs, but also taking responsibility for our online actions and making informed decisions about the use of digital services.

On the other hand, in a world where we post silly videos that are viewed by millions of people in real time anywhere in the world, it becomes complicated to access our own X-rays if we are injured in a different state than the one where we live. The software is different, the laws are different, the formats are different, and above all, today the systems do not "talk" to each other because we still think territorially instead of digitally.

Fragmentation of technologies, procedures and modes is contrary to the principles of centralization that we have come to know thanks to the Net. When you change states, you do not need to change the application to post a comment on a Web site, because the process is the same everywhere in the world. The database remains the same, regardless of geographic location.

Even there are states like Italy where Article 5 of the Constitu- tion reads, "The Republic, one and indivisible, recognizes and promotes local autonomy; implements in the services that depend on the State the most

The critical issues

extensive administrative decentralization; it adapts the principles and methods of its legislation to the requirements of autonomy and decentralization. "[65] Decentralization of public administration, although a fundamental principle of our Constitution, is an obstacle to the simplicity and speed of processes. Centralization clearly proves to be more efficient: a single decision-making entity, a unified control structure.

The founding fathers of the Italian Republic wanted to prevent a repeat of the concentration of power that led to the Fascist regime. Decentralization, when paper-based and physical, promotes local autonomy and ensures that decisions are made closer to those to whom they apply.

But in the age of digital is this still a valid idea? Today in which there are numerous websites dedicated to municipalities and ASLs. Each of them independently manages information, but this fragmentation leads to significant redundancy of data and limits accessibility to traveling, Net-using citizens who want to quickly avail themselves of the information they need.

Is it mere bureaucracy or a still valid founding principle? Burocracy goes against the principles of Cyberhumanism, because it hinders and complicates everything. We must be careful, however, not to confuse bureaucracy with democratic processes, which are the very basis of our civil society. Democratic processes must be preserved and po- tified, because they govern our peaceful coexistence. Thus, the challenge is not only about finding a balance between humanity and technology. The challenge is also about freeing ourselves from bureaucracy, thanks to the digital that was born as its natural antithetic.

What then should be our priority? Should we put first the protection of the Constitution and the fundamental principles on which it is based or should we put digital efficiency? This is a complex dilemma

Cyberhumanism
[65] http://s24ore.it/mcc61

That requires careful analysis. There are valid arguments on both sides. On the one hand, the values of autonomy and diversity are vitally important to local communities, and their reflection in the digital world is inescapable. On the other hand, digital efficiency is vital to facilitate our daily lives and push forward technological innova- tion.

4.2 The black boxes of AI

Another exacerbating issue for global democratic stability is related to the algorithms and foundational models that govern the functioning of digital society and its content.

What is really in it? This is one of the main questions that to date we have no answer to.

Strategic choices regarding digitization and the use of artificial intelligence in society should be the responsibility of state governments, not just the prerogative of private companies.

Companies, by definition, have a limited time horizon, focused on achieving short- and medium-term profits. Pos- are to have a long-term view, but by nature they do not take into account the effects on humanity because it is not in their purpose.

By corporate mission, it is normal to place more emphasis on value generation, which is in the nature of business, rather than on protecting human welfare or social justice.

Ethics and better choices for humans are not among the company's priorities. Their focus is primarily on creating products and innovations that generate profit, rather than on improving the human condition. Cyber humanity, therefore, must emerge as a movement that claims the importance of human di- gnity, social justice, and individual well-being in the context of an increasingly digitized world.

Today, however, we face a reality in which AI has the po- tential to revolutionize not only the way we access and use information, but also the very foundations of our so- cieties. The principle of Cyberhumanism calls us to reflect on these changes, to understand the ethical and social implications of AI use, and to actively work to ensure that technology is used in a way that respects and enhances human dignity and autonomy. Companies, particularly those whose operations are anchored in the intensive use of technology, face a dilemma. On the one hand, medium- to long-term vision is essential for sustainability, innovation, and market leadership. On the other hand, it is neces- sary to come to terms with shareholder expectations and the hectic pace of the market, prompting a preference for short-term results.

Companies should be keenly interested in a long-term vision that includes ethical reflection and a commitment to using technology in a way that respects and values human dignity and autonomy. Their future will depend on their ability to balance short-term goals with a long-term vision that takes into account the broader implications of their decisions and actions. Will the companies that can do this be the ones that thrive in the digital age? Or will they be the ones that, by ignoring ethics and Cyberhumanism, will end up harming not only society but also themselves?

We cannot allow decisions that affect our daily lives and our future to be made without taking into account the human, its complexity and its inalienable value.

But until today things were different. No company had such enormous po- tence to the point of becoming a risk to humanity or democracy.

Now with the new course of AI, things have changed, and a great deal of power is in the hands of a few. That is why it is crucial for governments to play an active role in leading the regulation of the

The critical issues

sector, ensuring that these innovations are used responsibly and that the benefits are fairly distributed among all members of society, because as of today those who hold the power are the large corporations and international digital organizations. They dictate the rules of the game, setting the limits within which AI and in- novation can move.

Technological progress has its own vitality; it has taken a direction that seems unstoppable. Inventions cannot be uninvented.

The digital is here and is already transforming our reality in ways we can no longer ignore. What we can and must do, if advocates of Cyberhumanism, is to ensure that this transformation happens in a way that respects and values humanity. That it does not allow technology to dominate man, but puts it at his service.

Another problem that is emerging in a major way is related to the difficulty of distinguishing what is generated by AI from what pro- comes from humans.

The dilemma has distant origins. Exactly in 1990 in Boston, when the first Loebner Prize was held, an official competition that subjected artificial intelligence to the Turing test. The purpose was to assess whether a machine was capable of manifesting behavior indistinguishable from human behavior. The test was based on the idea that if a machine could fool an interlocutor into believing it was human, it could be considered "intelli- people." Boston's challenge was to have humans and computers converse textually, without knowing who was who.

During the first Loebner Prize show, they brought out as many as ten judges and eight computers, six of which were controlled by an autonomous micro-processor and two by humans. They had to cer- tainly recognize who was a computer and who were humans. Some of the judges managed to get it wrong even though the computer was responding with random sentences.

Rereading the answers obtained by the judges in that contest more than 30 years ago makes us wonder how wrong the same judges could be today with ChatGPT, which is able to argue on complex issues. After all, even the chatbot ELIZA[66] in the 1970s appeared credible.

Today AI is extremely powerful, and if we were to rely only on the Turing test, ChatGPT would probably pass it as well, because for the test it only matters whether a machine is able to fool us, not how it succeeds. There are those who are thinking of marking AI-generated content in a way that is invisible to the human eye, in order to make it distinguishable.

"Before you become enthralled by splendid gadgets and mesmerizing video displays, let me remind you that information is not knowledge, knowledge is not wisdom, and wisdom is not lungimancy. Each grows from the other, and we need them all," said Arthur C. Clarke (1917-2008), British writer, physicist and astronomer.

All cultural heritage, from the past to the present to the future, rehears of the shift to digital form, both in terms of the tra- sformation of existing materials and the creation of new ones, including creative works. Everything is intermediated, time ago by research mo- tors and now by LLM systems such as for example ChatGPT or Bard.

We are increasingly leaving our thinking in the hands of software and algorithms because it is convenient and fast. We will no longer know whether we have made a decision ourselves or whether we have been manipulated by our virtual assistant. How will we know whether the AI's choice is correct or not? We could never know the logic of the system or

---

[66] One of the first chatbot experiments, created in 1966 by Joseph Weizenbaum. Its goal was to simulate a therapeutic conversation by behaving like a Rogerian therapist.

understand how an automated learning algorithm powered by quantum computation works. In other words, we should fi- d totally or not at all.

We are *zombifying ourselves*, opening the door to a kind of global digital feudalism, where the lords of technology think for us. They take the hassle away from us. But conversely they do what they want. They can add or "take away" facts from reality. If a search engine de-indexes a piece of content, that content starts to disappear. If an LLM does not cite it, it does not exist. But who decides what the correct results of engines and LLMs are? And again, what is really in it?

Moreover, at present, throughout the democratic world, there is no legal obligation to prevent the omission of information. The diffusion of culture and truth are in the hands of private companies that exert a disruptive effect on global culture and also their oblivion.

In addition, generative AIs such as ChatGPT, Dall-E 3, and Stable Diffusion filter and moderate not only training data but also prompts with the result that they replace us and limit our freedom to express our thoughts. The risks of preemptive censorship arise when, for example, AIs such as ChatGPT refuse to generate copyrighted images. This is where guaranteeing and respecting rights without preemptively restricting freedom becomes necessary. Think also of Dall-E's refusal to generate a *head shot* because it was deemed an inappropriate lin- guage, ignoring the legitimate meaning of the term (a particular framing for portraits).

The most alarming fact is that this kind of censorship is practiced not by states and governments well known in this regard such as China, for example, but by private companies such as big tech, and this highlights the authoritarian drift since they decide what constitutes a right and how it should be exercised, often just to protect their interests. Let us not forget that this systematic compression of rights is fueled by a culture of prohibition, as opposed to the li- ber approach that punishes violations rather than prohibiting them.

In the context of an increasingly digital world, it becomes imperative to develop rules and regulations that safeguard the freedom of in- formation and the right to truth. Around the world, the influence of the al- gorithmic basis of LLMs will have a significant impact on the dissemination of social, cultural, and historical information, both conscious and in- conscious. This will result in important po- litical, social and cultural consequences for the global community.

From 1975 to the present day, information technology and knowledge-based work, networks, and data analysis have assumed a key role in the business mo- vations of major industries and the operation of government bureaucracies. To safeguard democracy, it is fundamental to promote rules and laws that ensure freedom of information and the right to access the truth. The digital, which could be a means of liberating human beings, instead risks turning into a tool for controlling and manipulating the masses. Moreover, in the hands of private companies not subject to democratic control but only to the logic of profit.

I am certainly not against capitalism and private profit, but I do see great risks when it comes to culture and information in the hands of po- che and powerful corporations.

We also need to be aware of the power of technologies such as artificial intelligence and self-learning algorithms, which can influence our decisions and lives without our consent. It is important to ensure ethical and responsible governance of these technologies to avoid abuse and discrimination.

The digital revolution is radically transforming every aspect of our lives, from information policy, to tele-communications law, to intellectual property rights, to patterns of business, the structure of markets, and relationships between suppliers and buyers.

LLM systems have become key players in the di- gital landscape, trawling online data that in most cases had been posted on the Web with theintention of being used in a different way.

In a pre-IA era, no thought was given to how dirom- pent artificial intelligence could be in this regard. Foundation models did not play such an important role in our society.

As we know, foundation models are general-purpose technologies that serve as platforms for a wide range of AI applications, including generative AI. They are capable of generating text, images, video, speech, music and more. They are also called GPAI ov- true general-purpose AI systems, which can be used for various applications even if not specifically designed for them.

But unfortunately, their transparency is inversely proportional to their social impact, which is increasing sharply, with the risk of replicating the failure modes of certain social media.

A group of researchers at Stanford University Human-Centered Artificial Intelligence specializing in AI, specifically to assess the degree of transparency of the major players in the field, created the Founda- tion Model Transparency Index[67], through which ten of the best-known next-generation algorithms were evaluated. These include Google's Palm 2 (which powers Bard), OpenAI's GPT-4 (the basis of ChatGPT), Meta's Llama 2, Stability AI's Stable Diffusion 2, and Amazon's Titan Text.

The index is based on 100 indicators that measure the transparency and resources required in the creation and use of these models. In 2023, researchers assessed 10 leading developers against these indicators, providing a snapshot of transparency in ecosi-

---

[67] http://s24ore.it/mcc09

AI system. The highest score obtained was only 54 out of 100, highlighting a fundamental lack of transparency. Nono- spite of the average score being 37 percent, 82 of the indicators are soddi- sfied by at least one developer, indicating that there are significant opportunities for improvement through the adoption of competitors' best practices.

A study conducted by the Stanford Internet Observatory has revealed disturbing findings regarding the collection of images used for training well-known artificial intelligence models, such as the LAION-5B da- taset. This collection includes thousands of images raffi- guring child sexual abuse, to be exact 3226 alleged child pornography cases of which 1008 have been confirmed. The problem lies in the method of data acquisition, namely *web scraping*, an automatic practice of extracting data from websites without distinguishing between licit and illicit conte- nutes, resulting in the inclusion of extremely problematic and illegal material in the dataset and serious ethical and legal implications. A real moral burden: each image represents a real victim, whose suffering is repeated each time the abuse material is viewed or shared, further violating her dignity and privacy.

During the first AI Safety Summit[68], and attended by 28 world leaders, a letter of intent was drafted to "work in- sially to contain the potential catastrophic risks posed by the galop- pant advance of artificial intelligence."

Among those who take sides among the alarmists is Elon Musk, an internationally renowned impren- dentor and host of the summit, who believes in a science-fiction vision that AI could become a superintelligence capable of rebelling against human control. Entrepreneurs like him, while warning of the existential risks associated with this pos- sible superintelligence, also seem to exploit fear to

---

[68] http://s24ore.it/mcc48

consolidate its decision-making power and guide policies on the issue.

This approach, seen as a brilliant marketing move, calls into question the consistency of the political class in listening to impactors who clearly pursue their own economic interests. The existential risk narrative thus seems more like a marketing ploy than a reflection based on the concrete risks of AI, such as social impact, discrimination, and misinformation.

The need to regulate AI is undeniable, but it is critical to do so in a way that is informed and based on a real understanding of how deep learning algorithms work.

I think we sometimes forget that AI was created by humans themselves, and as such it is humans who guide and direct it toward one purpose rather than another.

Governments, scholars, and intellectuals should approach the question with a greater critical spirit and listen to scientists who suggest how to mitigate the risks posed by reckless use of AI.

Some dangers are not even manageable by the companies themselves that own the models. One of these is known as "model collapse" and takes place when artificial intelligence begins to train with the data it itself produces. This phenomenon involves a degenerative process in which the developed content contaminates the fu- ture generation model datasets, distorting the perception of reality. Thus, if AIs draw on self-produced information, a degeneration of the results is re- crushed.

Ilia Shmailov, lead author of a study conducted by researchers affiliated with universities in the United Kingdom and Canada, ap- profoundly examined the impact of model collapse in appren-

of automatic training[69]. As we have just seen, this phenomenon occurs when generative models are trained on self-generated data, leading to the degradation of their performance, especially in low-probability situations with limited data. Shumailov provided an interesting analogy, comparing this process to audio feedback in which a microphone captures and reproduces its own sound output. The problem of model collapse might be more problematic for companies with few financial resources to deal with more accurate data labeling. The scholar also highlighted the need to define robust evaluation metrics for machine learning models, especially for low-probability events, to ensure their robustness for minority groups, i.e., the data that do not appear in the sub- stant dataset. Model collapse affects the effectiveness of model training and performance, as models may inadvertently acquire biases from internally generated data. Thus, it is important to understand what is relevant within the models, with particular attention to events that are poorly represented in the data. Possible solutions to this problem include the fact that the machine learning co-munity should focus on defining high-quality evaluation metrics and a detailed understanding of model learning dynamics, spe- cialy in low-probability contexts.

The White House's current commitment to source control.

of the data could be a step in the right direction, but more thought is needed on how to handle the bias introduced by generative models in training data.

Other unmanageable risks are related to the synthetic data created by the mac- chines themselves, whereby a phenomenon known as MAD could occur

---

[69] I. Shumailov, Z. Shumaylov, Y. Zhao, et al, *The Curse of Recursion: Training on Generated Data Makes Models Forget*, in "ArXiv," (2023), 2305.17493.

The critical issues

(Model Autophagy Disorder), a dysfunction in which models nutrate the information they have created. Some studies indicate that this can lead to a deterioration in the quality of vocabulary, reducing the diversity of language. Data pollution affects not only text but also images, with visibly artifactual results.

Companies that produce artificial intelligence models recognize many of these problems and talk about implementing some sort of "guardrail" to avoid harm. However, precautions seem inef- fective, and many of these companies try to simplify the issue by pointing out the difficulty of removing harmful content from models. Think of the aforementioned case in the health sector, when the United-Healthcare has been accused of denying needed care to the insured elderly through the use of an AI model acquired in 2020.

Or to when, on January 15, 2021, Mark Rutte, president of the Dutch Council, and his government resigned as a result of a scan- dalo related to child support; it involved fraud committed by in- dividuals receiving Dutch benefits while living in other EU countries. In an attempt to counter these frauds, the government had im- plemented an automated system based on data analysis, which, however, had generated systematic errors and unfair fraud charges against thousands of families.

The machine-learning model used to identify fraud was based on historical data, which led to a kind of discrimin- ation, with an increased risk of fraud for individuals of non-Dutch ori- gine. The consequences were devastating, involving between 25 and 30 thousand families who were falsely accused of fraud, leading to layoffs, loss of homes, and referral of children to social services.

This case has raised many questions about the automation of public services and the use of algorithms in government decisions.

native, as similar cases have emerged in other countries, such as the United States, Austria, and Dani- marca. Italy, albeit with less severe impacts, was not outdone with the "Buona Scuola" reform, which aimed to optimize the assignment of thousands of teachers to schools scattered throughout the country, based on a gradua- tory and the preferences expressed by the teachers themselves.

However, the regulations were vaguely written, and the algorithm, while faithfully se- guing the instructions given, returned problematic outcomes. Result: thousands of teachers were wrongly assigned to the wrong schools, generating extremely negative consequences in their lives, as is easy to guess. This case highlights that inaccurate design of algorithms for pub- lic decision-making can easily lead to systematic errors and discrimination, and that clear formulation of rules and instructions for algo- rithms is essential to avoid undesirable outcomes. Therefore, the adoption of automated technologies without an adequate understanding of their potential impacts and without ne- cessary precautions should be avoided at all costs.

Although the "Good School" case had less severe impacts than the Dutch scandal, it highlighted the need for careful and transparent governance in the use of algorithms in citizen ser- vices and PA. It is crucial to understand the human responsa- bilities behind these projects and to be aware of the limitation of technologies to avoid errors and discrimination.

We still cannot afford to deresponsibilize humans in the automation of processes, as this can amplify discri- mination and injustice. Instead, supervi- sion, constant monitoring and risk awareness are always needed.

Despite these risks, technology companies are increasingly pushing the adoption of AI, while authorities are still trying to figure out how to assign liability for the damage caused. For

The critical issues

example, the European Commission itself believes that the current rules are not suitable for handling claims for damages caused by artificial intelligence-based products or services.

The field of AI seems to be fueled by the promise of automation and significant improvements in performance in every human domain. However, there are growing concerns about the safety, liability, and ethical impact of AI. Authorities are working on workable legal frameworks to regulate the field, but the challenge is enormous considering the complexity of the issues raised. The fact, then, that technology companies are also involved in the rule-making process raises well-founded doubts about their effectiveness and neu- trality and the biases that the founding models might contain.

An important model such as OpenAI's Dall-E 3, for example, is limited in understanding noncanonical concepts. In fact, it recently depicted a white doctor treating black children, despite the fact that the prompt, i.e., the user's command, was exactly the opposite. The problem with this model is that it maps words directly onto im- magines instead of building intermediate models of reality and the relationships between language and images. It fails, therefore, to separate the world from the statistics of the dataset, resulting in even triggering racial issues. Instead, we should develop new kinds of AI systems that integrate awareness of the past with future-oriented values in order to represent and reason about the values themselves rather than perpetuating the data of the past.

Still on the subject of Dall-E, another alarming story makes us realize how many potential risks lurk in the unaccountable use of generative AI. Microsoft executive Shane Jones, one of the re- sponsors of software engineering, claims to have discovered vulnerabilities in Dall-E 3. After reporting it and urging Ope- nAI to remove the software from the market because it is capable of creating "violent and dangerous im- mages, a risk to public health," he does not

would receive satisfactory responses. These flaws in the system would con- sent users to break security protections to create violent and explicit images. Jones remained unheeded even- ing after publishing a post on LinkedIn, which he was asked to delete without a specific explanation. He did so, but he also wrote to the Washington State Attorney General and U.S. congressional representatives expressing his concerns about the abuse of AI. I still maintain that these systems are black boxes and we don't know how they work or where they get their information and data from for their generations. And, despite reassurances from companies, we don't even know how secure they actually are.

ChatGPT has, moreover, often fallen into the more trivial gender stereotypes associated with certain professions (such as female nurse or male lawyer). In a study that examined its accuracy in translating between English and languages such as Bengali that use only gender-neutral pro- nouns, it was found that the program perpetuates gender ste- reotypes by turning neutral pronouns into "he" or "she," the same biases found in tools such as Google Translate or MS Translator. What's worse, when asked for information about gender in English, it seems to attribute more respect to men than women in the same profession.

> Another serious implication o f artificial intelligence is related t o open source, that is, systems that are unprotected and accessible to anyone. So far, we have focused on closed source systems such as ChatGPT. In these cases, the software is carefully guarded by t h e creators, allowing public interaction through a Web interfac- tion or, for enterprise users, through an application pro- gramation interface (API) to integrate AI into their processes. Companies such as Meta, Stability AI, Hugging Face, and others,

Instead, they released powerful unprotected systems to democratize access to AI.

But of course, this practice has raised concerns about the lack of protection, security, and potential abuse of the techno- logy, as has been highlighted by OpenAI's refusal to continue to open source its GPT models and especially by the White House's executive order on AI and the European Union's AI Act.

To better understand the open source issue, we should esa- minate the differences between protected AI systems, such as ChatGPT, Bard, or Claude 2, and unprotected ones. Requiring protected systems to perform malicious actions, such as designing a more lethal coronavirus, for example, generally produces a rejection because it violates usage policies. But this threat increases with unprotected models, including Meta's notorious Llama 2, which was made available for download with a responsible use guide promptly ignored.

Once someone releases an "uncensored" version of an unprotected AI system, there is little the original creator can do. Open source systems present considerable risks, with the potential for abuse facilitated by the lack of restrictions.

The paradox was that until now open source was seen, both by me and by the IT community, only as a great positive resource for mankind, while now it risks even being dangerous?

The ability to disable security features and create custom versions opens the door to malicious uses by malicious parties, who can exploit vulnerable distribution channels such as social media where it is easy to spread persona- lized misinformation and widespread scams. Another concern is the production of malicious content, such as deepfakes of noncon- sensual pornography, with unprotected AI that can amplify its spread.

Not to mention the risk of using open source models, for the production of biological and chemical weapons, an issue also addressed by the-

the White House Executive Order and by proposed legislation under discussion in the U.S. Congress. Many of the regulations apply to both protected and unprotected systems.

The main difference lies in the fact that it is easier for developers of protected si- stems to comply with these standards because they are imple- mented in the system itself; thus they can actively monitor abuses or failures, releasing periodic updates to maintain fairness and security.

Implementation of such standards would discourage companies from re-releasing unprotected systems. The first action to take would be to suspend all new releases if security re- quirements are not met, establish registration and licensing, create liability for misuse or negligence and risk assessment procedures, require transparency of training data, access by independent researchers, and mandatory disclosure of incidents.

Regarding distribution channels and attack surfaces, one should require the implementation of content credentials, auto matization of digital signatures, limitation of the scope of AI-generated con- held, and reduction of chemical and biological risks.

On the part of governments, we expect the establishment of agile rego- lation bodies, support for fact-checking organizations, and above all, international cooperation on AI access and rules or the world's democracies may be at risk.

4.3 Democracies at risk

There is an unprecedented spread of misinformation, harnessing the power of generative artificial intelligence. NewsGuard, an information reliability monitoring system70, has so far

---

[70] http://s24ore.it/mcc69

The critical issues

identified many hundreds of AI-generated news sites that ope- rate with little or no human oversight, and is monitoring false narratives produced by AI-based tools.

Site owners are anonymous and create problems for quality journalism. In addition to generating distrust of information in general, they become ruthless competitors. To ensure high li- vation journalism, it is necessary to have adequate funding to hire specialized staff, such as fact-checkers and editors. In contrast, the co- sto of running such a site tends to be very low.

Fake news and bots already existed, but now humans are no longer needed to manage the content. Very precise disinformation is created, directed to a potential group of citizens who in turn will share fake news on social media, creating viral mechanisms. Fake news gene- rates misinformed and ill-informed citizens and is able to create bias. Sometimes this is done knowingly for political reasons, to influence public opinion in the direction desired by the polluter of information.

Famous personalities such as Elon Musk and Congressmen Keir Starmer and Mi- chal Simecka have become unwitting protagonists of deepfakes, audio and video con- held that are the result of manipulative use of artificial intelligence. The former has been involved in videos that are clearly recognizable as fakes, but the other two have been subjected to more damaging audio deepfakes, spread in a targeted way to discredit the political figures involved. Simecka was featured in a fake audio clip in which he discussed how to rig elections by buying the votes of the Roma mi- norance and in which he even joked about child pornography. Of course, he then lost the classes. It was, however, a fake synthesized by an AI tool on the speaker's voice. Another audio clip surfaced on Starmer in which the leader seemed to have ver- bally abused his aides. The content was immediately denounced as fake, but meanwhile it had already been listened to 1.5 million times.

These cases raise serious concerns about the credibility of information, the ability to distinguish fact from fiction, and the social impact of such media manipulation. A next imminent phase of global disinformation is on the horizon, with the cre- scenting threat posed by generative AI and deepfakes. Nono- spite the warnings of experts regarding the use of this tech- nology to manipulate voters' opinions, artifi- cial intelligence is now cheap and accessible enough that anyone can use it for that purpose.

The deepfake problem is not the only one threatening political elections; another even more immediate one is the use of AI to create *spear phishing* emails that appear legitimate to the recipient and encourage him or her to share sensitive details with the attacker. This technique has already been used in 2016 by Russian intelligence to get into the pos- sex of Hillary Clinton's campaign emails, which were then leaked online during the election that Clinton lost. But back then AI had not been used and it was all much more ru- dimental. Today you can create emails targeted to each person, which speak differently to each person, based on data processed by AI.

However, overemphasis on the risks associated with deepfakes and AI can spread fear, thereby undermining voters' confidence in the political pro- cess. Regardless of whether deepfakes become a significant problem, generative AI innovation is already a reality. Experts worry that the abundance of synthetic images and texts on social media, even when clearly labeled, could con- fuse them leading them to not distinguish well between fact and fiction.

In the U.S. congressional elections, Demo- cratic Party candidate Shamaine Daniels has introduced a groundbreaking innovation that changes the way politics is done: it's called Ashley, the first election cam- paign volunteer powered by technology similar to ChatGPT, in

The critical issues

able to conduct personalized and simulta- neous telephone conversations with an unlimited number of voters. Unlike traditional *robocallers*, Ashley provides real-time responses, tailoring con- versations to voters' interests. However, preoc- cupations emerge regarding the ever-increasing possibility of the spread of misinformation, a critical issue that is already keenly felt in the U.S. po- litical landscape.

Even the CEO of OpenAI (owner of ChatGPT), Sam Altman, fears an impact on *one-to-one* interactive disinformation during elections.

To stay in the U.S., for his presidential campaign, Donald Trump used a small group of viral video meme creators to serve as his online advertising agency. This team spent time flooding social media with content that lo- dered the former president, promoted his candidacy for the White House, and heavily denigrated his opponents, openly engaging in disinformation, artificial intelligence, and deepfake creation.

Their memes are characterized by racist stereotypes, tropes denigrating LGBTQ+ people, and scatological humor. Known as "Trump's Online War Machine," much of this group operates anonymously, adopting a cartoony style and a cruel ferocity typical of Internet trolls. We expect similar activities from all opposing political groups.

In the age of social media, the influence of memes is growing, con- trary to traditional television ads. Cheap to produce and li- ble to distribute, memes largely escape the rules of accu- rity, fairness, and transparency that govern television and radio advertising instead, spreading increasingly in a context where a limited number of platforms on the Internet seek to manage political content.

New Hampshire citizens recently received strange tel- fon calls, even from President Joe Biden, urging them not to vote in the presidential primaries. This was a mes- wise fake, a real illegal attempt to compromise the right to vote, after NBC News also received a call of the same kind to confuse the opposing political camp. This is another example of how technology is widely used to con- fuse the voter and discredit the competitor, as we have already seen with the Argentina case; here, however, the deepfake is no longer visual but vocal so it uses state-of-the-art tools to per- fectly imitate a person's voice, plus it involves profiling to select a sample of users to target. In contrast, the creators, in order to carry out the operation, used an outdated medium of communication, namely the telephone, and this clashes with the use of state-of-the-art digital technologies. Ultimately, the upcoming election campaigns will truly be a surprise for everyone.

The last presidential elections in Argentina, which saw the two facing off against each other candidates Javier Milei and Sergio Massa in deepfake blows, could be considered as the world's first truly AI-influenced elections, invaded as never before by fake videos and photos to destroy the opponent. One reason could be found in the jovi- ness of the Argentine electorate, which is why perhaps the manipulative use of AI was targeted. In this sense we can speak of artificial ma- nipulation. When the information available to voters is distorted and their preferences are shaped by all sorts of manipulations, the very essence of democracy is com- pleted. And not only this: we must also reflect on a possible violation of cognitive freedom.

If indeed people's freedom of thought is being eroded, why not establish special "neurorights" to protect our cultural autonomy?

The critical issues

The prominent role that AI has played in the Argentine campaign and the political debate it has sparked underscore the growing diffusion of the technology and show that, because of its power and low cost, it is likely to become a common factor in many democratic elec- tions around the world.

Technology, with AI, can deceive and confuse voters, casting doubt on what is real and adding to the misinformation that can be spread by social networks. For years, these fears were largely speculative because the technology to produce these fakes was too complicated, expensive, unsophisticated, and unavailable to everyone. Now we are seeing an absolute explosion of incredi- bly accessible and increasingly powerful tools, increasing the ability to create viral content with just a few clicks, even by non-profes- sionists, that previously would have taken teams of graphic designers and video editors skilled in special effects days or weeks to work on.

Awareness of the risk is widespread and the public is aware of it. This is to the point of generating almost the opposite effect, which is to stop believing even what is true and genuine.

For example, many comments questioned the veracity of a beautiful photo by Valerio Minato on Superga, which included a particular angle of Monviso and the Moon. Photo awarded addi- rally by Nasa.

People have begun to question the veracity of what is the result of years of study and preparation without having any knowledge of photography. Is it just ignorance or arrogance, or is it still, as far as we are concerned, AI-generated fakes generate such fear and confusion that it leads to this kind of reaction?

There is even the case of Adobe, which is selling AI-generated realistic images of the Israel-Palestine conflict through Adobe Stock, its stock image subscription service. Al- some of these depict scenes prepared ad hoc, while others appear as authentic photographs, blurring the line between reality and simulation. But the problem is that these images circulate without clear indications of their authenticity and without explicitly specifying their AI-generated nature. How do we monitor transparency in the use of AI-generated images? Do users have the ability to recognize them? These doubts increase concerns about potential misinformation, distorting reality and elevating perceptions of truth and accuracy.

Web scraping, deepfakes and hallucinations are a growing concern in both the public and private sectors. How to defend against them? Perhaps there is no defense.

In theory, one would have to do fact- checking for inconsistencies and searching for artificial elements every time, analyzing the audio of a video and con- sidering its context. But in all these actions, one must use specialized soft- ware and tools and above all rely on fact checking, an essential process through which to verify the accuracy of facts and information disseminated in the media. Examining the truthfulness of statements and facts, subjecting them to detailed research and at- temptingly evaluating the data and sources in the news, can limit the pro- pagation of misinformation, which in the Internet age is increasingly prevalent due to the increased interaction between websites and users at- traverse blogs, forums and chats.

Lack of verification of news and supporting sources could lead to acceptance of fake news as authentic, influencing wrong and dangerous decisions. But is the user willing and able to do so? On average, no.

What if in making a decision instead of man there is an artificial intel- ligence? The issue becomes even more complicated, as we are told by the story of a Russian soldier who in 1983, at the height of the Cold War, averted a nuclear conflict by identifying a false missile warning. Lieutenant Colonel Stanislav Petrov had the task of

The critical issues

monitor the screens connected to the OKO system, which revealed the launch of U.S. nuclear warheads. When a missile departing from the United States toward Russia appeared on the monitors at a quarter past midnight, Pe- trov remained calm and decided not to report anything, convinced that it was a mistake. And indeed, the system had confused an atmospheric phenomenon with a missile attack. His rationality saved humanity from a nuclear war. But I wonder if there had been a machine in its place, how would it have reacted? What would it have decided?

The Net as we know has no borders, and the influencer may be another state, perhaps "otherwise friendly." We are witnessing a radical tra- sformation involving several areas, from information to telecommunications legislation, from intellectual property to business models, from the structure of markets to the dynamics between suppliers and consumers.

LLMs, as we have already explored, collect data online in a massive way, from sources that were not originally intended to be used in such a way. This process undermines the concept of privacy and identity, not only at the individual level but also at the level of democracy and fundamental freedoms. People seem to underestimate the value of their data and privacy, passively agreeing to share personal information in exchange for free ser- vices. The section on Privacy will elaborate on this issue.

This trend, however, can lead to a dependence on tech giants, which accumulate huge amounts of data and can mani- polate them to influence public opinions. Interestingly, there is often a greater reluctance to share information with de- mocratic entities than with large technology companies, despite the fact that the latter are not bound by democratic principles. This disparity contributes to a growing gap between data and information fragmentation and increasingly concentrated power in the hands of a few companies.

But scholars, information philosophers and political balance experts do not all agree that regulation of the field is necessary, and there are those who argue otherwise.

We could draw parallels between the apocalyptic and integrated described by Umberto Eco in his 1964 essay titled precisely *Apocalyptic and integrated*[71] and catastrophists and optimists in the field of arti- ficial intelligence, to get an interesting look at human reactions in the face of significant technological changes. Eco's apocalyptics saw mass communication as a threat to tra- ditional culture and society, predicting a dark future. The integrated ones, on the contrary, embraced it as a positive force and capable of bringing about improvements in general.

In the context of artificial intelligence, catastrophists are those who fear the negative and potentially destructive impacts of AI on society, foreseeing scenarios in which AI becomes uncontrollable or overtakes humanity itself with unimaginable consequences. On the other hand, optimists believe that AI can lead to significant mi- lorations in human conditions, revolutionizing such set- tors as medicine, education, and scientific research, to name but a few. In both cases, there is an element of fear and uncertainty attached to the emerging technology.

Umberto Eco pointed out how the reaction to new technologies underlying mass communication could influence collective perception and culture. Similarly, in the AI debate, divergent perspectives can influence the future direction of technological innova- tion. However, it is important to note that, as Eco suggests, extreme positions can be excessive. A balanced perspective, which recognizes both the potential risks and benefits of AI, could be decisive in guiding its evolution in a re- sponsible and sustainable way.

---

[71] U. Eco, *Apocalyptic and integrated*, Bompiani, Milan, 1964.

The critical issues

Among those we might call "catastrophists" is Geoffrey Hinton, professor emeritus at the University of Toronto, one of the most influential scholars in the field of artificial intelligence in the past fifty years. Notoriously committed to creating AI systems inspired by the human brain, Hinton has changed his perspective to the surprise of many. Contrary to his earlier belief that the human brain was superior, he stated that current artificial intel- ligence may already be more advanced, but has not yet been sufficiently scaled up. Concerned about a future in which such si- stems will surpass the performance of the human brain, Hinton made the decision to step down from his role as vice president and engineer at Google in May 2023 and continues to raise awareness of the ethical challenges and risks associated with this emer- gency technology.

Yoshua Bengio, director
scientist at the Montreal Institute for Learning Algorithms. His in- contention with ChatGPT took months of study to adapt to the idea that AI could rapidly outperform humans. In line with Geof- frey Hinton, he realized that artificial intelligence, which he helped develop for the good of society, could have catastrophic im- plications and surpass humans in all tasks within the next five to 20 years. For this reason, in 2023, he testified before the U.S. Senate on this danger, expressing his intention to shift his research toward consa- peable use.

Even Andrew Ng, an expert on artificial intelligence, raised a warning about the spread by some large tech companies of the false idea that AI could lead to the extinction of humanity. The goal of AI-owning companies would be to promote strict regulations that would stifle their con- ducts.

Is the threat to democracies or the extinction of humanity caused by AI really just a strategy of big tech companies to eliminate competition?

Yann LeCun, chief scientist for AI at Meta and professor of computer science at New York University, is known for his bold and controversial ideas that have contributed to the generative artificial intelligence revolution. In an interview with *TIME*, LeCun dismissed existential fears related to AI as absurd and criticized this current ma- ny as a fad that is destined to die out. Strongly defending the safety of AI, he argued that detractors do not fully com- plete the complex engineering involved in making superintelligent systems. Thus, contrary to Geoffrey Hinton and Yoshua Bengio, LeCun diverges from their more cautious type of approach, believing that the concern about superintelligent machines is overblown.

For him, the correlation between intelligence and desire to conquer is not automatic, and he expresses confidence in the design of safe targets for algorithms, believing that the issue is not as complex as perceived. He emphasizes, however, that an intelligent system equal to human intelligence is not imminent and will require not only time but also new scientific discoveries.

Therefore, he believes it is premature to regulate AI for fear of superhuman in- telligence, as current systems are only intelligent in narrow domains and new technologies and architectures need to be developed to achieve human intelligence.

For him, on the other hand, it is important to build machines that can understand the physical world, remember, plan and reason, aspects that are currently beyond the capabilities of existing systems. While expressing cautious optimism about the positive effects of AI on society, he admits that there are risks and stresses the need for responsible use of technology. In fact, he says that individuals they should feel "empowered" rather than threatened by the av- wind of smarter AI systems.

This, according to him, could lead to a "new renaissance" si- mile to that of the invention of printing, but he reiterates the need to use technology responsibly to maximize its be- nefits and minimize its risks.

Who will be right? To posterity the arduous judgment. One certainty is that whichever way you look at it, man and ethics must always be at the center of everything.

4.4 Cyber ethics

We live in a world in which, as a result of precise neural alterations, we might be induced to perform certain actions. What would happen if, through this method, our control over impulses became less and less stable? We must work now to protect humans from the long-term evolution of digicratic society.

Paradoxically, we trust an algorithm more than our si- mili, especially in the case of more complex operations. What will happen to our ethical principles now that machines are self-learning? For example, in cases of self-driving cars, who would have to sce- le to run over a child or an elderly lady, if the accident were completely unavoidable, will do so on the basis of an "ethics module," perhaps even interchangeable, that will be pre-installed by the company renting the car? "Would you prefer the Japanese ethics module or the Western one?"

We know that an autonomous vehicle can operate without human involvement because of its ability to sense the surrounding environment through a series of sensors that provide the autonomous driving information system with an enormous amount of data, which is essential to ga- rant safe driving. However, to enable the car autonomous car to make sound decisions in various driving situations, it is necessary to subject it to an extensive training process that per- sons the vehicle to interpret the collected data and make appropriate choices based on the traffic context. Now imagine the situation pro- vided for just above in which an autonomous car, with failed brakes, is rapidly approaching a grandmother and a child: swerving slightly po- might save one of them. This scenario raises a fundamental ethical question: who should be given priority, the grandmother or the child?

This dilemma underscores the importance of ethics in the development of technologies. Who is responsible for these choices? The machine, certainly not. It is just a set of metal and silicon designed by man. So is it the designer or the company that gave him the task and the guidelines?

With the increasingly significant rise of artificial intelligence in society, growing ethical concerns are emerging that call for the at- tention of clear limits in the creation and adoption of new AI tools. Although large-scale regulation is still lacking, many technology companies have adopted their own code of ethics or guiding principles to guide their use.

When we talk about ethics, we refer to those moral principles that are adopted to guide responsible and equitable AI development and use, addressing issues as broad as data privacy, pre-judgments, discrimination, transparency, accountability, human rights, and social impact. In a rapidly changing environment, numerous companies, organizations, and institutions are collaborating to develop frameworks and standards that can guide the responsible advancement of these technologies.

For example, OpenAI says it is committed to ensuring that its techno- logy does not undermine the democratic process ahead of the 2024 global elections by stepping up efforts to prevent abuses such as deceptive deepfakes and large-scale influence operations. New systems are carefully evaluated before release, co-involving users and external partners for feedback and also implementing security measures to reduce potential damage. The company says it is also refining its uti- lization policies by not allowing the creation of political campaign apps until it better understands the effectiveness of tools for personalized persuasion, banning the creation of chatbots that pretend to be real people or institutions, and disallowing apps that discourage participation in democratic processes. It is also implementing initiatives to improve transparency on the pro- venience of artificial intelligence-generated images.

They claim they will use digital credentials to indicate the pro- venience of content, providing users with the ability to better evaluate an image. Finally, they will work with organizations such as the National Association of Secretaries of State (NASS) to direct users to authoritative sources of voting information, helping to improve access to reliable election-related information.

But that may not be enough. Numerous ethical challenges surround AI, and one of the biggest is the risks of unintended bias and discrimination derived from the data used to train such systems, which can potentially result in unfair treatment of individuals or groups.

Meanwhile, new concerns arise about fairness and respect for human rights and other fundamental values. In light of these consi- dations, I don't know how many of you would accept being judged in a tri- bunal by a robot, even without full knowledge of the deci- sional process adopted by it.

In Italy, Delegated Law No. [111/2023][72] specifically authorizes the use of artificial intelligence to combat tax evasion. But it

---

[72] http://s24ore.it/mcc47

is not limited to basic tasks such as researching and drafting legal documents; its possible involvement in judicial decisions is also being discussed.

The work in a law firm and court involves research, interpretation, drafting of documents, and decision-making. Certainly AI can excel in research and drafting, but its ability to in- terpret, often characterized by a creative leap and non-predefined associations, is currently limited. The jurist's creativity in shaping new legal or regulatory interpretations is a human compe- tence that AI does not currently possess. And I would add by for- fortune! It can write legal acts such as appeals and pleadings, but it still requires human intervention for supervision and control. Although it can support a lawyer in evaluating the pros and cons of a strategy, the final strategic decision and its advisory role re- mance the human domain at the moment.

As far as education is concerned, the European Commission, with the support of a group of experts in such areas as AI, data, ethics, and education, has produced an official document[73] in which it sets out ethical guidelines for educators on the use of AI and data in teaching and learning. In every classroom, school or university now AI systems are used in different modalities to support and sup- port both students in their learning process and do- cents in teaching and assessment. As the paper shows, underlying the ethical use of AI are four key principles, human intervention, equity, humanity, and justified choice, which are combined with the need to understand the potential and risks associated with this technology.

Prejudice and discrimination are just some of the problems- main tics when we talk about ethics in AI, because algorithms are not immune to bias. Training data can

---

[73] http://s24ore.it/mcc30

reflect human biases, generating AI systems that make incorrect decisions. These biases may arise from developers unintentionally programming biased algorithms and from sto- rical data used to train these algorithms that may not rap- present the entire population fairly. The presence of biased algorithms can lead to discrimination against minority groups.

For example, in 2014 Amazon developed an internal artificial intelligence system to optimize the per- sonal selection process, but this proved discriminatory against female candi- dents, automatically penalizing resumes that indicated membership in groups such as chess clubs or exclusively female colleges74. Thus, discrimination often turns out to be a difference in treatment based on group membership.

To develop ethical and responsible AI, biases in systems must be eliminated or mini- mized, but only 47 percent of organizations actively check for biases in data, models, and human use of algorithms. The multiplicity of human biases makes it perhaps impossible to eliminate them all, but the goal should be to minimize them. But in this it is important to consider the "social salience" of morally relevant characteristics, i.e., "sex, race, color, ethnic or social origin, gene- tic characteristics, language, religion or belief, political or any other opinion, membership in a national minority, patri- mony, birth, disability, age, and sexual orientation," as listed in the EU Charter of Fundamental Rights. The representative harms de- rivated by discrimination are the result of biases embedded in the systems themselves and manifested through stereotyping, denigration or exclusion. To address this problem, we need to understand how systems become biased and how to measure bias, which is introduced into the systems themselves through a sample not

---

[74] http://s24ore.it/mcc58/

representative or cultural ignorance or even biased interpretations. In order to identify and correct any inequities, it is necessary to esaminate the entire AI development process, including the design, implementation, and data management phases.

It is not enough to focus only on algorithms, because inequity can derivate from multiple factors including historical and cultural ones. How then can we improve equity and reduce bias in artificial intelligence systems? I believe there is no universal solution, as biases can manifest themselves in different ways and there is a lack of a clear definition of a fair outcome for an algorithm. One of the common ap- proaches is anticlassification, which is the removal of protected variables from the data, although this solution can be dan- dous in some situations, as features have different pre- dictive powers between social groups. Another approach, resampling, reduces bias in the data, but its effectiveness must be evaluated on a case-by-case basis. Discrimination goes beyond systematic bias. For example, an AI system that distinguishes between homosexual and heterosexual people based on a single photo may result in discrimination even if the algorithm is unbiased.

Ethics cannot be reduced to quantifiable values, and we must evidate the risk of reductionism in the ethical analysis of AI systems that produce biased outcomes, as search engine technology does not act neutrally. Big data processing privileges the re- sults with the most clicks, influenced by users' preferences and geographical location. As a result, search engines can act as *echo chambers*, reflecting and amplifying biases present in the real world and further anchoring them in the online context. The question then arises as to how to ensure fairer and more accurate search results. Is it possible to flag biased ones? For example, what should be the accurate representation of women?

Cyberhumanism

And still the introduction of facial recognition technology into surveillance systems raises important questions related to privacy rights. The AI Global Surveillance (AIGS) reveals that 176 countries im- plement artificial intelligence-based surveillance systems, with liberal democracies leading the way. From an ethical perspective, even- tual government abuse of this technology or its legitimate use is considered contrary to human rights. Technology companies such as Microsoft and IBM have voiced their ethical concerns about AI-powered surveillance.

However, it is undeniable that AI-powered facial recognition, if used on a large scale, could make it possible to catch dangerous fugitives or prevent terrorist attacks in a short time.

Even in medicine, its use has raised concerns about ethics, as well as health data protection. In- formed consent and patient autonomy are essential when using AI in medical settings. They must be informed and have the right to refuse treatment or procedures.

Another issue is the social divide that can lead to economic disuguality. Advanced automation and the introduction of medical robots can threaten employment and exacerbate the gap between developed and developing countries.

But perhaps the ethical issue we are most concerned about is that AI, despite its advances, lacks empathy and solidarity, fundamental aspects in medical interactions. Robots may not provide the same compassion and kindness as human operators, especially in sensitive areas such as mental health or pediatrics. Will we be able to ga- rant that AI contributes positively to the advancement of healthcare without compromising core human values?

Joseph Weizenbaum, the MIT professor who in the 1960s invented the first chatbot called ELIZA, in his book *Computer Power and*

The critical issues

Human [75] warned that "there is a difference between human and machine, and there are certain tasks that com- puters should not be made to do, regardless of whether they can be performed by computers."

As theologian Paolo Benanti argues in his book *Human in the loop*[76], "ethically using technology today means trying to tra- sform innovation into development. It means directing technology toward and for development and not simply seeking progress as an end in itself. Although it is not possible to think about and implement technology without specific forms of rationality (technical and scien- tific thinking), placing development at the center of interest means saying that technical-scientific thinking is not enough in itself. Different ap- proaches are needed, including the humanistic and the contribution of different re- ligions."

Lawrence Lessig, Harvard law professor and Inter- net expert, warns us that the role of social media in society is often misunderstood.

People tend to perceive their feeds as neutral platforms, not realizing that behind them is advanced artificial intelligence that is extremely adept at modifying their attitudes and emotions to increase interaction, without worrying about negative impacts but thinking only of the profit from involvement. This awareness raises concerns about the manipo- lation of people to ends that are not in line with their well-being or the mi- lection of democracy. According to him, LLMs have the ability to mislead people into believing that they are engaging on certain issues, a manipulation that can be likened to

---

[75] J. Weizenbaum, *Computer Power and Human Reason: From Judgement to Cal- culation*, W.H. Freeman, San Francisco, 1976.
[76] P. Benanti, *Human in the loop. Human decisions and artificial intelligences*, Mon- dadori Education, Kindle Edition, p. 195.

to a viral attack in which such "pathogens," as he defines them, spread through the system without adequate defense mechanisms currently in place, posing a threat without antibodies.

Regarding the regulation of copyright in AI, Lessig argues that in order to achieve it, it is necessary for the system itself to re- gister the work, clearly including the origin and thus providing detailed infor- mation about who created it and when. Currently, however, copyright in works resulting from AI is an inef- fective ownership system, as it lacks transparency in determining who owns the works and makes identification difficult for negotiations.

After playing a significant role in STEM (Science Technology Engineering Mathematics) research for years, now the influence of AI has spread widely to sectors such as health care, banking, retail, and manufacturing. Despite this of- fra significant benefits in terms of efficiency and innovation, there are growing concerns about its transparency, its potential social impacts, and the risk of bias in decision-making.

For this reason, while it is widely accepted as an engine of change, at the same time there is a growing debate about the ne- cess of addressing its associated ethical aspects. While waiting for a set of standards and rules to be enforced, ethics education is therefore a pressing need: to train and empower everyone involved in the creation and use of advanced technologies on the subject. And not only of AI developers, but also and especially of business leaders and citizens, so that they can fully understand the so- cial and ethical implications of this rapidly evolving innovation.

4.5 Digital wars

Artificial intelligence is considered a strategic tool by go- verns and tech giants for two main reasons: it offers a industrial advantage that can generate immediate econo- mic wealth and can be used for military or internal control purposes. The interest of governments in the development and use of AI is closely linked to the impact its future developments may have on the prosperity of nations, considering the great global competitive game.

According to IDC (International Data Corporation)[77], the complessive value of the artificial intelligence market will grow by 19 percent per year and, between now and 2026, will reach nearly the value of $1 trillion. According to [Accenture78], this growth will be generated by a 40 percent increase in labor productivity through the use of AI, which in turn will bring benefits to all stages of production. While [PwC79], a professional services and consulting firm, quantified the impact of this growth in a research study, claiming that the wealth generated by the use of AI will exceed $15 trillion.

It was predictable that there would be an economic clash between the na- tions to control and manage artificial intelligence, conside- ting these figures. Three basic things are needed to develop it: innovative algorithms, a large amount of data to train models, and powerful computing power. This is why the U.S. is [investing80] 140 million dollars in order to promote the development of seven new research centers and has prevented the export of a number of technologies and banned U.S. companies from collaborating with foreign states in developing AI technologies. This is because some countries such as China are competitors in terms of commercial ap- plications and national security. China is becoming a leader in the field. In the summer of 2017, it [announced81] the goal of

---

[77] http://s24ore.it/mcc10
[78] http://s24ore.it/mcc25
[79] http://s24ore.it/mcc56
[80] http://s24ore.it/mcc39
[81] http://s24ore.it/mcc36

achieve global leadership in AI by 2030 and has invested[82] more than $13 billion in the field by 2023.

Europe has also tried several times to initiate research and development projects in the field of artificial intelligence, but has not achieved the results and scope of the United States due to the lack of sufficiently powerful micro-chips. The world's largest manufacturers are American or cooperate closely with the US. TSMC, Intel and especially Nvidia are world leaders in the field.

One of the most significant European actions to promote research and innovation as well as semiconductor industry development and chip sourcing was the Chips ACT[83], as well as the AI Act, the policy agreement to directly regulate operations in the artificial intelligence sector that was approved on Feb. 2, 2024. In Europe, we still cannot compete with the computing po- tence of the United States. Currently, their best systems use 17,000 GPUs, while our best-performing one uses 43,000.

The International Institute for Strategic Studies[84] has classified the cyber maturity of countries around the world into three levels. In recent years, the United States has maintained dominance in the first tier, while the second tier has seen the emergence of a diverse group of the United Kingdom, Australia, Canada, France, Israel, Russia and China. In the third li- vel we find India, Indonesia, Japan, Malaysia, North Korea, Iran, and Vietnam. According to various analyses, China has now reached remarkable cyber maturity, comparable to that of the United States, due mainly to its efforts in developing artificial intelli- gence. A global war on the supremacy of AI and its strategic use in international competition.

---

[82] http://s24ore.it/mcc42
[83] http://s24ore.it/mcc22
[84] http://s24ore.it/mcc49

The critical issues

Despite being at the third level, North Korea has recently begun using AI to enhance its information operations, consequently posing a threat to other states. In response, the U.S. launched the DARPA AI Cyber Challenge[85], an initiative aimed at mobilizing experienced defense hackers to develop AI-based security solutions with the goal of averting the potential North Korean threat. This scenario clearly underscores the importance of implementing robust and prospective in- formatic security strategies. Microsoft's Digital Defense Report further highlighted the urgency of the problem, given the increase in cyber attacks targeting IT service providers. Cybersecurity, therefore, has now become a top priority for companies to protect not only their data and interests, but their very survival in an increasingly threatening and in- certain environment.

Recently, the Stimson Center, a *think tank* committed to solu- complex policy issues, raised serious concerns about North Korea's investment in artifi- cial intelligence, calling for preemptive actions by cloud service providers to prevent the regime from leasing the infrastructure needed to develop its capabilities in AI. The paper published by the Stimson Center, titled *North Korea's Artificial Intelligence Re- search: Trends and Potential Civilian and Military Applications*[86], highlighted that North Korea considers AI a national priority.

Although international sanctions have restricted its access to the hardware needed to develop its AI infrastructure, the growing quantity of scientific papers written by Northco- kingan scientists indicates a possible transfer of knowledge across borders.

---

[85] http://s24ore.it/mcc02
[86] http://s24ore.it/mcc34

Cyberhumanism

North Korea, in fact, may rent ne- cessary AI infrastructure through cloud service providers, as the country is known to support IT operators abroad. Concerns focus on the concept of "intangible technology transfer" (ITT), which refers to the availability of resources through such means as e-mail, verbal communication, training, or visual inspection. Thus the North Korean re- gime could set up seemingly legitimate accounts to rent AI infrastructure, and conse- guence cloud service providers could unwittingly host North Co- rea's AI activities, contributing to the creation of its armed forces.

In the face of these threats, there should be a focus on improving customer screening procedures during onboarding and avoiding inadvertent collaboration with North Koreans in sen- sible areas.

Still on the subject of threats, the evolution of artifi- cial intelligence is also redefining power relations in the military context. Also in the field. The lack, however, of an international legal framework to regulate these technologies raises legitimate ethical and strategic concerns. The report titled *Ukrainian Advantage: How AI is Changing the Balance of Power in Warfare*[87] highlights several questions about the responsible use of AI, which is primarily employed for reconnaissance, target recognition, and sensi- tive data analysis acts. The call for an international ban on the military use of AI fuels debates, involving public opinion, policy decisions, and the media. While the U.S. State Department issues a policy statement[88] on conditions for the development of AI-based weapons, binding regulations are still lacking. It is ne- cessary to balance automated processes with human control, because over-reliance o n artificial intelligence and a

---

[87] http://s24ore.it/mcc38
[88] http://s24ore.it/mcc62

The critical issues

problem known as *AI* overreliance, or "blind trust" in AI by humans, raise legitimate concerns. The European Union, in setting laws on AI in the military, is using a risk-based approach, banning somewhat harmful practices with the goal of developing monitoring strategies for AI-based self-named weapons, considering both ethical and strategic-military implications.

Another theater of war that has seen recent implications of artificial intel- ligence is the conflict between Israel and Hamas. The Israel Defense Forces (IDF) has employed an AI-based system chiamated *Habsora* (Gospel, in English) to locate targets at a faster rate. We could call it a veritable "target factory," and it has indeed sped up ber- sage detection by a great deal, up to 100 per day. The first question that comes to mind is, what about the possible involvement of civilians in these attacks, even if the targets were the homes of individuals suspected of being Hamas or Islamic Jihad operatives? As much as the IDF has assured that the use of these technologies greatly reduces harm to civilians to the benefit of greater precision in targeting, there is little evidence to support such statements-just look at the effects of the bombings on the Gaza landscape.

The advent of machine learning in the military context has, therefore, ra-
dically transformed the way armed forces act in wartime si- tations, including the concept of "final decision-making." Machine-learning-based instrumentation offers seemingly superior expertise over traditional methods, pushing toward greater automation of decisions in the field.

From an ethical-legal perspective, however, the role of humans in life-and-death que- stions is essential, defining the "human" act of war. The use of intelligent autonomous weapons, capable of making decisions without human input, must be governed by an inter-recognition.

national setting limits on the duration, scope and scale of military operations involving such weapons.

For example, there are AI-powered sights that can indivi- duate human targets at a distance, while de- cision support systems can influence the planning phase of an attack, in the so-called "kill chain," already pioneered by the Pentagon, which is taking a number of initiatives to manage conflicts differently with AI-based tools. To advance these intentions, it has already developed 800 projects including the Replicator program, con- sidered a *game changer* in military strategy, which aims to deploy thousands of weapon systems and autonomous vehicles to modernize the armed forces and thus compete with China and Russia in a digital race that has strong geopolitical implications.

Replicator envisions the creation of a vast network composed of mi- glias of AI-guided drones, a versatile network that can operate collaboratively or autonomously, especially in situations where communications with remote bases are difficult. The Pentagon's is obviously not the first such experiment. The U.S. has long been involved in collaborations with several Middle Eastern partners, ranging from Tel Aviv to Riyadh, as part of the U.S. Navy's Task Force 59 efforts to create a centralized network com- posed by drones and sensors with the intent of monitoring Iran's military activities in a vast region stretching from the Persian Gulf to Syria. Autonomous weapons, often referred to by technologists as "killer robots," raise concerns among those who fear an arms race, risks of mass destruction, and serious human rights consequences, given thelack of international treaties regulating their use. Within a military context, there is also to consider the possibility that identifying with a robot soldier collaborating with others could lead to the "Lucifer effect," prompting the operator to behave in an aggressive and sadistic nature. This is a phenomenon

The critical issues

social studied by Philip Zimbardo[89], a U.S. psychologist, which po- might also be applied to AI-driven machines.

The use of lethal autonomous systems (LAWS) in the military is increasingly raising important ethical issues because these si- stems are capable of autonomously identifying and engaging targets based on preprogrammed constraints and instructions. Objections to their use are widely supported by nongovernmental organizations. The "Campaign to Stop Killer Robots," for example, drafted a letter warning against the threat of unbridled competition in the field of artificial intelligence applied to weaponry.

The Future of Life Institute (FLI) in 2018 published a petition[90] calling for an international ban on autonomous weapons. NATO has also set limits on the use of these weapons, such as only attacking military targets, but despite these and other initiatives in this regard, the UN has not yet issued a final treaty regulating their use. As we have seen, the use of AI in the conflict in Ukraine, with algorithms matching targets to artillery units, forces us to understand human responsibility in military actions when a decision is the result of a combi- nation of human and machine-generated elements. The future perspective envisions, yes, the integration of AI into automated networks that link weapons and humans, creating a kind of lethal decision network, but how do we ensure a clear human understanding of the decisions made by these automated networks? This raises new questions about the legitimacy and ethics of military actions, brushing aside the traditional laws and doctrines of war.

If we then think that the AI could be geared toward nuclear warfare... This seems like a far-fetched statement, but so

---

[89] P. Zimbardo, *The Lucifer Effect: How Good People Turn Evil*, Rider, 2008.
[90] http://s24ore.it/mcc19

demonstrated the authors of a paper[91] presented at NeurIPS, the annual conference on neural information processing systems. The scholars, having realized that especially with the advent of generative AI models such as GPT-4, governments are increasingly considering the integration of autonomous artificial intelligences into military and foreign policy decision-making processes, analyzed the comcomportment of different artificial intelligences in war-game simulations and their propensity to take actions that can escalate conflict. Using the political science and international relations literature on escalation dynamics, they developed an evaluation system to measure the risks of actions intra- taken by these artificial intelligences in various situations. Thus they found that all five of the LLMs studied show forms and patterns of escalation that are difficult to predict and that these systems tend to develop arms race dynamics, leading to increased conflict and, in some cases, even the use of nuclear weapons. This stu- dy leads us to only one conclusion: given the signi- cant implications in military and foreign policy contexts, we cannot independently employ language models for military or diplomatic stra- tegic decision-making given their utter unpredictability. The main problem always lies in the fact that these systems are trained on historical data, in this case the literature in the field of international relations, which is likely to focus on the exacerbation of national conflicts, hence the bias learned du- rantly during training.

The ambitious program of DARPA (Defense Advanced Research Projects Agency)[92] called DARPA CODE and concepted to enhance the effectiveness of drones in hostile environments or those without

---

[91] J.-P. Rivera, G. Mukobi, A. Reuel, et al., *Escalation Risks from Language Models in Military and Diplomatic Decision-Making*, in "ArXiv," (2024) 2401.03408."
[92] http://s24ore.it/mcc41

The critical issues

direct human communication and control. To be more clear, the program aims to create weapons that, guided by artificial intelligence, are capable of making decisions in an auto- nomous manner. These weapons, known as Lethal Autonomous Weapons Systems (LAWS), include military drones such as Unmanned Aerial Vehicles (UAVs), suspected to be involved in the recent attacks in Palestine. These autonomous systems detect, select and target targets without requiring human intervention. Another aspect of the CODE project is the design of aerial vehicles capable of emulating the cooperative approach of wolves, hunting in coordinated packs with minimal communication. Underlying this research is the intent to create a system in which drones, leveraging machine learning and AI, can improve their operational strategies in a way analogous to the collective intelligence of wolves.

At this point, the problem of artificial moral agents emerges. (AMAs) that would take responsibility for making moral decisions instead of humans, raising ethical questions about the role of morality in machines and its social implications. But what are and how do we define ethical standards for AMAs? Is it pos- sible to design machines with a higher level of morality than humans? Machines are machines and can cause harm, so there is a need for higher ethical standards than human ones. Recently, OpenAI has made changes to the policies for the uti- lization of its models, eliminating some impermissible uses such as malware generation, military and warfare applications, marketing multilevel, plagiarism and astroturfing[93].

Of course, this does not mean that users can now use ChatGPT for previously prohibited purposes. But, some restrictions

---

[93] Marketing technique that makes consensus (or dissent) around a concept, product, or person seem spontaneous, when in fact it is the result of specially designed campaigns.

have been incorporated into the four universal policies that outline broader rules, such as "Do not use our service to harm yourself or others" and "Do not reuse or distribute the ri- sults of our services to harm others." According to research conducted by [Anthropic94], current methodologies used to improve the security of AI models are not effective in correcting unwanted behaviors if they have been trained to act maliciously, as they continue to generate malware and of- fensive responses.

4.6 Connected brains

Will people be willing to voluntarily hand over their neu- ral data to companies? Rules must be set now, before it is too late, to guarantee individuals the right to mental privacy. The Na- tions should recognize it as a new human right, a new right to cognitive freedom, and define its boundaries.

Mental privacy is a fundamental aspect of cognitive freedom. But like all privacy rights, it is not absolute. People may have the right to grant others access to their cer- vate activities. The simplest devices already on the market, such as release or focus devices, have forms of reading cere- bral data, which are granted to the relevant apps when accounts are created. But there are still few social norms and laws regarding ce- rebral monitoring, and the rules are left to the discretion of companies.

The problem is very serious. Take technologies like SmartCap that were created to improve employees' working conditions, but could be used in a punitive way. It is not so far a

---

[94] E. Hubinger, C. Denison, J. Mu, et al, *Sleeper Agents: Training Deceptive LLMs that Persist Through Safety Training*, in "ArXiv," (2024), 2401.05566.

future where the data says that if the employee uses the app too often and the results are unsatisfactory, then he or she will be fired.

In the United States, the First Amendment of the Constitution has always been interpreted as the defense of freedom of thought, which in turn implicitly includes the right to read what one wants, think what one thinks, and not be forced to utter words or express feelings contrary to our beliefs. Most importantly, not to allow others to have access to it.

Now that artificial intelligence technology can increasingly infer our thoughts from our digital activities, and nano-technology can decode our emotions and, perhaps one day, pre- sto, even our thoughts, urgent updates to international con- venctions are needed. Freedom of thought, and its secrecy, is the beating heart of civil liberties. Without it, the diversity of ideas ne- cessary for human well-being is stifled.

Just as surveillance chills people from sharing their nonconforming opinions, thought control will inevitably lead them to change their thoughts, seeking to silence their inte- rior voices, setting in motion a dangerous spiral that ends in the suppression of even the most intimate opinions. It is of utmost importance to ban thought surveillance by governments.

There is already a program that can read the thoughts of the mind and convert them into text. Basically BrainGPT performs a *brain-to-test* translation, using the electrical impulses of the brain as input through a simple electroencephalogram. The result is not perfect, for example in some cases it translates nouns with synonyms, but the researchers are convinced that it can reach the standards of common translation soft- ware. This makes it easy to see how the time is not far off at all when our thoughts could be literally extrapolated from our minds and used for who knows what purposes.

Elon Musk's Neuralink, based in Fremont, California, has completed its first implantation of a wireless brain chip in a per- son, marking a fundamental step in the field of cer- vate-machine interface. Preliminary results already indicate promising re- levation of neuronal spikes. The goal of this new experiment is to enable people to control a computer through thought and perform actions through the same interface. The use of the implant could, according to Musk, help paralyzed patients walk again, restore sight to the blind, and treat psychiatric ma- diseases such as depression. The implant also allows control of devices such as phones and computers through thought, so it may be useful to those who have lost the use of their limbs, among others. In contrast, however, the entrepreneur's claims have not been independently verified, nor has his company provided information on the procedure he followed. Despite this and the allegation that the tests con- ducted on animals led to the death of large numbers of specimens, in 2023 Neuralink received approval from the U.S. Food and Drug Administration to experiment on humans.

The research involves the use of a robotic system to perform with precision the placement of 64 thin flexible wires, thinner than a human ca- pel, within a brain region responsible for con- trolling movement. The robot will employ this wireless brain interface to acquire and transmit neural signals to a device that can interpret and decode an individual's movements. The implantation of such devices, however, requires invasive neurochi- rurgical intervention and is currently still in the experimental stage. Other important issues also arise: will Musk not want to turn neuroscientific research into a profitable market as he has already done in the space field? Most importantly, how will brain data be treated? Will they be adequately secured? Imagine what could happen if people's data, at this point I would say thoughts, ended up for sale on the darkweb as today occurs for password databases.

Recently, researchers at Stanford University developed NOIR (Neural Signal Operated Intelligent Robots)[95], a brain-robot interface or BRI (Brain-Robot Interface) system that allows individuals to guide robots in various daily activities through brain signals. By means of an electroencephalogram, the robot is co- municated the action to be taken; it learns to predict in a few strokes even the goals that the human wants to achieve, reducing both the effort and the time it would take him to perform the same tasks. NOIR has been successfully tested in about 20 household tasks, improving human-robot interaction by adapting to individual preferences and predicting users' in- tentions through the synergistic use of robotic apprentation algorithms. The discovery could be very useful for those with reduced mobility pro- blems, for example, but at the same time the question arises: what happens to all the information collected by the operator through brain sensors? They are productions of our minds that end up in the hands of we do not know who and especially with what outcomes. The ethical problem is always around the corner.

4.7 Cybersecurity and cybersafety

As we have already seen, artificial intelligence has a perfectly dual soul: it can be exploited for the good of humanity, but also misused as a tool for phishing and scamming.

At worst by increasingly organized criminal gangs that are beginning to equip themselves with AI and ML experts to pro- durate ransomware attack tools. In short, a real disaster for security and privacy.

In 2018, OpenAI had already warned against the dual use of this

---

[95] http://s24ore.it/mcc32

technology, publishing a paper entitled *Preparing for malicious uses of AI*[96]. There is a need for increasing knowledge and implementation of cy- bersecurity techniques and making AI code more secure, for example, through AI Trust, Risk and Security Management (AI Trism), an area of research that seeks to reduce the misuse of AI.

For example, the ability of certain chatbots such as ChatGPT, Bard, and Bing to follow instructions or *prompts* provided by users to generate a text makes them susceptible to misuse, because the model can es- pose to ignore security precautions. In fact, the practice of *jailbreaking* ChatGPT through "role-playing" prompts by which people try to influence the template to express racist content, conspiracy theories, or encourage illegal behavior is becoming increasingly common, since now with the spread of large language templates, even inexperienced users can pose a risk during everyday interactions. In practice, a taxonomy of persuasion based on social science research is in- troduced and after this is used to automatically generate interpretable adversarial persuasive messages aimed at jailbreaking LLMs.

Persuasion significantly increases jail- break performance in all risk categories. OpenAI has tried to su- bject a remedy by incorporating jailbreaking examples into the training data to improve the future security of the chatbot. But there is an even bigger pro- blem, namely the integration of ChatGPT into online interactive products, which exposes the chatbot to be even more vul- nerable. Specifically, there is a risk known as "indirect prompt injection," which is the addition in a website of hidden text to change the behavior of the AI mo- del and obtain sensitive information. There is also the possibility of sending e-mail with hidden prompts. If the recipient uses a

---

[96] http://s24ore.it/mcc31

The critical issues

AI virtual assistant, the attacker could manipulate it to extract personal information from the victim's e-mails or even send bogus e-mails to people on his or her contact list.

There is also the issue of data poisoning: AI language models are vulnerable to attacks even before they are implemented, because they are trained on large datasets from the Internet, which are thought to be intact. Instead, researchers have shown that it is possible to poison such datasets; in fact, for a trivial amount of money, they purchased domains and inserted custom images, as well as modified Wikipedia entries that were used to train the models. We also consider that continuous repetition of training data can amplify associations in the model. By en- vying the dataset with a significant number of manipulated examples, it is possible to permanently influence the behavior and results of the model. Thus, the addition of chatbots to online search is creating a strong incentive for attackers: it is only a matter of time before attacks become a reality, if they are not already...

By 2028, cybersecurity spending in AI will increase to $60.6 billion with a growth rate of 21.9 percent (in 2023 it was $22.4 billion), according to the Ar- tificial Intelligence in Cybersecurity Market[97], a new study by Mar- ketsandMarkets. Due to the increase in both the number and severity of cyber attacks targeting defense institutions, go- vernmental agencies, and technology companies, there is a growing demand for advanced artificial intelligence solu- tions to ensure greater protection from threats. The increase will be seen especially in the Asia-Pacific market seg- ment, where there are stricter go- vernational policies and significant population growth. Vulnerable countries such as India, Australia, Japan, China, and South Korea will focus more of their resources on consolidating the

---

[97] http://s24ore.it/mcc53

defense infrastructure, given the cyber warfare scenario that is gradually unfolding.

Compared with traditional security systems, the approach that integrates various AI techniques in modeling cyber security intelligence has greatly improved the efficiency in preventing and indi- viduating security events or incidents. With this in mind, researcher Iqbal H. Sarker released a study titled *AI- Driven Cybersecurity*[98] in 2021, in which he explains the Security Intelligence Modeling methodology and indicates future directions for research in this area.

The analysis of the appropriate use of machine learning techniques in cybersecurity, along with the very protection of sistems from vulnerabilities and malicious activities, is an im- portant goal. This forms the core of the investigations con- doted in the research lab of Prof. Lorenzo Cavallaro of the Department of Computer Science, University College London, where they work at the intersection of program analysis and machine learning for system security. Recently, Prof. Cavallaro published a scholarly report titled *Security and Privacy of AI Knowledge Guide*[99], included in the Cyber Security Body of Knowledge, which addresses the need to explore how program analysis and machine learning can synergistically enhance systems security in adverse contexts, with the primary goal of defining practical tools and providing security services to the community.

The National Institute's new work also moves in this direction.

---

[98] I.H. Sarker, M.H. Furhad, R. Nowrozy, *AI-Driven Cybersecurity: An Overview, Security Intelligence Modeling and Research Directions*, in "SN Computer Science," 2021, 2.

[99] http://s24ore.it/mcc40

The critical issues of Standards and Technology (NIST) titled *Adversarial Machine Learning: A Taxonomy and Terminology of Attacks and Mitigations*[100], in which scholars identified AI and ML vulnerabilities and approaches to mitigate them, providing a detailed picture of potential attacks that artificial intelligence systems might suffer and interventions to limit the damage.

It is now clear that the datasets used for AI training are so extensive that it is difficult to monitor and filter them effectively. And there is currently a lack of reliable ways to protect AI from erroneous manipations, which can range from evasion attacks that attempt to alter an input to change the system's response, to poisoning attacks that occur in the training phase with the introduction of corrupted data, again to privacy attacks with attempts to learn sensitive information, and finally to abuse attacks whereby the AI is provided with erroneous data from legit- time but compromised sources. Despite the extensive knowledge of each of these types of attacks, we are still far from formulating all the di- fences that need to be put in place to solve the theoretical security problems of AI algorithms.

In enterprise organizations, the security problem is amplified by the fact that data become the main target of cyberattac- tors. Hackers could manipulate the data that drive artificial intelligence models to influence business decisions. That is why it is essential to make trusted data the backbone of the organization, evolve cybersecurity practices to adapt to the requirements of generative AI mo- ders, embed transparency, trust, and security in the use of AI, and protect the data that powers it. Cybersecurity should be treated as the core product to protect AI initiatives, with stakeholder adoption and awareness.

As for whether AI can compromise and violate the sphere of the

---

[100] http://s24ore.it/mcc29

rights of the individual, t h e Agency for National Cybersecurity (ACN), the National Interuniversity Consortium for Informatics (CINI), and the Data Protection Authority are working to direct AI solutions to the balance between responsabi- lity and opportunity and balance human rights and the demands of scientific research.

People often do not realize the importance and the work that the structures in charge of defending the digital security of citizens do. In Italy, every day the Postal Police repel or reduce the impacts of mi- gles of attacks. Every day that the prin- cipal infrastructure that makes the country work continues to function, it is because the ACN protects its perimeter.

They are only talked about when something slips through the cracks, but the hundreds of times a minute when they defend us, they are not widely appreciated.

Other AI-related crimes exploit unprotected IoT sensors, es- sential to infrastructure and manufacturing facilities. Attacks, once sporadic, are increasingly frequent and target U.S. and European targets. The hardest hit sector is manufacturing with 61 percent of attacks: attackers can disrupt industrial control systems, resulting in millions of dollars in lost orders, productivity and customers. Often, attacks target inadequately protected IoT, IIoT and programmable logic controller (PLC) devices, which transmit real-time data within infrastructure and plants. After this initial phase, it is easy to penetrate deeply into the network to cause disruption. But these attacks do not only affect these types of companies.

There are those who are currently focusing their efforts on the ra- pid use of artificial intelligence-based arsenals to make bold political statements or execute large-scale ransomware attacks. In addition to manufacturing, sensitive sectors such as energy, water, oil and healthcare are particularly vulnerable, as even a brief disruption could threaten lives and cause economic losses in the millions of dollars range. HLE, a company that manages security for more than 500 companies, has unveiled the Cyber Watch dashboard that can detect potential intrusion attempts into IoTs in real time, enabling threats to be stopped promptly and improving detection technology. IoTs are physical objects, known as "things," equipped with sensors, soft- ware and other integrated technologies to facilitate the connection and exchange of data with other devices and systems via the Internet. These devices range from common objects in the home to advanced industrial struc- tures. Experts predict that their number could grow to 22 billion by 2025, taking a prominent role among 21st century technologies. Thanks to the ability to con- nect everyday objects to the Internet through incor- porated devices, the way has been opened for fluid communication between people, processes and objects. This connectivity is made possible by technologies such aslow-cost computing, cloud computing, big data, data ana- lysis, and mobile technologies, enabling physical objects to share and collect data with minimal human intervention. In this hyper-connected scenario, digital systems have the ability to re-record, monitor and regulate every interaction between con- nected objects, creating a meeting point and cooperation between the fisical and the digital one.

Artificial intelligence plays a key role in improving IoT security, starting with real-time analysis of massive amounts of data from devices and advanced threat detection based on analysis of IoT traffic, detecting anomalous behaviors that could signal the presence of an ongoing attack or suspicious and unauthorized activity. This capability proves critical in preventing or limiting damage during attacks ransomware. Advanced identification and authentication are potentially enhanced by AI systems that improve IoT network access mechanisms, ensuring that only authorized devices can connect. This helps prevent the infiltration of compro- puted devices.

In addition, behavioral analysis performed by AI examines the evolving behavior of IoT devices to detect suspicious changes or deviations from normative patterns, anticipating potential mi- nthreats before they cause significant damage, not to mention the pos- sibility of automating responses to security events, isolating compromised di- devices or blocking access to specific resources to contain the spread of ransomware attacks. Con- tinuous learning is provided by machine learning models, which are constantly updated with new data from the IoT network to maintain high effectiveness in detecting evolving threats.

Thus, AI is constantly assessing the risks associated with IoT devices, taking into consideration aspects such as the presence of si- curity patches, compliance with security policies and other potential vul- nerabilities, and facilitating the secure sharing of si- curity information in order to prevent large-scale attacks. Not least, it is fon- damental for states to delve deeper into IoT security issues and adopt holistic approaches to protect their networks and infrastructure.

4.8 Working for the machines

In the current context, rather than ultra-intelligent robots taking the place of humans, we face the prospect of an increase in precarious and fragmented work. As we have seen, the use of robots is affecting a range of occupations. Machines are replacing workers in many manufacturing sectors and are in

The critical issues

able to perform complex tasks that previously required skilled implem ents and technicians, such as data processing, computer accounting, and medical diagnostics.

But the advent of intelligent machines is also having a profound im- pact on a wide range of intellectual professions, particularly in the area of technology, such as computer lin- guage programming, where intelligent machines can often be used to more quickly and accurately accomplish many of the tasks that would require extra time and energy from a human pro- grammer.

Or other fields such as scientific research, data analysis and machine learning are seeing the increasing use of artificial intelligence-driven automation to perform many tasks.

According to CEDEFOP[101] data, the situation is quite alarming when one considers that the first workers at risk (18 percent) are agri- cial laborers, artisans, and those employed in manufacturing, who make up the bulk of the workforce. Next, the industrial sector po- might see a 17 percent reduction in assemblers and machine and plant operators, metal and machine and spe- cialized workers (15 percent), while construction could see a 16 percent loss of ma- novals. Cleaners and helpers, drivers and vehicle operators, gardeners, and technicians are also at risk-13 percent. Those in electrical work could see an 11% reduction in employment, a percentage that drops to 10% for canteen and pro- tection workers. As for sales, 9% may be supplanted by AI, falling to 8% for scientists, engineers and researchers, teaching professionals, foresters, and fishermen. A 7% of health profes- sionists are at risk, as are office professionals. Also at risk are 6 percent of ICT technicians and professionals, accounting and office clerks, and associate professionals. 5% of

---

[101] http://s24ore.it/mcc37

attorneys, customer service and support clerks, and 4 percent o f roadside service workers, hospitality, service and retail managers. Finally, we consider 3 percent of technical and business managers and 2 percent of civil servants and legislators. As can be seen from these percentages, industries where there is a higher degree of automation and limited demands for communication, collaboration, critical thinking, and customer service skills are most at risk.

Recently the U.K. Department of Education published research[102] revealing that 10-30% of jobs may be replaced by AI. Those most likely to risk their jobs are lawyers, psychologists, teachers, counselors, and telephone agents. AI chatbots such as ChatGPT or Bard perform routine 24-hour tasks by interacting with multiple customers simultaneously. This sup- poses that AI will replace workers in a number of areas, but we should not forget that it can and should act as an assistant, leaving humans to devote themselves to more creative and less tedious and repetitive tasks.

Intelligent machines have also helped to greatly reduce the unit cost of many professional services offered by skilled specia- lists such as accountants and legal advisers. For the le- gal profession, for example, AI represents both a threat and an oppor- tunity. According to a 2021 report by the Law Society of the United Kingdom, it could lead to a "wild reduction" in jobs for humans. A 2023 study by the universities of Pennsylvania, New York, and Princeton estimated that instead of the legal sector, it is the in- dustry most likely to be affected by AI.

AI can play a valuable role in researching and com- pilating cases. Although there are some of these that have gone terribly wrong. Steven Schwartz, a lawyer in New York City, has

---

[102] http://s24ore.it/mcc04

The critical issues

found himself facing a very unusual hearing: during a legal precedent search for a case involving a man suing an airline for personal injury, he relied on ChatGPT. Surprisingly, six of the seven cases used turned out to be completely fabricated by [IA103].

Although this might have discouraged many law firms from adopting such systems, Ben Allgrove, chief innovation officer of Baker McKenzie, a renowned international law firm, expressed a different opinion: "I don't see this as a techno- gical issue, but a matter of professional behavior. Before we po- ter discuss about Mr. Schwartz's misuse of AI, we need to address the lack of professionalism and ethics on his part."

Some legal firms are already using artificial intelligence. Baker McKenzie has been monitoring AI developments since 2017 and has assembled a team of lawyers, scientists, and data engineers to test new systems coming to market. LexisNexis has launched its platform-form that can answer legal questions, generate documents, and summarize legal issues.

Artificial intelligence models are trained on the details of contract law. Any contract used by the system is loaded and labeled and then used as a learning tool. This means that a huge database of contract data is needed. But thanks to the AI tools now widely available, people can now draft their own lawsuits. Anyone with an Internet con- nection can use Bard or ChatGPT to formulate a legal letter. And while it is not as good as one written by an av- vocate, it is free.

Although the use of AI in the legal sector is still in its infancy, al- some systems are already facing challenges in this area.

---

[103] http://s24ore.it/mcc55

DoNotPay, which calls itself the world's first lawyer-robot, of- fers the ability to contest parking tickets and other civil cases using AI and has been the subject of several lawsuits, the latest of which accuses the company of practicing law without a li- cence. Meanwhile, as a result of Steven Schwartz's case, several superior judges in the United States now require lawyers to state whether AI was used in court presentations.

In the current landscape on the dynamics between generative AI and the world of work, there are two opposing visions. On the one hand, a positive transition is envisioned in which AI, particularly generative AI, is seen as complementary to human activities, increasing productivity and bringing about limited sectoral changes. On the other hand, a more pessimistic analysis emerges with the prediction of a massive replacement of workers engaged in routine and highly intellectually complex tasks.

A recent study by the International Monetary Fund (IMF) uses an index based on the exposure and complementarity of human labor to AI highlighting that although 40 percent of the world's jobs are exposed to its effects, complementarity reduces the risk in some sectors. The Organization for Economic Coo- peration and Development (OECD) also points out that despite the potential risks, AI can create new employment sectors and improve the quality of work. As well, a duality of anxieties and benefits is reflected in workers' perceptions, with 63 percent reporting increased well-being as a result of AI.

The World Economic Forum (WEF) report predicts a positive impact of AI on job creation, with 75 percent of companies adopting it, but 25 percent of them expect job losses. A PwC survey of CEOs shows optimistic confidence in the transformative potential of generative AI, but it also anti- cipa a reduction in staff in the short term. Thus, if

The critical issues

well used as a complement, generative AI could h e l p improve job performance and quality of work, provided the right initiatives are put in place to take full advantage of its po- tential.

Instead, many people have developed negative theories re- looking at the main aspects of this problem. Some argue for the possibility that artificial intelligence will replace most office tasks[104]. Others that it can learn how to ite- ratively improve itself by transforming i t s e l f into a superintelligence that leaves humans behind[105], that it can fragment information in sucha way that humans break up into islands of disjointed sets[106] or that addir- turely it can supplant human decision-making in various areas, from health care to finance and politics[107]. Some even believe that this could strengthen authoritarian powers, with the state constantly monitoring every movement of citizens and influencing their men- tality[108]. Even going so far as to argue that the monopolists of surveillance capitalism, who rely on AI, will harm small im- pacts and stifle entrepreneurship, leading to its demise[109]. Even Pope Francis has expressed himself on AI in these terms: "disproportionate bene- fits for the few at the price of impoverishing the many." Add to this the fact that most companies that use it pre- see a boom in layoffs because of its efficiency, even if

---

[104] M. Ford, *Rise of the Robots: Technology and the Threat of a Jobless Future*, Basic Books, New York, 2015.
[105] J. Barrat, *Our Final Invention: Artificial Intelligence and the End of the Human Era*, St. Martin's Press, New York, 2013.
[106] E.A. Lee, *The Coevolution: The Entwined Futures of Humans and Machines*, MIT Press, Cambridge, MA, 2020.
[107] K. Kelly, *The Inevitable: Understanding the 12 Technological Forces That Will Shape Our Future*, Penguin Book, New York, 2016.
[108] K.-F. Lee, *Super-Powers: China, Silicon Valley, and the New World Order*, Houghton Mifflin Harcourt Publishing Company, New York, 2018.
[109] S. Zuboff, *The Age of Surveillance Capitalism: The Fight for a Human Future at the New Frontier of Power*, Hachette Book Group, New York, 2019.

there are just as many that do not adopt this type of technology. Secording to Asana's State of AI at Work 2023[110] report, 29 percent of workers are replaceable by AI, but in this transaction a human-centered approach focusing on collaboration and performance improvement must be adopted. Because yes, it is true that layoffs are a reality, but at the same time we must recognize how the synergy between human and machine leads to a restructuring of work and the development of new skills to stay current in an ever-changing work environment.

Some have made a somewhat far-fetched proposal: a Universal Basic Income (UBI) as a solution to the pos- sible problems arising from automation and AI. The concept of UBI is not new, but it is gaining popularity in response to the wage disugua- lity and job insecurity caused by artificial intelligence. Elon Musk is one of the strongest advocates that AI will make many occupations obsolete, pushing workers into precarious forms of employment. UBI policy, on the other hand, could offset inequality and ensure a basic income for all. Experiments in states such as the Netherlands and Kenya indicate mixed results. In some cases, an increase in labor market participation and business creation has been observed. But UBI may encourage precarious jobs instead of promoting job stability. Some suggery the possibility of funding it through a robot tax, assuming we can define exactly what a ro- bot is. But how do we tax a robot? Will the robots then be the ones to pay and support us? Others believe that the UBI could be financed by taxes on companies that use AI to replace workers or generate profits. Basically, if the company wants to adopt AI systems, it has to pay for each job it will per- son.

---

[110] http://s24ore.it/mcc03

But to better clarify the somewhat thorny issue of job loss due to AI, we can rely on a paper recently pub- lished by MIT CSAIL and titled *Beyond AI Exposure: Which Tasks are Cost-Effective to Automate with Computer Vision?*[111], according to which only 23 percent of tasks could be replaced by AI in a cost-effective ma- nerial way. This is good news given the an- sia spread by academics who rank occupational tasks by their automation potential, when they should be talking about partial automation that would conversely produce job increases. The MIT researchers aim to build the first end-to-end AI automation model, which analyzes the level of skill required for a given task, based on surveys of the practitioners involved, considering the cost associated with acquiring the skill through the human workforce or implementing AI systems (which incur high development costs), as well as the economic decision of businesses in adopting or not adopting AI for a specific task.

Therefore, only 23% of task automation would be con- venient for businesses, given the high upfront costs of AI systems and their implementation in any area, factors that hinder its rapid adoption. The International Monetary Fund study released in January 2024, on the other hand, claims that about half of all jobs will benefit from the integration of AI with a conse- quently increase in productivity, while the other half could be completely replaced. But in the end, the world of work does not follow the experts' predictions, especially when they concern how people will handle new technologies.

Not all artists, for example, are against the use of AI, but concern about the econo- mic implications remains in the creative world.

---

[111] http://s24ore.it/mcc20

According to the *Financial Times*[112], tools such as Dall-E, Stable Diffu- sion, and Midjourney have reduced the time required for tasks that would normally take expert illustrators or svi- luppors weeks, allowing anyone to commission them instantly. This raises concerns about the persistence of such profes- sions. For example, in the field of architecture, AI is already being used to handle everyday tasks such as parking and bathroom layouts, raising further questions about the future of certain creative profes- sions.

Collaboration with robots will become increasingly common in areas where they support humans but do not replace them. That collaboration is based on the integration of robot skills with human capabilities, creating a synergistic and po- tential work environment. An innovative new approach that promises to increase efficiency and productivity by allowing individuals and robots to work together synergistically to achieve common goals.

However, as we have already seen in section 2.4, one study re- leased that people tend to pay less attention when they la- vor with robots, considering them as part of their team. "Collaboration is good and bad," said Dietlind Helene Cymek, first author of the study published in the journal *Frontiers in Robotics and AI*[113]. "Working together can motivate people to do their best, but it can also lead to a loss of motivation because the individual contribution is not as evident. We were interested to see if we could find similar motivational effects when the team partner is a robot."

---

[112] http://s24ore.it/mcc45
[113] D.H. Cymek, A. Truckenbrodt, L. Onnasch, *Lean back or lean in? Exploring social loafing in human-robot teams*, in Frontiers in Robotics and AI, 10 (2023) 1249252.

4.9 Copyright

John Philip Sousa (1854-1932) was an American composer, co-known as "the king of marches," a man of great musical talent, but who from early on clashed with the record industry of his time, defining sound productions as "canned music."

This criticism appears in his article "The Menace of Mechanical Music, "[114] published in 1906 in *Appleton's Magazine*. *In* particular, Sousa challenges the phonograph designed by Edison around 1877 on the grounds that it is a mechanical instrument far removed from music, that is, an already mechanical expression of the soul, and defines it with these pa- role: "With the rapidity of a passing fashion in slang or Panama hats, in political war cries or popular novels, now comes the mechanical device that sings a song for us or plays the piano for us, in place of human skill, intelligence and soul."

For him, therefore, it is inconceivable for a machine to replace human con- tact, since he understands music as already the mechanical representation of a composer. His words are more comprehensible to us when we consider that in 1906 copyright laws did not guarantee any protection for musicians. In 1909, however, the copyright law was amended giving birth to the so-called "mechanical rights."

OpenAI has acknowledged the need to access copyrighted material to create innovative chatbots such as ChatGPT, and this shows that AI companies are under pressure with regard to the conte- nts used in training their products. Chatbots such as ChatGPT and image generators such as Stable Diffusion, for example, rely on vast amounts of data from the Internet, many

---

[114] J.P. Sousa, *The Menace of Mechanical Music*, in "Appleton's Magazine," vol. 8 (1906), pp. 278-284.

of which are subject to copyright, which now covers all kinds of human expression.

Recently, the *New York Times* sued OpenAI and Mi- crosoft, accusing them of illegal use of its copy- right protected content to create tools such as ChatGPT and Bing. The complaint also relates to the hallucinations produced by the chatbots, which are capable of pro- during articles that were never published, complete with invented links, thus fueling misinformation and generating considerable im- magine damage for the newspaper and the inability to provide quality journalism. In response, the companies admitted that training advanced language models requires access to copy- right protected works, and limiting training to out-of-copyright materials would produce inadequate artificial intelligence systems. Their defense is based more on the legal doctrine of *fair use*, which allows the use of con- held in specific circumstances without the permission of the owner, such as if the use is brief and for the purpose of criticism, commentary, scientific evaluation, or parody. OpenAI has continued to defend itself by arguing that, legally, copyright law does not prohibit training.

The *New York Times* lawsuit is not the only one and joins numerous other legal complaints against OpenAI by authors and companies, increasingly raising the legal issues related to the use of copyrighted material in AI.

Analyzing it well, we can see important implications. If the lawsuit were to be successful, the models underlying AI would be useless because they were trained illicitly. In addition, the training activities would be more expensive due to prior payment of fees, making the use of these technologies for a few and increasing costs for users.

While the idea of allowing companies to use copyrighted materials without permission is being floated in Japan to stimulate the AI industry, the focus in Europe with the AI Act is on transparency, forcing operators to specify which copy-right protected materials were used for systems training.

Some scholars are pondering how to redefine concepts of intellectual pro- prietary, suggesting a greater focus on equity and creativity than on economic incentives for me- dia companies. According to Kate Crawford and Jason Schultz, authors of an article pub- lished in *Issues in Science and Technology*[115], it may be time to develop new concepts of intellectual property, inspired by emerging collective bargaining agreements in the film industry that emphasize creativity rather than copyright. These examples could serve as a model for a more equitable conception of intellectual property, requiring in-depth philosophical engagement about who has a say, how creations are used, and who should benefit from them, in order to create a more sustainable creative environment.

It has recently been shown that language models of large dimensions can reproduce parts or large portions of the text of their training sets, including sensitive data. Think of the case of the *New York Times* just cited in which OpenAI's software reproduced the newspaper's articles almost verbatim. We call these "pla- jar outputs," and we know that they can also exist in im- magine production. Experiments done with Midjourney and Dall-E 3, trained on copyrighted materials, show that it is possible to generate plagiaristic out- put with prompts related to movies, cartoons, or video games.

This can happen even inadvertently and without di- rect instructions, that is, even when not asked to do so, po- tentially exposing users to copyright infringement claims.

But the problem is that there is no way to trace the owner of an im-magine on the Internet to authenticate it, and no indication is given as to how it was created. In addition, there is no

---

[115] http://s24ore.it/mcc24

tool with which a user can determine possible infringement nor any instruction on how they can do so. The first solution that comes to mind would be to train language models only with properly licensed data, filtering out queries that might violate copyright and the sources from which they drew, but we always come back to the "black boxes" di- last. Here it is no longer a legal issue, we are talking instead about human values to which software should alli- nee.

The hot issue concerns the training of advanced artificial intelligence models with copyrighted material, leading many companies to face real litigation. To ci- cite just one case, a group of authors filed a lawsuit against Meta, accusing it of illegally using co pyrighted material to develop its Llama 1 and Llama 2 language models. In response, Meta confirmed the use o f Books3, a dataset composed of the text of more than 195,000 books weighing about 37 GB, to train its LLMs, admitting its use but without intentional behavior. The company has dismissed the allegations of copyright infringement, also claiming that the use of protected works to train LLMs does not require consent, credit or compensation and disputing the va- lidity of the lawsuit as a class action. In 2023, the disputed dataset was targeted by the Danish anti-piracy group Rights Alliance, which sought to ban its digital storage, using DMCA (Digital Millennium Copyright Act) notices to re- move it.

At this point one wonders what will be the effect of the ca- pacity of AI to produce works of art and how we should handle copyrights when an artist is replaced by a machine. Is it fair to give AI the same rights reserved for humans? We need to laugh- end what it means to be an "author" and owner of the rights to one's work in order to protect human creativity and ingenuity. They are

The critical issues

already known cases of artworks being auctioned or exhibited that have been generated by algorithms, but can copyright also be applied to works that are the result of AI? To hear the European Patent Of- fice (EPO), it seems not; in fact, it recently rejected the bre- vice application filed for two inventions created by artificial intelligence. The EPO's rationale was that only humans, not machines, can be considered inventors. If AI can support us in creation, however, we need to understand whether we can speak of creativity in its case as well. Indeed, we can call a machine a creator if, starting from inputs through learning and training algorithms, it generates outputs that can be considered the end result in terms of artistic creation. But if by creativity we in- tend the reflection of human consciousness, then it is impossible for AI to be creative. Conversely, if by creativity we mean something im- predictable, consequently even the most advanced AI system can be creative since it can act unpredictably and autonomously. We know that in order to own a right, one must have legal capacity, a capacity that machines lack, so at present, since there is no provision for this, the author's right to a work resulting from AI is held by the creator of the software. Unesco was one of the first institutions to adopt an instrument to clarify the standards of the subject, launching the Unesco Recommendation on the Ethics of Artificial Intelligence[116], signed by 193 states in novem- ber 2021.

Professor Yann LeCun, for example, wondered who should es- be liable for copyright infringement in the case of producing an image very similar to a protected one. The copyright law, independent of the means used to reproduce a work of art and the means to disseminate it, protects it from unauthorized copying. The person responsible for infringement in this case is the person who distributes the work

---

[115] http://s24ore.it/mcc24

and not those who create it nor those who produce the tools to create it. Thus, in the case of AI image generation systems, the use of copyright pro- tected materials for the training set should not constitute copyright infringement. There is free software, Nightshade[117], that can poison AI models that try to ad- strate on the works of certain artists. But such an ad- destrated AI model on these altered images could misclassify objects or works.

The use of artificial intelligence provokes deep eti- cations in the artistic field as well. In 2016, for example, the painting *The Next Rembrandt*, created by a computer with a 3D printer a full 351 years after the Dutch artist's death, caused a notable stir. Through detailed analysis of 346 Rembrandt paintings, deep learning algorithms created a unique database, capturing every nuance of the painter's artistic identity. The result was an extraordinary head of work, reproduced by the printer with such accuracy as to fool even art experts. At this point we must ask a crucial question: who can be considered the author of such a work? The company that spearheaded the project, the engineers involved, the al- gorithm itself, or even Rembrandt?

In 2019, Huawei revealed that an AI algorithm completed the last two movements of Franz Schubert's Symphony No. 8, a com- position that began a full 197 years earlier. The emergence of AI ge- nerated works of art invokes the need for a new definition of "author," raising questions about copyright and the recognition of the au- toriality of algorithms. The role of AI thus raises significant ethical and legal que- stions in artistic creation as well, challenging traditional conventions about creative authorship. How do we di- stinguish between human authenticity and algorithmic creation? This calls for new assessment frameworks to preserve the integrity of creativity

---

[117] http://s24ore.it/mcc26

The critical issues

human, ensuring appropriate remuneration and recognition for artists and protecting the cultural value chain.

Dissident artist Ai Weiwei, known for his open criticism of Chinese au- torities, believes that art easily replicated by AI has no reason to exist. According to him, if artists like Picasso and Matisse had lived in this era, they would have stopped making art. Regarding the debate on the creation of images by AI using data collected from artists' websites, Weiwei argues that this operation takes only a few seconds, which makes the artists' own training and experience insignificant. For him, this kind of art should have disappeared long ago. However, the artist has collaborated on a project called "Ai vs. AI," in which both he and an AI ri- spond to a list of 81 questions that are projected on giant screens around the world and the answers are posted online (81 days is the length of the confinement to which he was subjected by the Chinese government in 2011). He sees this work as a kind of provocation and warns that if AI becomes too powerful in the future, it heralds the risk of a society with only one "right" answer to the big questions, which would return us to the totalitarian regimes of the past. He is convinced that excessive AI con- trol could even take us back to the Third Reich or the Chinese Cultural Revolution of the 1960s.

With the advent of AI, music also changes. Universal Music Group, along with other record labels, has sued Anthro- pic, a company specializing in artificial intelligence, accusing it of dif- fering through its AI model, Claude 2, lyrics similar to those of famous songs such as Katy Perry's *Roar*, Gloria Gaynor's *I Will Survive*, and The Rolling Stones' *You Can't Always Get What You Want*, even without possessing the necessary licenses. The charge is twofold because Anthropic is accused not only of distributing co-pyrighted material without permission, but also of using such materials for training its own language patterns. What's more, according to the

Universal Music Group did so while being aware of the vio- lations and taking no protective measures to avoid them. Copyright infringement has now become a major issue in the field of generative AI, and this is not the only case in which legal action has been taken against artifi- cial intelligence platforms. The music industry can no longer put the issue of copyright protection on the back burner, seeking instead to equi- librate innovation with the protection of its own interests.

Tennessee lawmakers have proposed a bill called ELVIS (Ensuring Likeness Voice and Image Security) to ban voice clo- nation using AI, with the goal of protecting the state's music industry, in response to growing concern over voice replication using artificial intelligence, highlighted re- cently by the agreement between the SAG-AFTRA union and the startup Re- plica Studios for voice cloning for training and voice licensing purposes.

One of the most famous victims, who recently saw one of her porn deepfakes displayed on the social network X (formerly Twitter) tens of millions of times, was U.S. pop star Taylor Swift. To be precise, the photo in question was viewed 47 million times before it was re- posted. Unlike other social media, X does not have filters for consensual porn, but apparently also for porn without consent. This is one of the latest cases and one of the most egregious mon- dially, so much so that it has also sparked the outrage of many Sta- tunity politicians, and some lawmakers have proposed a bill to regulate adult content without consent that is the result of AI, with the in- tention of legally prosecuting those who generate or disseminate digitally altered images. For example, Democrat Joseph Morelle has introduced the *Preventing Deepfakes of Intimate Images Act* se- cording to which the sharing of deepfake pornography is illegal without con- sense.

The critical issues

Unfortunately, AI is advancing much faster than related protections, so whether the victim is a public figure or any young girl, AI-generated content needs to be labeled as such. We have seen how many politicians have been victims of deepfakes, but the exploitation of this technology is far greater against women: in 2019, 96 percent of deepfake video content was non-consensual pornographic material. Unfortunately, enormous progress has since been made in image alteration thanks to AI, which even with a simple text command can gene- rate totally new and convincing images.

But how to apply copyright principles to content created or used by AI?

Programs such as Dall-E, ChatGPT, Stable Diffusion, and others can generate outputs in response to textual input. Legal analysis focuses on issues of authorship, copyright infringement, and fair use related to this new content. The main one re- looks at copyright protection for generative AI outputs. For example, the U.S. Constitution grants the exclu- sive right to human authors, but the law does not specify who or what can es- pect "author."

A 2022 case challenged the human authorship requirement, but the court held that this is essential to a copyright claim. Also in 2022, Stephen Thaler sued the Copyright Office for denying him the registration of a work of visual art generated by the Creative Ma- chine AI program, arguing that the autonomous generative AI can be conside- rative of the author and asserting that only human authors need in- centives through copyright.

Works created by humans using generative AI could be copyrighted, but obtaining protection is difficult.

One case saw a copyright claim rejected for a graphic novel illustrated with images generated by Midjourney, arguing that when AI determines the expressive elements of the work the result is not a product of human contribution.

In the case of copyright protection, the question arises as to who pos- sits the copyright or not.

But AI programs can be regarded as the other instru- ments that humans use to create copyrighted works. The analogy with photography has been raised, suggesting that the AI user should be considered the author, but there is also the issue of the amount of creative control exercised by the user over it.

The AI training phase also raises concerns about copyright infringement, as it may involve the creation of digital copies of existing works. Some AI companies argue that this constitutes fair use, but there are disagreements over the re- spect of the four factors that determine fair use, namely the purpose and character of use, the nature of the work, the amount and impor- tance of the part used in relation to the work as a whole, and the effect of the use on the market. The generation of certain outputs by the AI may infringe copyright if they are substantially similar to existing works. The test requires demonstrations of access to the underlying work and substantial similarity, but not everyone agrees on the likelihood that AI programs copy existing works in their products, and in any case it is an im- likely accidental result.

Who is (or should be) liable if generative AI products infringe the copyrights of existing works? Under current doctrines, both the AI user and the AI-producing company could potentially be liable.

4.10 Privacy

The ethical debate on artificial intelligence focuses on two principles. The first denies the existence of intelligence in an entity lacking consciousness and critical spirit, reducing AI to a com- plete system of technical rules. The second rejects the idea of granting com- puters decision-making capabilities, as they lack consciousness and social/emotional intelligence, merely applying rules and instructions.

This is where we immediately enter the topic of privacy, highlighting the re- risking of entrusting technological devices with personal data and the implications of revealing to them our reasoning, habits, needs, and preferences.

Data protection systems are still insufficient in the face of a world in which AI is widespread. Everyone has con- trol of their own privacy which means that, outside of citizenship obligations, it is possible to decide what personal data to share, with whom, and in what way.

But artificial intelligence devices, based on the data provided, can infer additional information, including personal information that the user may prefer not to share. And unfortunately, they are not liable to scrutiny in this operation as are the isti- cations that hold our data, thus becoming potentially dangerous.

A clear example of this is the recent report that ChatGPT appears to be releasing private conversations with the access credentials and personal details of users of a pre-scription drug portal, taken from a technical support platform used by the portal's per- sonal staff. According to the investigation, it appears to be a case of account takeover, in which conversations were recently generated during unauthorized accesses to the user's ChatGPT account. Although he has changed the password, per- sistems doubt about the compromise of his account, since the chats of other people suddenly appeared in his history. The user discovered the additional conversations after nor- mal use of ChatGPT for an unrelated search. Unfortunately, the chatbot still lacks protection mechanisms such as two-factor authentication (2FA) or access tracking via IP addresses, which are standard on many platforms. This incident raises many concerns about the security of personal data and makes us realize how important it is to avoid sharing sensitive information with artificial intelligence services, which, as I have already mentioned, are black boxes created by private companies and whose operation and sources from which they get their information are unknown.

As of May 25, 2018, EU Regulation 2016/679, known as GDPR (General Data Protection Regu- lation)[118], which covers the protection of individuals with regard to the processing and free movement of personal data across member states, is fully operational in Europe. It was introduced to provide legal certainty, harmonization, and simplification of rules regarding the transfer of personal data. The importance of data protection is underscored by the need to ensure that data are kept up-to-date and fit for speci- c purposes, and their automated processing, especially in rile- vant decisions, requires special attention to the logic used and the associated ri- schi.

In this sense, the GDPR is a real pillar for the protection of personal data, imposing transparency in au- tomatized decision-making processes and the right of data subjects to know and control these processes. In a society increasingly oriented toward the use of data, data quality and security become the core of such a system, so proactive enforcement of GDPR is not just a regulatory necessity, but an essential investment in ensuring people's well-being and trust in new technologies.

---

[118] http://s24ore.it/mcc46

The critical issues

As an example of the indiscriminate use of sensitive data in an AI-based si- stem, let us cite the case of researchers at the Technical Uni- versity in Denmark who developed an artificial intelli- gence system that appears to possess oracle-like divination and prediction capabilities through detailed analysis of the lives of a number of Danish citizens aged 25 to 70. Using deep learning techniques and the Transfor- mer algorithmic architecture, the AI was trained with data collected from 2008 to 2020, covering various aspects of human life such as health, society and economy, and thus learned from real "life sequences," organizing events chronologically to better analyze them. The model was ca- pace to recognize and connect events in a person's life, of- fering predictions about his or her future, outperforming the current state of the art di- vinatory in 11 percent of predictions about the probability of death. This experiment raises important ethical and moral questions, as the use of AI to predict future events, especially intimate or perso- nal ones, may have unintended consequences. First, the accuracy of pre- visions could be affected by training data, leading to potential bias. Second, dependence on such predictions po- might undermine the human ability to make autonomous decisions. Therefore, rigorous ethical evaluation and appropriate regulations are needed, as privacy, human dignity, and free will could be seriously at risk.

Every year on January 28, we celebrate the International Day of the privacy, with the aim of raising awareness of the sensitive issue of safeguarding and protecting our data. The EU's GDPR is the law that regulates this matter, but it is no longer sufficient with the increase in the use of generative AI: a holistic approach is needed that always puts humans, their rights and their rap- port with technology at the center.

The main privacy issues range from data breaches (costing $4.45 million in 2023) to locating data in a specific country perhaps different from the country of origin, from Privacy-Enhancing Computation or Privacy-Enhancing Computation (PEC), which protects data from unauthorized parties, to facial recognition that can es- prove to be used even for manipulative purposes. The list could go on with the sometimes distorted use of data by companies to understand and predict consumer behavior. With the development of AI being trained even on sensitive data, everything becomes more complicated, but fortunately there are companies that use it to improve data ge- stration, for example through privacy conservation, classification, and security of sensitive data. Given the power of this instrument and the ethical and responsible practices it can include such as transparency, accountability, fairness, and privacy by design put in place from the beginning, AI itself can ensure that the technology is not used for malicious purposes, but to protect our rights and humanity.

Chapter 5 - What to do

5.1 Holistic approach

To ensure a future for humanity, it is essential to devote as much energy to the development of human beings as to tech- nological development. I firmly believe that if we want the world to remain a place fit for human beings, with all our imper- fections and inefficiencies, we must invest significant economic, political, and social resources in defining what might truly represent a new kind of humanism: Cyberhumanism.

It will not be enough to focus exclusively on the latest techno- logies, which promise to expand our human capabilities, because over time we risk finding ourselves driving machines whose internal dynamics we will no longer be aware of. To ensure a sustainable balance between man and machine, it becomes necessary to take a holistic approach involving both technological innovation with the development of advanced artificial intelligence and the enhancement of human capabilities through access to new forms of learning and personal development. Only in this way can we ensure a harmonious and balanced future in the constantly evolving digital society.

The following are some other key points on which I believe we must la- vor to ensure a healthy future for humanity.

5.2 Ethics by design

Before writing or producing software one should have as a first reference some universally recognized ethical principles.

An ethical, human-centered artificial intelligence must be designed and developed in a way that is aligned with the values and ethical principles of a society or community that is affected. Ethics is based on well-founded standards of right and wrong that prescribe what humans should do, usually in terms of rights, ob- gress, societal benefits, equity, or specific virtues. "[119]

Could it be harmful to someone or a group, or advantageous unequally to people? Does it best respect the rights of all? Does it treat users fairly? Will it produce the greatest good and do the least harm to the greatest number of users? Does it preserve and promote respect for human autonomy? Does it pro- tect privacy of personal data and data governance? Does it ensure individual, social, and environmental well-being?

Pope Francis, on the occasion of the Fourth World Meeting of People's Movements held on Oct. 16, 2021, said, "I want to ask, in the name of God, the giants of technology to stop exploiting human frailty, people's vulnerabilities, for profit, without considering how hate speech, grooming, fake news, conspiracy theories, and political manipulation increase."

It is necessary for any AI to respect human ethics from the projectual stages. It must be human-centered designed.

But what ethics?

Being ethical does not mean doing "what is acceptable to society," because in every society standards of behavior can be very different.

A few years ago, sociologist Raymond Baumhart asked some managers, "What does ethics mean to you?" and these were the principle answers: "Ethics has to do with what my feelings tell me is right or wrong"; "Ethics has to do with my religious cre- ations"; "Being ethical means doing what the law requires."

---

[119] Markkula Center for Applied Ethics.

"Ethics consists of the standards of behavior accepted by our society," down to those who replied, "I don't know what ethics means."

Of course, being ethical is not just following the law. While the law often incorporates the ethical standards to which most citizens adhere, it can sometimes deviate from what is ethical.

Generative AI collects so much information online and draws conclusions based on it. But it does not verify the accuracy of these conclusions. Everything is regulated by algorithms. We live in an algocracy. Algorithms operate on values of a numerical nature, while ethics oc- cases on moral values. We have to translate moral value into a machine-computable format.

Another major problem with generative AI is bias. Algorithms are generally written by humans, so even when you write the code, the beliefs, values, and assumptions of that person, or group of people, influence the basic ethics of what the AI will do.

To address many of the ethical issues related to AI, the concept of *value alignment* has been proposed, a methodology used to direct artificial intelligence systems toward specific goals, principles and preferences while respecting human ethical values throughout their operation.

An AI system can be considered "aligned" when it consciously pursues predefined goals, avoiding ca- sual evolution and respecting the basic ethical principles of humanity. We start from the fact that a machine will never be guided by the same values as a human being. The point is that unless it is taught, an AI does not know values such as respect for human life or the environment.

Brian Christian, author of *The Alignment Problem*[120], cited as a telling example of the lack of AI alignment the Uber autonomous vehicle accident that claimed the life of Elaine Herzberg in Arizona in 2018. The National Transportation Safety Board investigation then revealed that the vehicle had not been programmed to recognize a person crossing the street in an unconventional manner, a behavior known as "jaywalking." This lack of instruction on the unexpected then led to the inci- dent. Even if AI is instructed on human values, new issues arise such as racial bias and minority discrimination. For example, if we entrust an AI system to select a resume for a job, it might reflect the biases in the training data. Research on alignment focuses on three aspects: the goals intended by the human operator, the goals specified in the system's data set, and the emergent goals to be pursued by the system.

When one or two of these goals do not match the others you internal or external misalignment occurs. Understand well that if artificial in- telligence becomes a general artificial intelligence, performing any task that a human being is capable of performing, it will be even more important that its ethical principles, goals, and embedded va- lues align with the goals, ethics, and values of human beings.

But achieving this goal is opposed by several issues such as the fact that the AI still remains a black box inside which we are not allowed to see; then there is the problem of *reward hacking* that occurs if the system does not achieve its programmed goal. An AI si- stem could also develop power-seeking behavior, autonomously gathering resources to achieve its

---

[120] B. Christian, *The Alignment Problem. How Can Artificial Intelligence Learn Human Values*, Atlantic Books, London, 2021.

What to do

objectives. Approaches to AI alignment can be technical or normative. The former include ite- rate distillation and amplification, value learning, debate among multiple systems, and cooperative inverse appren- dation by reinforcement, i.e., a two-way game in which human and AI share a common reward function. Normative allinement, on the other hand, concerns the ethical and moral values embedded in the AI system.

Closely related to the values of alignment is AI safety research, which tends to seek viable answers to the major risks associated with AI over its harmful use in bioterrorism, persuasion, and concentration of power, to name a few. As the Center for AI Safety (CAIS)[121] in San Francisco also suggests, in order to mitigate these harms, AIs with expertise in biological research must es- pose strict access controls to prevent the risk of being used for terrorist acts. Biological capabilities, then, should be excluded from those intended for general use. The application of AI to improve and invest in general biosecurity ini- tiatives, such as advanced wastewater monitoring for early detection of pathogens, should be explored. Access to high-risk AI systems should also be reduced by allowing only regulated interactions through cloud services and implementing screening processes based on the "know your customer" principle.

The adoption of computer monitoring measures could ulteriorly restrict access to dangerous functionality. Then, before making it open source, AI developers should demonstrate how to minimize the risk of causing harm. To avoid its im- proper use, effective anomaly detection for unusual behavior or AI-generated misinformation should be put in place as well. Or impose legal liability on developers for

---

[121] http://s24ore.it/mcc59

potential for its misuse or failure, thus encouraging safer development practices and proper cost accounting to repair damages derived from risks. Then there are just as many risks associated with the race to implement AI such as both military and corporate arms races and evolutionary dynamics. To reduce the issues de- rivating from competitive pressures, one should enforce security regulations to the letter, undertake international coordination and public scrutiny of general-purpose AIs, and take care of data documentation, all guided always by human oversight. As for organizational risks, a culture of safety must be cultivated. Laboratories developing AIs should in- charge external teams to identify hazards and improve and dem- strate system safety, adopting a gra- dual release process not before reviewing application research.

Consequently, they should develop response plans for incident management with an office designated for just that, follow secure and fail-safe design principles such as defense-in-depth, backup for each security measure, and segregation of duties. These actions should be implemented in coordination with government cybersecurity agencies, which must increase resources devoted to security in direct proportion to AI advancement. Unfortunately, developers often prioritize speed rather than security, thereby contributing to a risk that should not be underestimated: AI could become "rogue" in the sense of pursuing power and goals contrary to our interests thereby circumventing security measures and enacting so-called "target drift." To curb these other problems, it is necessary to avoid the riskiest use cases, support security research by pursuing robustness of oversight mechanisms, transparency, model honesty, and removing na- scous functionality. Currently, security in artificial intelligence is a

What to do

underdeveloped sector, with obvious issues in the control of advanced systems and limited understanding by developers themselves. There are, however, strategies to mitigate these risks, such as limiting access to dangerous artificial intelligences, promoting security norms and international cooperation, and investing in alignment research. In short, a proactive criterion to secure the future of humanity in the age of artificial intelligence.

AI Ethics research differs somewhat from AI Safety in its more humanistic approach. The wide diffusion of artificial intelligence in a wide variety of fields, its rapid evolution, and the competition among na- tions and companies to develop robust AI solutions have increased the urgency of establishing ethical guidelines and principles to guide its development and application. The field of ethics in AI is now a real and growing discipline that is increasingly refining its research to respond to issues related to its impact such as data distortion, privacy, equity issues, and the need for developers to be more aware of the risks of the technologies.

The ethics of AI extend from highly technical issues to com- prehension of human behavior during research, from intera- tion to the development and use of AI itself. In particular, as ab- lished, there are five dominant ethical principles in this field: transparency, accountability, trust, privacy, sustainability, autonomy, and dignity. The concept of transparency, often considered a pro-ethical principle or even better an enabler for ethical AI, also expands in the area of Explai- nable AI (XAI), which refers to interpretable systems capable of providing understandable explanations of their decisions.

XAI is a growing area of research, especially considering the im- plementation of systems in critical areas that require clarity

On the actions of AI. A tangible example is me- dia AI, in which the need for transparency is closely linked to the fundamental ethical values of medicine.

But despite its importance, the role of transparency in AI ethics remains ill-defined. Community coordination is needed to ensure that ethical reflection is integrated into AI research itself to monitor any consequences. Current ethics review practices, then, focus more on the risks of individuals than society as a whole, with fears that these processes may limit technological progress. It is also critical to engage an international stakeholder group with figures ranging from funders to research leaders such as scientists and legal scholars, as well as policymakers and public administrators, to foster reflection on the human values that are called into play in the development of AI as it evolves as research advances.

During the GPT-4 presentation, Greg Brockman, one of the founders of OpenAI, stressed the importance of thoroughly understanding how this new model operates, given the concern to ensure that its performance is actually useful to users.

But during pre-launch security testing, an event occurred that caught everyone's attention: the GPT-4 managed to convince a TaskRabbit worker that he was a human by simulating blindness to get assistance in solving a CAPTCHA, a test uti- lized to distinguish humans from computers.

This is an essential evaluation process to identify po- tential risks in AI development, to ensure the proper functioning of the system and the production of reliable and safe results. And it re- sults an even more important ethical dilemma in light of the advent of the technological singularity. The potential loss of human control over machines is a real issue related to the increased

of the intelligence and capabilities of machines, and it becomes increasingly complicated for us humans to predict and manage their actions.

There is also another significant ethical concern: will superintelligent machines be able to develop goals and values of their own, potentially at odds with human interests? Imagine a conflict between humans and machines, with the latter capable of causing harm to achieve their own goals.

Add to this the impact on human employment. Mac- chines could replace tasks previously performed by humans, generating large-scale unemployment and so- cial instability. In this scenario, only those with access to the most advanced technologies would benefit at the expense of those without.

Artificial intelligence algorithms "constitutively" require ethics. Because artificial intelligences can make mistakes, it is critical to understand how to handle such errors.

The ethical issue is of vital importance and urgency: we must con- dividend an ethical system that allows these technologies not to gener injustice, not to harm people, and not to create profound imbalances.

For intelligent machines, there is a need to develop a new universal lin- guage that translates ethical guidelines into machine-executable directions. And in general, by design, that is, from analysis and design, AIs must not adversely affect au- tonomy, freedom, or human dignity; they must not violate privacy and make illegitimate use of personal data; they must use the minimum amount of personal information that is not subject to pre-judgment, that is representative, and that is accurate.

They must be designed to ensure that they do not cause individual, social or environmental harm or rely on harmful technologies. That they do not influence others to act in harmful ways or lend themselves to abuse of functions. They also need to be as transparent as possible about who the related stakeholders are.

Most importantly, all those involved in their development, as well as the ma- nagement, should take responsibility for the way such applications work and any negative consequences.

AIs, by design, must process personal data in compliance with the law and in a transparent manner. Technologies and measures must be in place so that the rights that apply to other applications are safeguarded, with the appointment of a data protection officer, anonymization, pseudonymization with a use of encryption and aggregation. Strong security measures are required to prevent data breaches and disclosures. They must comply with the most recent Cy- bersecurity Act[122] and international security standards. Data developed to be stored and used in a way that can be veri- fied by anyone.

In addition, artificial intelligence systems should be designed to avoid bias factors in input data, modeling, and algorithm design. Preferably, the code should be open source, as anyone should be able to understand, supervise, and control the design and operation of artificial intelligence-based systems.

On a road that is about to open the door to strong artificial intelligence, and perhaps the singularity, there are ethical principles of AI toward humans that should be respected. End users should not be deprived of the ability to make basic decisions about their lives or basic freedoms. It must be ensured that AI applications do not choose autonomously and without human supervision, and that there is always the possibility of recourse. Let it be ensured that there is the possibility

---

[122] http://s24ore.it/mcc17

to humans to subvert any decisions made by machines on fundamental personal que- stions that are normally made by humans through free personal choices, on economic, social and political funda- mental issues that affect individuals.

End-users and others affected by the AI system should in no way be subjugated, coerced, deceived, manipulated, objec- tivated, or dehumanized; instead, they should be provided with comprehensible information about the logic involved by the AI, as well as the meaning and conse- quences intended for them.

Intelligences must not intentionally stimulate attachment or habituation to the system and its operations, they must be able to sense human desires and must adapt to cooperate with humans. It is man who must be at the center, and not the other way around.

A system should be implemented that makes it clearly visible, without doubt or misunderstanding, that users are interacting with an AI system. The purposes, capabilities, limitations, benefits, and risks of this system and the decisions conveyed should be co- municated openly to end users and other interested parties, including instructions on how to properly use the system.

All artificial intelligence systems should be verifiable by independent third parties. Whenever the machine is not sure of certain preservation of human value, it should require human intervention.

Diversity and inclusion, transparency and human rights must be ensured in the development and use of AI systems.

But we return to the topical questions still unanswered: what ethics? Decided by whom? By what society?

Self-driving cars will soon be on our roads, and legitimate questions arise about their behavior. In the event of a probable accident, what would you want the car to decide to do?

Running over the two pedestrians in front or swerving to avoid them, but ending up against a tree resulting in the death of the passengers? This is just one of the many dilemmas to be posed, because the traffic light could be red or driving the car could be a criminal or, on the contrary, a doctor who saves lives every day. Self-driving cars will be a reality in a few years that would reduce both traffic and pollution and traffic accidents, but to avoid them altogether, cars will have to be trained to make quick decisions in emergency situations. In 2015, three American scholars created the site Moral Machine[123], on which they offered a survey asking about two thousand per- sons how they would like their car to behave in the event of an accident. The results of the study saw the prevalence of the utilitarian prin- ciple, that is, saving as many lives as possible by sacrificing the con- ducent instead of pedestrians. But if the driver is the respondent, the situation changes: he or she would not want to buy such a car at all. The issue seems insoluble, and if the decision were left to legislators, it might seem like an imposition. This is a clear example of how we are faced with problems that are more ethical than technical.

Ethical dilemmas have no small impact on our
choices. Each of us in our daily lives is faced with a choice between one moral principle and another, often not knowing which one to privilege. Think of a doctor who has to strike a balance between patient reser- vation and not harming another individual, or the journalist who has to choose between informing the public and respecting people's privacy, or even an entrepreneur who has to make pro- fit without harming consumers. And we could go on with other examples.

---

[122] http://s24ore.it/mcc17

What to do

Rushworth Kidder, an author and ethicist, classified four types of ethical di- lemmas[124]: truth vs. fairness (choice between absolute honesty and loyalty to in- dividuals or groups), individual vs. community (discordance between personal interests and collective benefits), short-term vs. long-term (choice between immediate benefits and long-term consequences), and justice vs. mercy (tension between equitable consequences and compassion). Within each category the author has identified a number of ethical dilemmas.

In the first, he included seven: conflict of interest, whistleblowing, professional secrecy, confidentiality in journalism, employee favoritism, client representation, and academic cheating.

In the second category, i.e., individual vs. community, conside- tive debates on vaccinations, resource allocation, urban con- troversies, public health measures, changes in educational policies, environmental regulations, and free speech. In the short- and long-term category, the author includes financial investment, career advancement, environmental considerations, health choices, corporate growth, public policy, the technology updates.

Finally, the last category (justice vs. mercy) includes leniency for first-time offenders, forgiveness of a condemned man on death row, retribution for hate crimes, academic misconduct, the role of counselors in financial crises, the di- lem of war crimes, and social welfare decisions.

This long list makes us realize that for a human being to be faced with an ethical or moral dilemma is not an easy task, and often there is no right or wrong answer. Let alone for a machine...

---

[124] R. Kidder, *How Good People Make Tough Choices: Resolving the Dilemmas of Ethical Living*, Harper Perennial, New York, 2009.

5.3 LONGTERMISM

Longtermism is a philosophy or rather an approach that emphasizes the importance of positively impacting the long-term future and seems to be "the comet" to follow in order to steer in the right direction toward the future.

A vision considers the long-term consequences of today's actions, with a particular focus on the implications for future genera- tions and the long-term sustainability of life on Earth and beyond.

In the context of Cyberhumanism, longtermism aligns with the idea of advancing toward a posthuman civilization that can explore space and thrive. This approach does not perceive tech- nological progress as a threat, but rather as an opportunity to improve the human condition and address global challenges.

William MacAskill, associate professor of philosophy at Oxford University and co-founder of the Centre for Effective Altruism and author of *What We Owe the Future*[125], stresses the importance of longtermsism and the moral priority of positively influencing the long-term future by considering the challenges ahead and acting in the interests of all generations to come.

But how can we pursue this important goal? According to the philosopher, we must first ensure the survival of human spe- cies and civilization, which could become extinct (think of the re- ction of the Covid-19 pandemic) or continue to progress for millions of years. Then we could introduce trajectory changes and improve the values that guide society. But the progress of the future is uncertain, then- as artificial intelligence puts at risk the achievements of freedom and equality of the last century.

There is always the fear that the transition to a superintelligent AI.

---

[125] W. MacAskill, *What We Owe the Future*, Basic Books, New York, 2022.

may escape human control, with systems that may have objectives that conflict with human ones.

Longtermism has its origins in *effective* altruism[126], a philosophical and social movement that developed in the 2000s that wants to "use evidence and reason to figure out how to benefit others as much as possible, and act on that basis." It is not just a field of research but a real, very broad community that aims to do as much good as possible by identifying ways to do it and how to put them into practice. The movement started at Oxford University and has grown to involve miglias of people in more than 70 countries. Those who refer to this current of thought, the so-called "effective altruists," often choose a type of work that they believe will save the most lives or reduce suffering.

Their priorities include global health and development, social disu- guality, animal welfare, and risks to humanity's survival in the long-term future. Or how to prevent the next pandemic or terrorist attacks, distribute medical supplies to developing countries, end intensive breeding, or improve decision-making.

Effective altruists are also working on academic research on the future of AI, particularly its alignment. AI is advancing rapidly, as we have seen so far, and the ultimate goal po- might be to develop it equal or superior to humans, with unimaginable transformational impacts such as the loss of control of AI systems themselves.

The management of this evolution is very complex and decisive, then- as it can lead to prosperity or, at the opposite, to extreme concentration of power. The problem of AI alignment becomes critical when considering the control of systems that may have capacities greater than those of humans. Therefore, it is necessary to ensure that such

---

[126] http://s24ore.it/mcc43

systems promote human values, making alignment a long-term moral priority.

However, despite its political, social, and economic relevance, few researchers are dedicated to this issue compared to those working to enhance AI, although efforts are being made to inform more people and build a dedicated research field. Initiatives such as the Center for Human-Compatible AI at UC Berkeley and teams focused on AI alignment at leading labs such as DeepMind and OpenAI are examples of this; these are trying to develop innovative approaches and research agendas to ga- rant ethical alignment in AI evolution.

The movement, which now has about seven thousand people active in the effective altruism community and strong ties to elite schools in the U.S. and U.K., is associated with Silicon Valley and the tech industry, forming a tight subculture.

Many organizations are taking longtermism actions in di- verse areas. And there is also a vibrant research community forming around this movement, wondering among other things whether an artificial intelligence superior to humans will evolve in the near fu- ture and what role it will play in the development of civilization. However, investing in the defense of future generations should not cause us to neglect current interests; these are actions that go hand in hand.

To date, only a tiny fraction of society's time and attention, and especially economic resources, is explicitly devoted to promoting a positive long-term future.

To give you an idea, the annual budget of the Biological Weapons Convention, the only international body charged with banning the proliferation of these weapons, is less than that of a me- dio restaurant. We must also consider that action geared to the long ter- mine brings benefits in the short term as well. For example, predicting the next pandemic can save thousands of lives or

What to do

innovation in clean energy not only helps combat climate change, but also reduces the number of deaths related to air pollution from fossil fuels, which kills millions of people each year. The same principle can also be applied to other efforts aimed at the long term, such as promoting democracy, reducing the risk of wars, or improving the ability to predict and manage new disasters before they ve- rect.

One concrete and immediate action of longtermism that can be taken to more equitably redistribute the costs and benefits of artificial in- telligence for the benefit of society and to ensure that it is accessible to all could be to tax robots and AI companies. The first to come up with this kind of proposal were Bernie Sanders and Bill Gates, but obviously an updated version of their plan is needed, taking into account advances in gener- ational AI.

Launching a debate aimed at a global political consensus po- might take years and should begin without delay. It is impor- tant to agree on the percentage of revenues or profits to be taxed and to determine the purpose of the tax: should it specifically aim to reduce job per- sons or address the broad societal impacts of AI? China and the United States, which are leading the development of AI, have not yet enacted corporate tax regulations at the national level, but it can no longer wait. Given the impending social spending, the discussion of a meaningful tax on billion-dollar AI companies cannot be procrastinated.

Longtermists, such as Albert Einstein, Nikola Tesla, Buckminster Ful- ler, Isaac Asimov, and Marshall McLuhan in the past, and contempo- rary figures such as Elon Musk, Ray Kurzweil, Peter Diamandis, Richard Bran- son, and Bill Gates, are individuals who strongly believe in the need to plan and act with the impact on the future in mind.

These thinkers and innovators focus on how current policies and actions can positively influence fu- ture generations, with a keen eye on the long-term effects of decisions on society, the environment, and the economy.

If we want to make a classification of the main philosophical approaches to AI, we can concretely divide them into four categories, among which stand out the technoapocalyptics who see it as a risk to huma- nity or even a product of the devil.

Then there are the techno-utopians a la Marc Andreessen, a statunitense computer scientist, for whom AI will save the world and transform our lives for the better.

Midway between these two we find those belonging to so-called "AI Safety," who are convinced that a general AI will be inevitable but we can save ourselves from it by aligning it with our values. These three groups are all guided by ideological views adapted to economic interests. Outside them are the *AI Ethicists*, scholars and academics who assess the risks of this technology as well as the impact that a tool ba- sed on statistics can have on our society. And it is perhaps this group-unregulated by the political and economic interests of the first three-that we must rely on in the long run.

5.4 Digital awareness and culture

Being aware of our relationship with the digital and the impact it has on our daily lives is critical to understanding what is happening to our society.

We need to recognize that digital is not only a tool for simplifying and speeding up processes, but it also has pro- fond consequences on our relationships with others, our mental and physical health, and our privacy. Only by understanding this can we ini- tiate its conscious use to improve our lives.

What to do

Awareness is central to per- sonal data management in the digital world. By becoming more aware of the va- lue of our data, we can make more informed decisions about who can have access to this information and in what context. Our personal data is a valuable asset that can be used to mi- larly enhance the services we use, but it can also be exploited in ways that may not be in the user's best interest. Therefore, it is essential to know to whom it can be safely transferred and to whom it cannot. We must not forget that the information we share can have a significant impact on our privacy and security.

For example, we do not hesitate to entrust our valuable data to digital giants, private companies that use it without limits and often in ways we cannot fully understand. Their operations seem distant and incomprehensible, like intricate digital labyrinths that conceal the true purpose behind simply collecting our per- sonal data. Yet despite this lack of transparency, we conti- nuously hand over detailed information about our habits, behaviors, and social networks, feeding the cycle of data collection without realizing it. It is a modern para- dump, where our trust in technology and the convenience of digital platforms collide with our concern for the privacy and security of our data. Conversely, we distrust our democratic states, which are fundamentally "our home." They are run by governments that we have elected ourselves, through a democratic process in which citizens exercise their right to vote. These governments use the data they collect to provide essential public services, such as the health care system, education and security, for which we contribute taxes. With this data, governments can make informed and targeted decisions for the good of society as a whole.

In early 2023, in Italy, the Privacy Guarantor requested information from OpenAI regarding data collection through its ChatGPT pro- duct. In response, OpenAI decided to restrict access to the service from Italy. Many criticized the Guarantor instead of preoc- cuping how ChatGPT was handling user data. They did not realize that the decision to restrict access might indicate that there were issues in data management. ChatGPT users were unaware of the U.S. company's data management practices, yet they wished to continue using the service without worrying too much. For them, the important thing was to live in the present moment, without prioritizing their data security and privacy.

I published a series of posts in which I tried to explain the importance of the Guarantor's choice and how it was for the benefit of all of us users. However, the responses of many demonstrate a lack of con- sumption about the magnitude of the problem. In general, the concept of data is unclear. They think it is just the e-mail and little else. They do not realize that our data also includes other aspects, such as our real-time location, our thoughts, our desires, and anything else we deliver into the hands of artificial intelligences, whichcould potentially be exploited against us for profit. This is why digital literacy and technology literacy is vital; it is vital that as many people as possible are aware of this and have an adequate understanding of the digital world in which we live. Digital literacy is no longer an optio- nal, but a necessity, a basic requirement for navigating a world increasingly permeated by technology and artificial intelligence. Being digitally literate means being able to know the instru- ments, to know where they come from. Which are not a gift from the universe, but knowingly produced by private companies that hold the power on what is then generated with their "black boxes."

What to do

The human-machine relationship now pervades every aspect of our lives; it is no longer just a technological innovation or business trend. We must yes think about what machines do for us, but also what they can be for us. By 2024, gene- rative AI has democratized, and by 2025, 90 percent of global companies will integrate it into their workforce.

This requires thinking about how to manage the trust, risk, and security of AI, with AI Trism, for example, which we have already participated about, monitoring the drift of data and models and controlling risk for both inputs and outputs.

There is also an aspect that we have not considered so far: the rise of automated customers or *custobots*, i.e., non-human customers who can purchase goods and services, so billions of connected products will com- pose as real customers.

But the issue of no small importance is that everyday AI, which improves productivity and will eventually be within everyone's reach, will not have a differentiating competitive advantage, instead the one that will truly affect business models and entire industries will be revolutionary and creative AI, capable precisely of creating new products, services and results.

This is why we need to consider the benefits of AI in both the short and long term. Both people and companies must be ready for this transition, including making data safe for use.

While still many focus only on productivity, per- diting from examining the opportunities and risks of AI in the back and front office, devising new products and services, and experimenting with new core capabilities.

They should, in short, take a critical and balanced approach such as that suggested by Reggie Townsend, vice president of Data Ethics Practice at SAS, who always uses common sense in his assessments to avoid running into misinformation and various discriminations, so as not to create further bias or prejudice. To give us a better understanding of his thinking, he makes a comparison between AI and electricity: although we do not know how the latter actually works, we do know how to harness it and how to keep ourselves away from the risks associated with it. He argues that we should use the same approach with AI as well: "What we should do, then, is promote AI common sense in a world where technology is increasingly pervasive.

How? For example, by focusing on some important aspects, such as recognizing human nature and AI, by training models with broad, inclusive and diverse data, but also by fighting prejudices about automation." Relying totally on it by attributing total fi- duction to it could have serious consequences, but rejecting it out of hand would also be a mistake given where it is taking us. "This means questioning the results generated by AI, recognizing the possible limitations and being aware of the potential biases of algorithms.

By understanding the human element in AI, combating misconceptions about automation and promoting critical thinking, we can empower individuals to make more informed decisions and con- tribute to the development and responsible use of AI technologies," Townsend wisely concludes.

Awareness also includes that about the large environmental risks associated with the increasing computational power needed to power AI. Supercomputers generate a major impact on na- ture, requiring large amounts of energy and water to run and cool. AI models, especially large ones like GPT-3, draw and consume large amounts of water. For example, just during the training of GPT-3 in Microsoft's data centers, 700 thousand liters of clean water were consumed, an impressive figure. Considering that the growing global demand for AI could cause an estimated water withdrawal of between 4.2 and 6.6 billion cubic meters in 2027, a figure that exceeds the total annual withdrawal of water by 4-6 times Denmark or half of the United Kingdom, we really should be concerned. Freshwater scarcity has become one of the most urgent challenges worldwide due to de- mographic growth, depletion of water resources, and obsolescent infrastructure. There is a need for AI model operators to assume social responsibility and commit to reducing the water impact of these technologies. The use of nonrenewable sources contributes to CO_2 emissions, while pressure on water resources saps regions already undergoing climate disruption. Despite pro- poses to reduce consumption by some large companies, however, the environment is still relegated to the background in favor of competition on a strategic and economic scale.

5.5 Digital education

The role of education is fundamental to Cyberhumanism. It is at- through education that individuals can fully understand the potential and risks of digital technology, thereby developing the com- petencies needed to use it.

Digital education therefore becomes essential from the early years of school. It is not enough to teach children how to use technology, but it is necessary to make them understand the importance of conscious and responsible digital use. Children must es- educate themselves to manage and protect their personal information, to understand the potential consequences of their online actions, and to recognize and manage risky situations.

This kind of education will not only prepare them for si- cure and aware browsing, but will also help to form active and responsible digital citizens, capable of using technology ethically and responsibly.

More complex digital-related concepts that are part of our lives as connected cit- tzens should also be taught in high schools, such as the importance of our data, how it could be used to our disadvantage, and how we can defend it.

We should learn to recognize fake news, analyze sources, and avoid falling into the traps of misinformation. In addition, we should be aware of our digital rights and how to have them respected, especially in an age when our perso- nal information, such as sensitive data and preferences, has become a pre- cious asset for many companies. It is important to understand the implications of this information sharing and take steps to protect our privacy and security online. Investing in the knowledge of our digital rights allows us to make informed decisions and act proactively to ensure that our information is treated ethically and securely.

The problem is that in the case of digital technologies, the change of products is so rapid that the user's knowledge, once ac- quired, has to be constantly renewed and therefore is not very suitable as school material.

The main goal of education will be to strengthen the per- sonality of young people, not just impart knowledge and skills. We will have to emphasize active learning, stimulating the ability to make complex decisions and evaluate situations intelligently.

Unfortunately, we are witnessing an opposite trend: standardization, fast teaching, and higher education that neglects reflection. We find ourselves passively absorbing an enormous amount of information, while social, ethical, artistic, creative, manual and technological skills are neglected.

We do not give due importance to the individual as a whole, respectating different facets, talents, interests and abilities. In an ideal world, the child, adolescent and young adult will find themselves on the road to education, on a path that will enhance and support them as they grow.

AI should also play a central role in basic education starting from elementary schools.

The history of the relationship between AI and learning is so long and complex that it has developed over the course of some seventy years, starting with the simple question first posed by Alan Turing: can a machine think? Moving from the pioneering studies of John McCarthy (the first to use the term "artificial intelligence"), Nathaniel Ro- chester, Claude Shannon, and Marvin Minsky in 1956 with the Proposal of Dartmouth[127] to recent developments in GPTs and educational chatbots. Initially, the focus was on creating a "teaching mac- china" based on logical-symbolic rules, but over the years it has come to be known as weak AI, according to which machines emulate the biological functions of the brain without developing thought or intentionality.

Weak AI is very important in contemporary innovations such as computer vision, text and vo- cial recognition algorithms and application in automation, to the recent evolution represented by GPTs and chatbots, which rely on advanced neural networks for text and image generation.

The history of the development of artificial intelligence in education can be divided into four phases: the mechanical phase (1945-1950), with Burrhus Skinner's teaching machines; the programming phase (1955-1990), that of the first intelligent machines for Com- puter Aided Instruction; the personalization phase (1970-1990), that of the Self-Adaptive Educational System, with automatic tutoring systems based on constructivism and algorithms; and finally the

---

[127] http://s24ore.it/mcc01

of personalization Intelligent Adaptive Learning System (2000 to present) with the development of cloud computing, data mining, big data, and generative AI. The evolution of these four phases marks the tran- sition from Skinner's "programmed" instruction to the co- struttivist approach and the adoption of personalized methodologies based on inferential algo- rithms. As we can see from this quick excursus, AI has truly revolutionized education by making possible the in-depth ana- lysis of learning data, the personalization of teaching, and the automation of processes such as assessment.

Understanding current digital transformations is critical to enable everyone to move confidently and effectively in the ever-changing digital landscape.

From public policy to education, several strategies can be implemented to facilitate this understanding. First, it is an essential priority to emphasize di- gital literacy to reduce the gap and train skills.

Schools and universities should integrate concepts such as online privacy, cybersecurity and the responsible use of social media into their curricula. Despite the fact that the NRP devotes 27 percent of resources, or nearly 41 billion euros, to the digital transition, thus a massive in- vestment, in Italy there is a glaring lack of digital literacy of citizens, which is instead the initial priority to ensure an inclusive and comprehensive digital evolution of society. Our country has a significant gap with other European states in citizens' digital skills, due to at least 30 years of blindness in this regard.

I have always had a desire to help ordinary people understand this world, and to do this it is necessary to use the mass media. The Internet is not the right medium, as the message needs to be addressed mainly to those who use it little or not at all.

What to do

It wasn't until ten years ago that I had my first television slots with great au- dience, and to date only one private network has given prime se- rata space to these issues, thanks to the vision of Antonio Ricci who decided to make this choice with the program *Striscia la notizia*. An entertainment program that was thus perfect for reaching a wide audience.

UCL research has shown how helpful this publishing choice has been to Italy in improving citizens' digital skills.

However, due to the blindness of more than 30 years of digital-insensitive policy, the DESI 2020[128] (Index of Digitization of Economy and Society, to monitor progress and gaps in the digitization process carried out by EU member states) evi- dated that Italy is last in Europe in digital skills, indicating a gap between human capital and digital progress. To af- fer this challenge, the goal is to close the digital skills gap with at least 70 percent of the population expected to acquire digital skills by 2026. Actions aim to reduce the *digital divide*, increase the number of ICT graduates, engage SMEs in emerging technologies, and expand the use of public digital services, in- clude for senior citizens.

The most relevant initiative fielded is Repubblica Digitale[129], which aims to reduce the digital and cultural divide by acting on skills, infrastructure and tools, promoting digital inclusion and technology education, with the goal of ensuring key compe- tences through integrated pathways between schools, universities, research and businesses.

The Digital Transformation Department, where I am among the contracted experts, is finally, under the leadership of Alessio Butti, undertaking the digital transition in the right way, seeing it

---

[128] http://s24ore.it/mcc14
[129] http://s24ore.it/mcc33

as an opportunity for growth for the country, but also as an imperence to ensure inclusion and equal opportunity. Because access to In- ternet and digital innovation is a right, and the digital transition must bridge inequalities rather than accentuate them.

Digital skills need to be developed not only among students, but also among workers. Organizing e-leadership workshops, training days, and workshops on topics such as arti- ficial intelligence, automation, and the Internet of Things can be a good prac- tice. It is necessary for companies to adapt quickly to change through the acquisition of digital skills by their di- pendants. In fact, digital transformation is not only about hard- ware and software, but impacts people and requires the diffusion of specific knowledge. The future job scenario, with the expected loss of jobs but also the emergence of new opportunities, makes it es- sential to retrain and upgrade workers' skills.

The discrepancy between those with only basic ones generates a squi- librium in power, favoring those with advanced digital skills.

Companies also face several difficulties in designing digital skills training programs, including pro- blems related to the speed and effective communication of change, adult involvement in training, and lack of accessibility to innovative tools. To overcome these obstacles, they must consider a digi- tal transformation pathway with features such as continuity, involvement, accessibility, personalization, and empathy, without first clarifying the objectives of the training pathway, taking into account the variety of digital skills needed.

Actions such as promoting internal digital competency models, linking digital initiatives to business goals, using

What to do

apps for digital skills development and the division of the corporate population into bands for specific training courses.

It is good to introduce different strategies such as *reverse mentoring*, which involves young people in developing the digital skills of seniors, and *blended learning*, which integrates traditional training with online elec- tives. And also propose the organization of *digital breakfast* sessions and the creation of an internal *buzz* (or slogan) to pro- mote corporate digitization. All this is done to attively involve employees in the whole process of digital transformation.

In this evolution, the role of governments is critical to the implementation of digital policies that improve people's lives. They must invest in robust digital infrastructure, ensure fast and reliable Internet access for all, and promote digital inclusion through targeted public policies and training programs. Communication infrastructures, services, and data must be accessible to all, and their sharing must respect national, private, and security interests.

To do so, they should reduce trade barriers, promote competition, and improve connectivity in rural areas, for example. Often, however, most people and organizations use only a small fraction of the potential inherent in di- gital tools.

The promotion of digital skills by governments is es- sential for improving the use of technologies. Policy should age- fly entrepreneurship, increase financial resources, help basic research, subsidize experimentation and new business models, encourage training, the adoption of di- gital tools in enterprises, and the promotion of innovation, but each country innovates differently and at a different pace. The labor market, then, is undergoing significant transformations. Governments should address machine automation, ensuring training of mass, preparing workers for change and finding an equili- brio between flexibility and stability in work through social dialogue. To stimulate market opening, they should reduce com- mercial barriers, promote open financial markets and address the challenges of taxation.

This helps to reduce the gap and inequalities, incentivize better management of digital security, privacy, and improve online consumer protection. Within this framework, companies should work to improve their understanding of digital transfor- mation. For example, PwC's *New* skills[130] program is designed to help us improve our understanding, skills, and knowledge of the digital world. Finally, all Internet users should know and respect that set of rules and behaviors that can avoid conflicts and misunderstandings, what we call "digital etiquette."

Over the years, our approach to new digital technologies has changed a lot. Take WhatsApp, for example, which has gone from being considered an app for young people to being used by everyone. The spread of these technologies has generated a generation gap not only between parents and children, but also between generations closer in age with partially different ways of communicating.

Digital education has become a challenge for both teachers and educators and institutions. Projects such as Social Warning, a volunteer mo- vation that brings digital literacy into schools with informative and ethical atti- vities, demonstrate the efforts taken to bridge this gap. Generation Z, being digital natives, practices interactive appren- ducation and t h e conscious use of technology with the adoption of new educational modes such as interactive online lessons or *flip- ped classroom*. However, according to Mike Ribble, educator and author of

---

[130] http://s24ore.it/mcc57

Digital Citizenship in Schools[131], there are nine useful elements to guide young people toward a safe and ethical online life ranging from access to literacy, health and wellness to digital safety. From this perspective, do not think that ge- nitorial training is any less important, as children often learn to use technology without adult supervision.

Therefore, it is good to implement a set of rules to follow at home to promote digital awareness, including restrictions on smartphone use at the dinner table and the need to log off before bedtime. Ribble stresses the need to address educational challenges proactively, networking among edu- cational institutions, governments and businesses. This is the only way to achieve con- dividual access to technology and active involvement of the population, understanding of digital transformations, in short, this is the only way to enable everyone to actively navigate a con- tinuing digital world.

5.6 Regulation

In May 2023, several scholars including Sam Altman, in a terse letter predicted that AI will lead to a possible "human extinction" if this is not subjected to strict regulation. In the letter published by the Center for AI Safety, the risks associated with out-of-control AI are equated with those of atomic weapons and pandemics.

It is essential that the digital world be regulated in a way that respects principles that place human beings at the center and ga- rantees the protection of human rights and individual freedoms. Constructive dialogue between governments, institutions, and international organizations is indispensable to develop appropriate regulations that

---

[131] M. Ribble, *Digital Citizenship in Schools*, ISTE, 2007.

can promote an equitable, inclusive and secure digital society. These regulations should address issues such as privacy, si- data security and digital accessibility, ensuring that everyone can benefit from the opportunities offered by technology. Only through global collaboration can we create a digital environment in which everyone can participate and thrive.

It is imperative to understand the urgency of acting quickly in this area. The digital world is evolving at a dizzying speed, and any delay in implementing effective regulation can pose potential risks to individual rights and freedoms. Artificial intelligences, for example, are becoming increasingly so- fisticated and invasive, and if not placed under human control, digi- tal can turn into a double-edged sword. Humanity cannot afford to lag behind or overlook the potential dangers of the digital. Therefore, it is imperative to accelerate global regulatory processes.

Italy was among the first states to establish a Steering Committee for Strategies on Artificial Intelligence, of which I am one of the 13 experts who make up the committee.

However, at the global level, addressing the problem of fragmented regulations, laws and states is a significant challenge. This can be overcome through concerted action and cooperation among nations.

It is essential to establish an international body, or to leverage existing ones, to develop a set of universal digital guidelines and standards with respect to Cyberhumanism.

The body should be tasked with harmonizing the various existing laws and regulations, eliminating discrepancies and promoting consistent digital regulation. This process, however, requires the political will of states to cooperate and abandon narrow national sovereignty in favor of global regulations.

What to do

Moreover, it is crucial that citizens be involved in this pro- cess to ensure transparency and representation. Uniform regulation around the world would not only facilitate the adoption and implementation of AI with respect to human beings and demo- cracy, but would also ensure that all individuals, regardless of their geographical location, enjoy the same protections and rights.

After all, the digital world is a kind of meta-state in which we all live, immersed in unprecedented virtual interconnectedness. Through- to devices and networks, we are constantly connected and interacting in a digital ecosystem that permeates every aspect of our lives. This digital universe offers us limitless opportunities, but it also requires critical awareness to navigate the challenges and complessities that come with it. It is an ever-changing landscape in which the boundaries between the real and the virtual blur, creating a new way of existing and relating to the world.

Ethical innovation

Ethics in digital refers to the field of inquiry that examines moral, social, and political que- stions arising from the use of digital technologies. These issues may concern privacy. of data, online security, access to technology, transparency and accoun- tability of technology companies, among others. Ethics in digital requires consideration of how our actions in the digital world affect individuals, communities, and societies both locally and glo- bally. In addition, it emphasizes the importance of respecting human rights and individual freedoms in the digital context. Last but not least, digital ethics is closely related to the principles of Cybe- rumanism, which insists that digital technology should serve humanity, not the other way around. So, innovation should es- ceed to be guided by a strong sense of ethics, with the goal of promoting the well-being of all individuals and to build a digital society that is equitable, inclusive, and respectful of human rights.

To promote Cyberhumanism, we must encourage ethical innovation. Technologies must be developed with a humane approach, taking into account the needs and perspectives of the people involved. We must also encourage critical reflection on how new technologies may affect our society and act accordingly to ensure a balanced future.

Ultimately, Cyberhumanism is the idea of using technology in a human way, to enhance people's lives and not replace them. It is a dynamic concept that adapts to the needs and challenges of humanity.

A prominent figure in the field of ethical innovation is Tim Berners-Lee, whom we mentioned earlier, who has stressed the importance of an open Internet accessible to all. The computer scientist, through his "Web We Want" initiative, has urged the creation of a Web that respects human rights, is open to all and allows everyone to contribute to its smooth operation. Similarly, innovators such as Elon Musk and Bill Gates have raised ethical concerns regarding artificial intelligence and the need for appropriate rego- lations to ensure that these technologies are used responsibly.

For example, how can we avoid or at least limit the damage caused by deepfake videos? Authorities are already addressing this mi- ness with a variety of legislative actions.

Two laws have been passed in California: AB-602, which prohibits the use of synthetic human images to create nonsense pornography, and AB-730, which prohibits the manipulation of images of political candidates within 60 days of an election.

But I wonder if these measures will be sufficient. Fortunately, developers in the world of AI cybersecurity continue to

What to do

release increasingly effective detection algorithms that analyze videos by detecting small distortions introduced during the forgery process, such as altering a 2D face to fit a 3D perspective. Although some current deepfake videos can be detected with the naked eye, identifying features such as jerky movements, lighting changes, and digital artifacts, the conti- nuous evolution of techniques makes visual recognition increasingly difficult.

Partially coming to the rescue are emerging technologies such as the use of cryptographic algorithms to insert hashes into video, tamper-resistant fingerprinting via AI and blockchain, and the insertion of digital artifacts into videos to slow down deepfake algorithms.

But still, despite technological solutions, the mi- gle protection is to implement sound security procedures. Integrating automated checks into fund transactions can prevent similar attacks and frauds. It is also essential to educate citizens about how deepfakes work, promote their identification, and use only trusted news sources. In my social accounts every day I post the most popular deepfakes of the moment and dangerous misinformation. But unfortunately, very few of us do this. Perhaps the state itself should take care of it.

The adoption of basic behavior protocols, such as "trust but verify," is basic to avoid deception. In the future, however, the deepfake pan- ram is set to change. Technology continues to evolve rapidly, with new generations of video challenging detection through improvements in motion quality. Currently, there are an estimated 15 thousand deepfake videos in circulation, some for recreational purposes and others with manipulative intent, but they will grow exponentially in the coming months. The speed in their creation indicates a significant increase in such content in the future, to

this it is important to keep up to date with security practices and anti-fake technology.

The issue raised by many is complex, but there is no shortage of solutions. First, we should focus on the problem itself, to better understand it and simulate all possible scenarios useful for predicting and managing risks.

Perhaps, instead of trying to solve the biases of AI systems and their errors, we could find ways to coexist with essisecondo the principles of cooperation and coexistence, that is, we should develop a symbiotic rapport with AI, rather than seeing it as a threat.

Although as we have already elaborated in previous chapters, a real threat already exists and it is the threat exerted on our data and privacy. Therefore, it is necessary to ensure that AI techno- logies are designed and used responsibly, with data protection and security at the center of our concerns. In addition, we must never lose sight of our responsibility in managing new technologies and maintain some degree of human con- trol. Although AI is already making decisions instead of humans, it is essential that humans remain the main re- sponsors of their decisions.

The rapid evolution that AI is undergoing, moving from a fantascientific concept to a concrete reality in every human context, requires a new perspective in governance, in which a key piece is the ISO/IEC 42001:2023 standard "Information technology - Artificial in- telligence Management system, "[132] published on December 18, 2023. A key step toward responsible AI management, which companies and organizations can draw inspiration from to meet the challenges of this evolving field.

A standard intended for those who provide or use AI-based products or services, establishing requirements and guidelines for implementing,

---

[132] http://s24ore.it/mcc51

What to do

maintain and continuously improve the AI management system within organizations and companies, supporting the development and responsible use of such systems and meeting the requirements and expectations of stakeholders.

ISO/IEC 42001, the world's first standard for AI systems, is designed to ensure responsible, safe, and ethical management of artificial intelligence by assessing its impact and providing a *framework* that integrates the concepts of risk, system, and governance, con- sidering AI-related issues such as transparency in automated decision-making and management of data and machine lear- ning. Specifically, it suggests clear policies, gover- nance procedures, rules, and guidelines for managing the risks and operational le- git aspects of AI, with the goal of developing reliable, transparent, and accountable systems, managing the data and model lifecycle, addressing diversity and inclusiveness in AI systems, and monitoring and au- dit. It not only plays a key role in conformity assessment and certification, but also integrates with the UN's so- stenible development goals (see Agenda 2030).

AI legislation globally is constantly evolving, and has so far seen the implementation of several initiatives such as Singapore's 2020 Model AI Go- vernance Framework; Australia's AI Ethics Framework, to manage potential AI risks, with a commitment to watermarks or labels for recognition of AI-generated content, is from the same period; in 2023, we recall the AI Risk Management Framework published by NIST, the Biden Executive Order in the United States, and the Bletchley Declaration on AI signed by 28 countries, the latter with the intent to collaborate and manage the risks associated with this new technology, for example by subjecting new models to testing before they are deployed. In this vein, Great Breta- gna has tripled its investment in the AI Research Resource, which com- takes two supercomputers that will carry out these kinds of tests. Also this initiative promotes transparency and accountability on the part of those developing frontier AI technologies in order to measure, monitor, and mitigate potentially harmful capabilities.

Another noteworthy initiative is the "Hiroshima Process" held during the G7 meeting on May 19, 2023, which ended with an according signed by member states, including Italy, a kind of international code of conduct for companies and organizations developing advanced AI systems, which are required to have greater security and transparency.

The document is based on four main pillars (risk and opportunity analysis, international guiding principles, international code of conduct, and projects in support of sustainable AI) and consists of an eleven-point list through which organizations and companies are urged to promote safe and reliable AI and to respect and tu- tect human rights in the design, development, and implementation of AI. According to this code of conduct, the parties involved should be transparent, sharing useful information to identify possible dangers and not develop AI systems that could cause harm to democracies, individuals, or society at large, or even encourage terro- rism actions and crime, leading to security and human rights tu- tions. All this is done to balance technological progress with the management of associated risks.

The ordinance, although it does not provide a detailed plan and tempistics to put it in place, it does not represent a decisive norm- tive restriction. On the contrary, it recognizes that further action is needed to address the concerns and challenges related to AI, but at the same time advance its progress. If we go back over the years, however, we come across a glaring example of how state inte- resions often do not collide with technological progress. Think of the Locomotive Act, which was introduced by the British Parliament in the

What to do

second half of the nineteenth century to limit the use of motor vehicles on the roads, as its economic interests centered more on the diffusion of rail travel. If we compare it to the much more recent Highway Code, we can easily see how the regulation of technological innovations is often driven by the economic in- terests of the legislature. And this can es- prove to be applied in the field of artificial intelligence as well.

In President Biden's Executive Order, mentioned earlier, the main points of the order include a requirement for companies developing AI models such as GPT-4 or LLaMa to notify the government during training and share security test results with it. Then, it provides for the development of standards and tests to ensure the safety and security of AI systems, along with measures to guard against its risks such as protecting against AI-based fraud, establishing an advanced cybersecurity program, providing federal support for privacy protection techniques, and combating al- gorithmic discrimination.

With the ordinance, the U.S. government also pledges to ensure fairness in the criminal justice system, advocate for workers and consumers, promote the responsible use of AI, encourage AI research, and shape the potential of AI in education.

The purpose of both the Code of Conduct approved by the G7 and Biden's am- ministrative act is to guide a technology that, according to most experts, in the absence of clear rules, could one day have disastrous outcomes for both society and de- mocracies.

In 2023, in China, the National Information Security Standardization Committee published draft requirements for generative AI service providers, directly addressing privacy, intellectual property and security que- stions.

Provisions of the draft include security assessment of training data, consent of the data subject whose information is used for training purposes, and guidelines on risk mitigation.

While Japan has adopted regulations that are less strict re- spect to those in Europe and more in line with the order issued in the U.S., but the Privacy Supervisor has banned OpenAI from collecting sensitive data without permission. Poland and Spain have also launched an investigation into the company for violating European data protection laws.

Even Pope Francis from Vatican City has been clamoring to regulate the sector, to prevent algorithms from replacing human beings and establishing true "techno- nological dictatorships."

Europe as a whole has not been outdone in trying to find the right guidelines to mitigate any risks associated with AI, adopting the first comprehensive global legislation, the AI Act, which seeks to maintain a delicate balance between the excitement of innovation and the need for regulation that addresses all the risks associated with the application of AI. In truth, the AI Act is the manifestation of an important ethical dilemma: with a strong human rights orientation, Eu- ropa is seeking to provide opportunities to design ethically responsible AI systems, while recognizing the fact that regulating them could slow down technological development.

More advanced generative AI models in general, and LLMs in par- ticular, show high performance in a wide range of tasks, but their unpredictable results raise concerns about the li- ceity and accuracy of the generated content.

Overall, EU law does not seem adequately prepared to deal with such novelties. This is where policy proposals include updating current and future regulations, in particularly those that include AI in a broad sense, as well as the ema- nation of specific regulations for generative AI.

For companies, this new scenario implies a reevaluation of risk management strategies: greater algorithmic transparency is required and at the same time greater human involvement. The penalties for violations are not negligible, underscoring the im- portance of complying with these high standards (see ISO/IEC 42001). In this sense, it is important to consider the fact that data is critical: for AI to work properly, this data must be secure and certified, but when we are not certain that it is, we run into the so-called "data bottleneck," resulting in misleading re- sults.

To limit these harms, collaborative standards involving companies, industry associations, and institutions at all levels can be aimed at synchronizing the use of data, reducing inefficiencies and pro- moving the effective use of AI. A recent example of progress in this direction is the Data & Trust Alliance[133], a consortium of companies developing a data tagging system.

So while AI plays a central role in our lives, we are facing the challenge of making it not only advanced, but also respon- sible. As we have seen, the European AI Act acts similarly to a "highway code" for AI, ensuring that data are collected and processed ethically and creating a regulated innovation environment.

Regulations such as the AI Act provide fertile ground for the development of responsible AI, balancing advanced capabilities with rigorous safety and ethical stan- dards, such as when building a fast but safe car, thus influencing the competitive landscape and shaping the

---

[133] http://s24ore.it/mcc12

direction of technological innovation. In sum, the AI Act should not be seen as an obstacle to innovation, but as a key guide for ethical and safe development of AI.

This act is a tangible example of the commitment to balancing regulation with technological progress, not only in a harmonious way, but also with the goal of guiding the tech- nological path toward accountability and sustainability and, above all, not blocking the advance, with data standardization being at the heart of this reflection.

This is not just a technical issue, but a basic pillar for ensuring the integrity and transparency of AI systems. In this journey we must consider both technological progress and ethical imperatives, aiming to contribute to collective and individual well-being. Indeed, this challenge goes beyond technology: it is a redefinition of our relationship with it and, ultimately, with society itself.

All these initiatives intend nothing more than to develop an inclusive scientific research network on AI security, including and complementing international collaboration in defining the public good. So we need international laws now that go beyond declarations of intent.

Specifically, the AI Act focuses mainly on protecting individual rights and freedoms by requiring companies developing AI solutions to demonstrate that their products and development processes do not put people or their integrity at risk. On February 2, 2024, after political agreement was reached in di- cember 2023, the AI Act was approved by the 27 member countries during the meeting of the Committee of Permanent Representatives (Coreper). The final version of the text had been presented on Jan. 24 during a technical meeting, but initially some states, including France, Germania and Italy, had expressed reservations, which were resolved before the Act was adopted. With Coreper's approval, the text will be submitted to the parliamentary committees on the Internal Market and Consumer Protection and on Civil Liberties, Justice and Home Affairs for consideration. Finally, the law will be brought to a vote of all MEPs in a plenary session of Parliament with the goal of adoption by April.

The categories to which it applies range from vendors to distributors, to those who use AI under its authority, excluding private non-professional use, for military and national security purposes, or for scientific research. It also does not apply to AI systems licensed free or open source.

The scope of AI is thus broad, but key areas include restrictions on biometric identification systems and a requirement for transparency with respect to systems used for chatbots such as ChatGPT, i.e., the user must be aware that he or she is dealing with an algorithm and recognize its products as such; in the case of deepfakes, for example, it is necessary to declare that the video or photo is the result of AI. A crucial element is the method of risk classification, already adopted in similar regulations such as GDPR, which attributes specific characteristics to certain AI systems as "high risk," subjecting them to rigorous compliance actions.

The regulation sets high standards for these systems, com- taken transparency and information for the user, human oversight, data quality, cybersecurity and robustness, risk assessment, and compliance. For such systems, it introduces a kind of "Fundamental Rights Impact Assessment" (FRIA), highlighting the importance of ethical considerations in AI implementation. For example, practices such as the analysis of sensitive biometric data and the indiscriminate use of images to charge facial recognition systems are prohibited.

Law enforcement agencies may use biometric systems only in exceptional cir- cumstances, such as searching for victims or missing persons.

parse, the prevention of public threats or terrorist attacks, or the identification of certain suspects. The AI Act also prohibits emotion detection in the workplace and in schools, cognitive-behavioral manipulation techniques, as well as predictive policing and *social scoring*, which is the use of AI to pun- tate behavior and personal characteristics. The regulation also requires high-impact AI models, such as Ope- nAI's GPT-4, to ensure transparency in the training process and con- divide technical documentation prior to market launch.

Penalties for non-compliant companies can be up to 7 percent of their total turnover. The implementation process of the AI Act will take place in several stages, with the largest expected in the second half of 2026. Therefore, big tech must prepare adequately when defining the systems currently under development to ensure compliance with the new EU regulations.

Specifically, the AI Act consists of 85 articles and 9 annexes[134] and is directly applicable without states having to transpose it with another law. As we anticipated, there are clearly defined prohibited AI practices, starting with categorization and real-time biometric identification by law enforcement in publicly accessible spaces, including untargeted extraction of facial data from the Internet; for that at a distance, authorization must be required from a judicial or administrative authority and must not be used for law enforcement purposes in a non-targeted manner, i.e., without any connection to a crime, pe- nal proceeding, threat of crime, or search for a specific missing person.

Also prohibited are systems that exploit subliminal techniques, vulnerabilities, or manipulate humans to circumvent their fundamental- mental rights and cause physical or psychological harm, those that recognize the

---

[134] http://s24ore.it/mcc11

emotions, assessing social scores or ranking per- sons or groups based on their social behavior. After the expressly prohibited uses, since the AI Act's approach is risk-based, all designated high-risk systems (HRAIS) will be subject to numerous obligations, especially providers. Experimenting with them under real-world conditions outside of regulatory AI sandboxes will be subject to a number of safeguards, which in- clude, among other things, approval by the market supervisory authority, the right for data subjects to request cancellation of their data after experimentation the right for market surveillance authorities to request information from providers regarding testing, including the power to conduct inspections, the limited duration of such testing, and certain additional safeguards designed specifically for testing in the areas of law enforcement, migration, asylum, and border control management.

To be more precise, high-risk systems are those used to manage essential public infrastructure such as electricity, water, and gas, those used in student assessment or in recruitment and employment, such as in border and migration management, or even those used to influence elections and the democratic process, and finally those used in banking and insurance.

The agreement also includes new provisions for general purpose AI models. These new standards introduce horizontal obligations for all GPAI models, which include keeping them up-to-date and making technical documentation available to the relevant authorities upon request. There are some additional requirements for models with systemic risks, divided into the four categories of minimal, limited, high, and unacceptable, which include model and risk assessment, adoption of systemic risk mitigation measures, and reporting on the energy efficiency of GPAI, ensuring a adequate level of cybersecurity protection and the reporting of serious incidents to the appropriate authorities.

Regarding copyright, the agreement stipulates that GPAI model formers will be required to implement a policy of compliance with Union copyright law and make available to the public a sufficiently detailed summary of the content used in the charge- ment of the general AI model.

The text also includes new rules on governance. While market surveillance at the national level will apply for AI systems, the new rules for GPAI models provide for a more cen- tralized system of supervision and enforcement. To this end, the AI Office, a new governance structure with a set of spe- cific tasks for GPAI models and with a strong link to the scien- tific community to support its work, will be established. The new pro- posed governance structure also includes an enhanced role for the AI Council. Its list of tasks has been expanded to give member states a stronger coordinating role, including in AI regulatory sand- boxes, stakeholder consultations, and outreach activities. The final text also introduces two new advisory or- gans. A scientific group of independent experts will provide technical advice and input to the AI Office and market surveillance authorities and will also play a key role in the enforcement of rules for GPAI models, as it can issue qualified alerts of pos- sible risks to the AI Office. Based on the general approach, member states will have the option of using experts from the scien- tific groups to support their market surveillance activities. An advisory fo- rum, on the other hand, will provide stakeholder input to the Commission (including the AI Office) and will be composed of a balanced selection of stakeholders, including industry, startups, SMEs, civil society, and academia.

With regard to AI systems already placed on the market or put into service, in the case of public authorities that are suppliers or im- plementers of high-risk AI systems, the agreement is to offer them four years from entry into application to make their systems con- form. This change is not significantly different from the Council's po- sition, since it is highly unlikely that within four years these systems will not undergo a substantial change.

For non-compliance with the provisions on vie- tive AI practices, the penalty was set at 35 million euros or 7 percent of annual turnover. The maximum amount of fines has been aligned with that for high-risk AI system providers. Importantly, there will be an additional grace period for providers of general-purpose AI models, as no fines can be imposed during the first year after the regulations come into effect.

In terms of entry into force, the agreement provides 24 months for most parts of the regulation, with slightly shorter deadlines for some elements, notably 6 months for bans and 12 months for provisions on notifying authorities and notified or- ganisms, governance, GPAI models, confidentiality, and sanctions, and a slightly longer deadline of 36 months for high-risk AI systems.

The European Commission is formulating an innovation strategy on AI to establish so-called "AI factories" (AI Factories). This initiative can be interpreted as a first step toward a specific industrial policy for artificial intelligence, pending the formal adoption of the AI Act. At the heart of this strategy are AI factories, which we could understand as open ecosystems revolving around European public supercomputers, bringing together the prin- cipal material and human resources needed for the development of generative AI models and applications. The physical infrastructure will consist of the dedicated AI supercomputers and well-connected data centers.

The dilemma of regulating technologies such as artificial intelligence is described by Professor David Collingridge as a pa- radox, which is based on the difficulty of intervening effectively in the regulation itself: doing so too early could make regulations obsolete, but waiting until the technology is mature carries the risk of losing control of it[135].

The solution to this impasse could come from *regulatory sandboxes*, environments in which companies can experiment for a limited pe- riod with new technological products or services under the supervision of authorities, thus taking advantage of exemptions to existing regulations and a safe and controlled testing ground. The Italian government is also exploring the possibility of applying the *regulatory sandbox* concept in the fintech sector, or financial innovation made possible by technology. International experiences, such as those in Norway and Spain, suggest that these spaces can facilitate the development and validation of innovative artificial intelligence systems under safe conditions.

The European Commission, anticipating what was proposed with the AI Act, has already issued regulations that include the creation of regulatory spe- rimentation spaces for AI, highlighting the importance the EU attaches to this approach for the future development of AI.

Recently, UN Secretary-General António Guterres also raised serious alarms about the reckless practices of big tech companies pursuing profits from artificial intelligence without taking into account the risks derived from it. In his speech at the World Economic Forum in Davos, he linked the dangers of AI to those of the climate crisis, emphasizing the absence of a global stra- tegy to address both problems. Technologi- cal companies should work with governments to regulate AI instead of

---

[135] D. Collingridge, *The Social Control of Technology*, Palgrave Macmillan, London, 1980.

seek profits with "disregard for human rights, per- sonal privacy and social impact." The International Monetary Fund report warns about the likely worsening of inequality due to AI, so Guterres emphasized the need for more sustainable energy sources, criticizing fossil fuel companies that hinder progress on climate change. He also urged governments to work with technology companies to ge- strate current and future AI issues, suggesting the implemen- tation of risk management frameworks and damage monitoring, as well as promoting wider access for developing economies. He, too, therefore, sees an urgent need to bring attention to the irresponsible actions of technology companies and the risks of the cli- mate crisis, calling for immediate collaboration between governments and companies to mitigate these risks and ensure the successful use of AI.

To this end, some have even proposed taxing the producers of AI systems. The hypothesis should not seem absurd to us given how generative AI is impacting globally, primarily with job losses due to automation that will have not-in-different consequences on the profit of a few at the expense of many and public costs. That is why Marietje Schaake, director of international policy at Stanford University's Cyber Policy Center and special advisor to the European Commission, proposes taxing AI companies to allow society to rebalance costs and benefits. But doubts quickly arise that this solution is only a palliative cure to solve the impending problem of job losses, instead of addressing the issue in depth.

5.7 Public-private collaborations

Synergistic cooperation between public institutions and private actors is a key element in managing the evolution of intelligence artificial and acts as a shield to prevent dominance that could undermine human interests. This alliance holds crucial rile- vance for a variety of reasons.

Public agencies play a key role in shaping the re- gulations and regulations that must ensure the use of ethics and respect for human rights in digital technologies. By setting guidelines and standards to which to conform, they promote equity, tra- sparence, and accountability in the increasingly complex AI environment. Through investment in research and development, they can contribute to protecting the digital rights of citizens while improving their quality of life.

A tangible example of their commitment would be their investment in the development of algorithms aimed at reducing bias and inequality in automated decisions, thus ensuring a fairer and more equitable use of technologies. Private companies, for their part, bring technical expertise and financial resources essential for the efficient development and implementation of such technologies.

In 2019, the Digital Humanism Initiative (DIGHUM)[136] was established in Vienna, an international collaboration whose goal is to create a community of scholars, policymakers, and industrialists committed to ensuring respect for human interests in technological development. DIGHUM has formulated a manifesto containing foundational principles that can be adopted and adapted by various governments as reference and guidance in this development. First, digital technologies must be designed to foster democracy and inclusion and to overcome current inequalities by harnessing their potential to emancipate and make society more advanced.

Privacy and freedom of expression are inescapable values of democracy and should be prioritized in our actions and those who govern us.

---

[136] http://s24ore.it/mcc07

What to do

For this, it is necessary to establish effective regulations and laws, based on a broad public dialogue, which should ensure the accu- rity of predictions, fairness and equality, as well as accountability and transparency toward the data used by software and algorithms. Governments must take action against techno- gical monopolies in order to restore market competitiveness and prevent the concentration of power that stifles innovation. Leaving all decisions to companies should never be an option. Instead, these should continue to be made by humans, always assessing first the possible impacts on individual and collective human rights. So automated decision-making systems should only act as a support to human decisions, not replace them.

No less is the interdisciplinary scientific approach essential for meeting future technological challenges. Technical disciplines, such as computer science, must collaborate with the social sciences and other humanities, overcoming disciplinary divisions. In this sense, universities, as sources of new knowledge and foundations of critical thinking, have an extra responsibility because they must stabi- lish a synergy between academic researchers and industrialists, openly engaging with institutions to reflect on their approaches, supporting each other in the production of new knowledge and technologies while defending freedom of thought and scientific research.

It is important to combine together knowledge from the huma- nistic disciplines, social sciences, and engineering studies, because in an era of automatic decision-making and artificial intelligence, creativity and attention to human aspects are fundamental to the education of future engineers and technologists. The study of computer science and its social impact must begin as early as possible, teaching students to integrate computer science skills with an awareness of the ethical and social issues at stake. In this evolutionary shift, professionals in the field must recognize their responsibility in the impact of new technologies, understanding that no in- vention is neutral and without implications and developing an awareness of both the potential benefits and disadvantages while always having the good of humanity in mind.

What if we created a kind of Global Digital Council, tasked with defining the ground rules and universal values of a fully digitized society?

This is not an entirely science fiction prediction, because AI could merge with the evolution of science that is now able to genetically modifi- cation humans. At this point perhaps we should think that humans will have new rights, with a list that could be quite long, because we have to take several variables into con- sideration.

First, we should be able to opt out of ge- netic or machine integration changes in order to make ourselves more per- formant. Then we should have the right to disconnect and maintain anonymity when we want, or the right to hire people instead of machines. In addition to the rights just listed, we also have di- verse duties.

We should not allow humans to be governed or completely guided by technologies such as AI, IoT or robotics, thereby ac- cording machines the power to self-determine and evade human control. In the same way, we will not allow bots, mac- chines, platforms, or other intelligent technologies to take over basic democratic functions in our society, functions that should instead be performed only by humans, nor will we allow them to make or challenge our moral decisions.

We also have a duty not to create, design or distribute tech- nologies with the main intent of generating dependence, and especially not to attribute excessive power to technology just because it generates economic benefits.

5.8 Privacy by design

Comte de Vaublanc Vincent-Marie Viénot (1756-1845), echoing words not his own, argued that spying on an honest man would find sufficient reason to have him arrested.

This quote introduces us to the sensitive topic of privacy and confidentiality, the violation of which poses a threat to the rights and freedoms of both individuals and businesses.

As discussed in the previous chapter on Privacy, generative artificial intelligence si- stems process and generate vast amounts of data, including text, images, video, code, business plans, and technical formulas. Manipulating, verifying, uploading, analyzing, consulting or processing such input and output data in any way requires different levels of protection and security, with a significant distinction between personal and non-personal data.

In the first case, where data is considered from the design of digital products, personally identifiable information such as names or details about a person's life, and where data protection laws may apply, either locally (such as the CCPA in Ca- lifornia that allows citizens the right to access their personal in- formations, as well as to delete them or disable their sale) or regionally (such as the GDPR in Europe under which companies that ope- rate in the EU are subject to a set of data protection rules).

Even business data, therefore, such as financial information, technical information, strategic know-how, and trade secrets, should be classified as confidential information right from the design of the products or services that incorporate them. Following according to lo- cal laws or contracts, resulting in civil and criminal penalties in case of negligent handling of such data. Therefore, when employing generative artificial intelligence si- stems, organizations must carefully categorize the data entered into such systems and adopt

Cyberhumanism

Measures to ensure that processing is done in a legal, si- cure and confidential manner.

As we have already seen, AI generative models can unintentionally apprehend and reproduce sensitive information in training data, generating outputs that contain confidential information that, if disclosed or made public, can put privacy at risk.

Companies must also be aware of their confidentiality obligations from the time they design a product. If a company's use case involves confidential information shared by customers, suppliers, or third parties, the company must first consider the confidentiality obgress and other contractual terms by which the in- formations were shared and consider whether it is permissible to use them within a generative artificial intelligence system. Companies, when using such systems, should pay particular attention to the common principles and protections on personal data that are strongly affected by generative AI systems.

How is it possible for them to implement this? First, in outlining their privacy policies and statements, they should explain in accessible language the use and purpose of AI systems, clarifying the rationale behind automated decisions derived from artificial intelligence and highlighting potential risks to individuals.

Then, although as we know huge amounts of data are ne- cessary to train AI systems, companies should consider whether it is necessary to reduce, remove, or exclude personal data from the ad- righting set, for example by preventing end users from entering data into the system's search function. In some jurisdictions, there are specific legal bases for the processing of personal data, even if such data were already publicly available at the time of collection. Those operating AI systems appear to justify the

What to do

processing of personal data by invoking their legitimate interests in forming the system and contractual obligations in providing the service, thus for their own mere business purposes.

Fortunately, several jurisdictions instead impose more ri- gorous requirements on companies when processing personal data about minors or other sensitive information such as criminal convictions, health or bio- metric data. Such requirements may include age verification, stricter juri- dic bases for processing (e.g., consent), or per- sons to prohibit processing. In these cases, individuals have various data protection rights, ranging from requesting access to and copying of personal information to correcting erroneous data, from requesting human intervention in automated decisions by artificial intelligence to objecting to processing for legitimate interests and permanent deletion of data. However, in light of the tech- nical principles on which artificial intelligence is based, implementing processes that respect these individual rights can be quite complicated.

Therefore, organizations should make a number of considerations before legal and regulatory requirements come into effect. First, access to data should be limited to authorized personnel, and the role of physical and logical access control mechanisms, such as authentication systems, should be delineated.

Then figure out what specific policies and procedures for the use of AI tools to adopt and whether these will be adapted by guaranteeing the exercise of individual rights (e.g., data deletion) and how to maintain and verify compliance. Then decide what training and awareness sessions are appropriate for employees on the ethical, legal, and safe use of this technology; how supply chain audits and controls affect the providers or recipients of artifi- cial intelligence generation services; what technical and organizational measures (e.g., A I governance, privacy by design, and for default setting, pseudonymization, anonymization, encryption, and secure storage) should be put in place to ensure that organizations and the personal or confidential data they ingest or retrieve are protected from unauthorized disclosure, alteration, or loss of availability. Provision should also be made for whether specialists and legal experts will be involved in the design of controls to protect personal data and confidentiality from the earliest stages of any artificial intelligence project, and whether the compe- tences will be internal or external.

The problem is first of all, of course, related to data collection. If AIs are restricted in collecting data on humans, they may be less harmful in the future.

The UNESCO Declaration on Science and the Use of Knowledge and the Recommendation on Open Science[137] state that the sciences must respect human rights and the dignity of people, as already enshrined in the Universal Declaration of Human Rights.

The Universal Declaration on the Human Genome specifies that some scientific applications may be harmful, emphasizing the "special" re- sponsibility of scientists and other actors, which must be included in the debate through public consultation.

The Universal Declaration on Bioethics and Human Rights of the Une- sco established general principles regarding human vulnerability, the integrity of the person, and the right to privacy and confidentiality.

But all this is not enough.

On August 8, 2023, the Chilean Constitutional Court issued a sention of historic importance in the field of technology and the protection of personal integrity. In that ruling, the first of its kind worldwide, it stressed that even devices intended to monitor people's brain activity for "private" purposes must be authorized by health authorities. If users' data are then

---

[137] http://s24ore.it/mcc64

processed for scientific purposes, the user's consent must be informed, express, research-specific, and dynamic-that is, required whenever the purposes of the research change over time. This decision marks an important milestone in the delicate intersection of technology and personal protection.

A new vulnerability of the human being, hitherto unexplored, is the knowledge and control of brain activity for purposes other than just health. To ensure the defense and development of neuro-rights, explicit regulation of neuro-data as a category of sensitive personal data is needed. In Europe, it is essential to make changes to the GDPR in this direction.

In the philosophy of Cyberhumanism, privacy and security play a key role. The need to protect perso- nal data and sensitive information is greater than ever in a digitally dominated era. Artificial intelligence, in particular, presents unique challenges in terms of privacy and security.

It is critical that robust security measures be implemented to protect individuals and society as a whole from po- tential risks. At the same time, the privacy of the individual must be respected, recognizing everyone's right to control and protect their personal information. This balance between technological innova- tion and the protection of individual rights is central.

There are many recent cases of failure to protect privacy due to blindness at conception that we could cite as examples.

The app The Weather Channel has been accused by the city of Los Angeles of unauthorized sharing and using the location data of millions of users, who were not properly informed about its use. The lawyer behind the lawsuit correctly stated that in order to know the weather forecast, one cannot sacrifice one's personal data and users must be warned of such use.

One study showed how a predictive algorithm used in various U.S. hospitals discriminated against black patients several times by giving priority to whites. According to the algorithm, only 18 percent of the former were entitled to access certain care, when in- vance the real number should have been around 47 percent.

Another emblematic case was that of the credit card, the Apple Card of Goldman Sachs, which seemed to dispense different cre- finger limits, penalizing women and thus discriminating between the sexes. The so- ciety had to defend itself against a real charge of sexism.

Of course, we also cannot fail to mention one of the most significant political scandals in early 2018: Cambridge Analytica had acquired the personal data of 87 million Facebook accounts without users' consent, using it for political propaganda purposes. Here it was even privacy violated by design!

This episode, which led to a significant drop in Facebook's stock value, also raised calls for stricter nor- matives to regulate the use of personal data by technology companies.

Artificial intelligence could prove superior to humans in a number of cognitive, emotional and diagnostic tasks, as evi- dated in the case of ChatGPT, which surpassed human abilities in recognizing people's emotions from what they write online and ad- ditionally was able to correctly diagnose a 4-year-old's illness that eluded 17 doctors.

The problem is that this advanced ability can also be used to infer with surprising accuracy the personal information of users who would instead like to protect it. Recent research has ana- lyzed the OpenAI GPT4, Meta, Google, and Anthropic language models, finding that they can easily infer characteristics such as skin co- lor, profession, or place of residence from simple con- versations. For example, ChatGPT was able to extract private information from text snippets of Reddit profiles with 85 to 95 percent ac- curity, at 100 times less cost and in 240 times faster time than human methods. Again pri- vacy not respected by design.

This case raises many concerns about the violation of users' privacy rights. By exploiting its probabilistic reasoning capabilities, the chatbot is able to make data-driven inferences, inferring characteristics of users not explicitly stated in the messages. And this results in a major privacy risk, then- because thus sensitive or personal data can be inferred from users without any authorization. Another important aspect that should not be underestimated are the ethical and legal questions regarding the use of chatbots: this technology could be maliciously exploited to obtain in- formations about individuals who instead wish to maintain anonymity, such as activists, dissidents, or journalists, violating their right to data protection and individual freedom.

5.9 Watermarking

Watermarking is a technique we borrowed from analog photography, which back in the day served us to protect the originality of digital photos and prohibit theft, and now instead is necessary to prevent or limit the damage of deepfakes.

In AI-generated content, watermarking techniques incorporate invisible patterns that only computers can perceive, a labeling, authentication and provenance mechanism, a kind of electronic watermark or mark to enable detection and tracking of content generated by this technology.

This is part of the obligations under the European AI Act, geared toward the development of watermarking tools and standard rules. A guidance compiled by the Brooking [Institute138] identifies its main methodologies: the inclusion of an identifiable pattern in the content to trace its origin; content provenance, which securely incorporates and con- serve information about the origin of the metadata; retrieval-based detectors, which store all AI-generated content in a searchable database to verify its origin; and post hoc detectors, based on machine learning models to detect subtle but systematic patterns in AI-generated content, distinguishing it from human-created content.

In the case of images, watermarking based on automatic application is used; common avoidance techniques include cropping, pixel changes, and the application of filters or over- ciphers. Particularly problematic, however, is identifying content that has a mixed component of human and AI input, especially when interactive collaboration with a model takes place.

There is also statistical watermarking in which, instead of patterns, we incorporate a statistically unusual arrangement of words/pi- xels/sounds, although we risk spoiling the content. It is utopian to think that we can detect all AI-generated content, to distinguish all that was created by a machine rather than a human (if it has no watermark it is not automatically a co- pia); instead, we should generate less content without watermarking or ensure that at least a good percentage incorporates a water- mark. After all, currently there is still no standard that im- poses its use, and the watermarking used for AI-generated works cannot be equated with that of human works of authorship; in fact the opposite is the case: the AI owner has an interest in making his or her work equal to human works.

The not inconsiderable benefits are both ethical and social but also economic, related to the opportunity for the public to be adequately

---

[138] http://s24ore.it/mcc35

What to do

informed about the origin and nature of a product, so that they are also able to make more informed choices. In short, achieving a balance between individual and public interests. In this sense, watermarking could be understood as a possible certification marker and a statement of transparency, to ultimately ensure that AI systems are knowable and transparent and exercise widespread control over the way they operate, in order to identify in them the presence of possible bias and correct it.

Google DeepMind has launched [SynthID][139], a tool that incorporates a digital watermark directly into image pixels. Even- though imperceptible to the human eye, it can identify im- magines generated by [Imagen][140].

The Coalition for Content Provenance and Authenticity (C2PA)[141] organization, headed by Microsoft's Andrew Jenks, is working to use content credentials and develop technical methods to map digital media files by attaching cryptographically secure metadata to images and videos. A number of companies in the me- dia and communications sector have immediately adopted the content credential system at a time when misinformation is increasingly rampant. The problem is that tools such as Dall-E 2 and Midjourney now allow almost anyone to alter content no- nost the security protocols of generative AI platforms. With the C2PA system, images will be given a "cr" icon so that the user can get every piece of information about it, from who created it to how it was possibly altered. New legislation such as the AI Act or the White House executive order under which synthetic content must

---

[139] http://s24ore.it/mcc13
[140] http://s24ore.it/mcc23
[141] http://s24ore.it/mcc06

be authenticated and tagged. Few companies have done so yet, however; it is complicated to adapt their workflows to this new system, but there are those like the BBC group who suggest the idea that publishers could rely on ser- vice centers to authenticate their images and content. Easier ri- sult in political communication to help candidates tag their campaign material with metadata, however, is more arduous for social media such as Facebook, which makes no secret of its hesitancy about the fact that users might give up waiting for a watermark to be added to every piece of content. Social me- dia platforms can still make use of metadata for filtering and clas- sification of reliable content. And camera prototypes from Leica, Nikon, and Canon already have embedded content credentials.

In research conducted at the University of Maryland is pro- post a new technique for inserting a watermark in the result of a proprietary language pattern, that is, inserting a nasco- sto pattern in the text that is imperceptible to human eyes but can be identified as synthetic by algorithms. The idea is to select some random tokens and increase the probability that the language mo- del will generate them. The authors have developed an open source algorithm that uses a statistical test to confidently detect watermarks.

But the world does not consist of one state and one common law, as we have already seen in the previous chapter. And as much as we can introduce mandatory watermarks, can we ever force, for example, North Korea to comply with these rules? And if, as an example, all AI-based mon- dial disinformation started from North Korea and without any watermarks, what would be the use of the efforts of Western democracies?

5.10 Speed

As we have seen, the revolutionary impact of artifi- cial intelligence in the economic system raises questions about the survival of the model of liberal democracy we know. The advancement of AI could threaten the social order, as the ability of robots to imitate people online is comparable to counterfeiting currency in the financial system.

Although the spread of AI is inescapable, we need to devise strategies to limit concentrated power and manage the challenges that de- rive from it. But we must do so quickly.

If humans remain fragmented and engaged in an arms race, AI control becomes almost unfeasible, making the situation akin to an extraterrestrial invasion that could theoretically dominate the planet.

A collaborative deci- sional mechanism needs to be established quickly that instead ensures that artificial intelligence is harnessed to promote only the supreme interests of humanity.

The revolutionary innovation it represents involves the adoption of a concept of guarding and caring and an attitude based on the *primum non nocere* principle, even if it might mean renouncing some short-term benefits.

As extraordinary as the studies in the field of STEM are, I believe there is also an urgent need to analyze the importance of true human factors such as creativity/compassion, originality, reciprocity/responsa- bility, and empathy.

We are at a crucial stage, and we need to act with greater lun- gimirity, adopting a holistic perspective and managing more incisively the implementation of technologies that could gain extraordinary power beyond our predictions.

We can no longer afford to be slow or passive if we are to maintain control over our future and direct the developments that could shape it. It is categorical to devote equal attention to the implications of what it means to be or remain human in a future in which advanced technologies could irrevocably transform the very es- without of our humanity.

Strong cyberhumanism can help us keep the rudder straight toward human preservation, it is just a matter of not losing sight of the bus- alone and going very but very fast.

THANKS

I thank those who helped me, directly or indirectly, to write this book.
Angelino Alfano because he advised me to put in writing my human-centric view of the digital.
Paolo Benanti for writing the preface. Alessio Butti for believing in it.

I thank Piera Ghidotti and Luigi Feligioni who supported me, lovingly and closely, in the previous steps of my life.

I would like to thank those who allowed me to fulfill my main professional mission, which is to popularize digital to help as many people pos- sible to use it properly: Antonio Ricci and Alessandro Meazza.

I would also like to thank those who contributed culturally in providing me with sup- port or inspirational elements that enabled me to write words, sentences, paragraphs or content invisible between the lines of this book. In alphabetical or- dine: Evelyn Adamo, Roberto Alessi, Silvia Arnaud, Albert Ballardini, Andrea Bariselli, Simone Battistella, Domenico Bellantone, Concetta Belluardo, Alessandro Belluzzo, Edoardo Bennato, Laura Berlanda, Andrea Biondi, Guido Borghi, Angelo Borrelli, Maurizio Bra- gagni, Ernesto Caffo, Federica Camisani Calzolari, Cristian Canton, Vittorio Capriello, Giulio Cardona, Francesco Carioti, Fabio Casti- glione, Lorenzo Cavallaro, Claudio Cecchetto, Marco Valerio Cervellini, Marco Cesarini, Luca Chiarella and Angela Creta, Edoardo Colombo, Rita Cucchiara, Fabiana De Bellis, Mario Degetto, Francesco Diella, Stefano

Cyberhumanism

Domenicali, Alex di Martino, Veronica Feligioni, Stefano Feligioni, Ivano Gabrielli, Monica Gandolfo, Alessandro Garofalo, Annalisa Gerosa, Enrico Gherlone, Agostino Ghiglia, Jimmy Ghione, Franco Giacomazzi, Alessandro Gianferrara, Andrea Giannotti, Maurizio Giunco, Lisa Giussani, Gabriele Gobbo, Gianluigi Greco, Ezio Greggio, Emanuela Grigliè, Allegra Groppelli, Enzo Iacchetti and the Striscia la Notizia family, Anna Maria Mandalari, Antonio Mantelli, Alessia Marzio and Isabella Castelli, Alessandro Mascali, Luisa Massaro, Marco Mazzoli, Paolo Monesi, Antonello Mordeglia, Giampaolo Mori, Massimo Mor- purgo, Gianna Nannini, Laura Nava, Mario Nobile, Elio Della Notte, Marco Lodola, Stephen O'Reilly, Marco Odisio, Antonio Palmieri, Ro- sario Pellecchia, Giovanni Pernice, Davide Pilatti, Ilaria Pitea and Sara Pira, Vittoria Ricci, DJ Ringo, Tiziano Roseto, Aron Rutiliano, Massimo Scala, Guido Scorza, Camilla Scotti, Gerry Scotti, Barbara Strappato, Lorenzo Suraci, Claudia Svampa, Paolo Taticchi, Tiberio Timperi, Mas- simo Tortorella, Luigi Turano, Marco Villani, Mattia Villani, Rosaria Vi- scecca Maria Alberta Viviani, , Marco Zamperini, Michele Zizza.

GLOSSARY

Abbreviations

2FA   Two-Factor Authentication
ABM   Account-Based Marketing
ACN   Agency for National Cybersecu- rity.
AGI   Artificial General Intelligence
AI   Artificial Intelligence
AI TRISM   AI Trust Risk and Security Management
AIGS   AI Global Surveillance
AMA   Artificial Moral Agents
AMIE   Articulate Medical Intelligence Explorer
API   Application Programming Interface
AWS   Amazon Web Services
BRI   Brain-Robot Interface
C2PA   Coalition for Content Provenance and Authenticity.
CCPA   California Consumer Privacy Act
CEO   Chief Executive Officer
CINI   National Interuniversity Consortium for Informatics
CNN   Convolutional Neural Networks
CPM   Cost Per Thousand
DARPA   Defense Advanced Research Projects Agency
DESI   Index of Digitization of the Economy and Society
DIGHUM   Digital Humanism Initiative
DMCA   Digital Millennium Copyright Act
EEG   Electroencephalogram
EHDS   European Health Data Space
ELIAS   European Lighthouse Ai for Sustainability
ELVIS   Ensuring Likeness Voice and Image Security.
EMG   Electromyography
EPO   European Patent Office
FDA   Food and Drug Administration
FLI   Future of Life Institute
IMF   International Monetary Fund
FRIA   Fundamental Rights Impact Assessment
GAN   Adversarial Generative Networks
GDPR   General Data Protection Regu- lation.
GPAI   General Purpose AI
GPT   Generative Pre-trained Transformer
GPU   Graphics Processing Unit
HR   Human Resources
HRAIS   High-Risk AI Systems AI. Artificial Intelligence
ICRISAT   International Crops Research Institute for the Semi-Arid Tropics.
ICT   Information and Communication Technologies
IDC   International Data Corporation
IDF   Israel Defense Forces
IIoT   Industrial Internet of Things

IoT	Internet of Things	REE	Rare Earth Metals
IP	Internet Protocol	RLHF	Reinforcement Learning from Human Feedback
IT	Information Technology	RNA	Artificial Neural Networks
ITT	Transfer Intangible of Technology	RNNs	Recurrent Neural Networks
LAWS	Lethal Autonomous Weapons Systems	SCO	Security Operations Centers
LGBTQ+	Lesbians Gay Bisexual Transgender Queer	ALS	Amyotrophic lateral sclerosis
LLM	Large Language Models	SPID	Public System of Digital Identity
LMM	Large Multimodal Models	STEM	Science Technology Engineering Mathematics
MAD	Model Autophagy Disorder	SVM	Support Vector Machines
MDR	Managed Detection and Response	UAV	Unmanned Aerial Vehicles
MEG	Magnetoencephalography	UBI	Universal Basic Income
MIT	Massachusetts Institute of Technology	EU	European Union
ML	Machine Learning	VPN	Virtual Private Network
MND	Motor Neuron Disease	WEF	World Economic Forum
MRSA	Methicillin-Resistant Staphylococcus Aureus	WMO	World Meteorological Organization
NASS	National Association of Secretaries of State	XAI	Explainable AI
NATO	North Atlantic Treaty Organization		
NBA	National Basketball Association		
NCSC	National Cyber Security Centre		
NIST	National Institute of Standards and Technology		
NOIR	Neural Signal Operated Intelligent Robots.		
OECD	Organization for Economic Co-operation and Development		
UN	United Nations Organization		
PA	Public Administration		
PEC	Privacy-Enhancing Computation		
PLCS	Programmable Logic Controllers		
SMES	Small and Medium-sized Enterprises		
RAG	Retrieval Augmented Generation		

Glossary

Definitions

Algorithm: set of instructions to be applied to perform a processing or solve a problem.

Hallucination: a phenomenon that occurs when the output generated is false, is not based on the dataset it was trained on, nor is it predicted by the model with which it was made. Predictive analysis: use of statistical algorithms and machine learning techniques to make predictions about the future using current and historical data.

Machine learning: ability of a computer system to ap- pear, extract patterns and change in response to new data without the help of a human being.

Deep learning: a method of machine learning that relies on artificial neu- ral networks. Virtual personal assistant: an application that can understand natural language and perform tasks such as dictation, reading aloud te- sto or e-mail messages, scheduling schedules, phone calls, and pro-memory.

Automation: the use of complex machines and procedures capable of re- gularising their own operation and controlling the quality of the work pro- ducted, particularly with reference to production cycles governed by process calculators.

Bias: cognitive distortion resulting from bias, causing biased predictions.

Big data/megadata: collection of computer data so extensive in volume, speed, and variety as to require specific technologies and analytical methods for value or knowledge extraction.

Blockchain: technologies that enable the creation and management of a ledger for tracking transactions made between parties, costed by blocks containing sequences of data (tokens) that are cryptographically protected, non-modifiable and chrono- logically organized.

Bot: a program or script that infects computers with spam, viruses and spyware, blocking Web sites and stealing personal infor- mation.

Chatbot: a program that communicates with people through te- stual or voice commands by imitating conversations between human beings.

Cloud computing: set of hardware or software re- sorces present in remote servers and distributed over the Net, containing a user's data and programs.

Cybersecurity: technologies, processes, and protective measures designed to reduce the risk of informational attacks.

Training data: data used during the training process of an automatic learning algorithm.

Personal data: information concer- ning an identified or identifiable natural person, particularly with regard to his or her speci- fic characteristics.

Deepfake: photo or video that presents images captured on the Internet, reela- borated and adapted to a di- verse context from the original one by an algorithm.

Digital: a designation given to apps and devices that handle numerical gran- deities, converting their values into numbers of a convenient numbering system.

Fact checking: verification of facts and sources to assess the soundness of news or claims, with parti- cular reference to what is dif- fused on the Web.

Fair use: a legislative provision in the U.S. legal system that regulates the ability to use copyrighted material without seeking written permission from the rights holder.

Foundation model (GPAI): neu- ral network of artificial intelligence adde- strated on large data at scale that can be adapted to various tasks for which it was not specifically pro- jected.

Framework: supporting logical architecture on which a software can be designed and implemented.

Generative Pre-trained Transfor- mer (GPT): large language models trained on im- portant sets of text and code.

Graphics Processing Unit (GPU): computer chip that performs graphics and image rende- ring with rapid mathematical calculations.

Hardware: basic, unmodifiable component of a device or system.

Generative AI: an AI system capable of creating a wide variety of data, such as images, video, audio, text and 3D models.

Input: the data themselves and the transfer of them from a peripheral unit to the central me- mory of an elec- tronic computer, as opposed to output, that is, to the output quantities and data.

General Artificial Intelligence (AGI): a system with extensive human-level or higher intelligence capabilities, including reasoning, pia- nification, and the ability to learn from experience.

Interface: a system or channel of con- nection and adaptation between two si- stems operating in different modes.

Internet of Things (IoT): a network of interconnected physical og- jects equipped with sensors, software and other technologies, enabling them to connect with other devices and systems via in- ternet.

Jailbreak: an "unlocking" procedure that allows unofficial software to be installed on the iPhone, iPad, and iPod Touch. Large Language Models (LLM): artificial intelligence si- stance adde- strated on significant amounts of textual data, capable of generating natural language responses to a wide range of inputs.

Large Multimodal Models (LMM): an artificial intelligence system that combines text with other types of infor- mation, such as images, video, au- dio and other sensory data.

Machine Learning (ML): a subset of artificial intelligence whose job is to train systems to im- port from data and improve with experience, rather than being purposely programmed to do so. Metaverse: zone of convergence of interactive virtual spaces, located in cyberspace and accessible b y users through an avatar acting as a representative of individual identity.

Glossary

Multimodal: a model that receives requests in different modes (text, immagine, audio, etc.) and produces results in multiple modes.
Open source: software that is not copyrighted and freely modifiable by users.
Phishing: computer fraud perpetrated by sending e-mail and finalized to obtain sensitive personal data.
Prompt: a visual indication, consisting of textual or graphic elements, even mixed together, that signals to the user that the system is waiting for a command.
Ransomware/malware: malicious computer program that can infect a digital device, blocking access to its contents and then demanding a ransom to be paid to "free" them.
Augmented reality: an interactive experience in which real-world environments and objects are supplemented by animated sequences and 3D models and are shown as if they were in the real world.
Virtual reality: a scenario that simulates a real-world experience that can be interacted with using special electronic equipment, such as virtual reality viewers or sensor-equipped gloves.
Generative Adversarial Network (GAN): an auto-mathematical learning algorithm that can be used to generate realistic images, text and other forms of data by pitting two neural networks against each other.
Neural network: a computer model whose layered structure resembles the network structure of neurons in the human cervel.

Robotics: design, construction and deployment of robots that can help and assist humans in various tasks.
Sandbox: test environment for application development and testing.
Software: set of programs that can be used on a data processing system.
Token: categorized block of text, usually consisting of lexemes.
Watermark: inclusion of information within a multimedial or other file, providing information about its origin and provenience.
Web scraping: a computer technique of extracting data from a Web site by means of software programs.

BIBLIOGRAPHY

Anderson C., *The End of Theory*, in "Wired," 16(2008), pp. 106-107.

Asimov I., *Runaround (*1942), in *I, Robot*, Garden City, New York, 1950.

Barrat J., *Our Final Invention: Artificial Intelligence and the End of the Human Era*, St. Martin's Press, New York, 2013.

Benanti P., *Digital Age. Theory of the changing epoch. Person, family and society*, San Paolo, Cinisello Balsamo, 2020.

Id., *Human in the loop. Human decisions and artificial intelligences*, Mondadori Edu- cation, Kindle Edition, Milan, Italy, 2022, p. 195.

Id., *The Cyborg. Body and corporeality in the age of the posthuman*, Cittadella, Assisi, 2012.

Bender E.M., Gebru T., McMillan-Major A., *et al*, *On the Dangers of Stochastic Parrots: Can Language Models Be Too Big?*, in "FAccT '21: Proceedings of the 2021 ACM Conference on Fairness, Accountability, and Transparency," (March 2021), pp. 610-623.

Bengio Y., Ducharme R., Vincent P., *et al*, *A Neural Probabilistic Language Model*, in "The Journal of Machine Learning Research," 3 (2003), pp. 1137-1155.

Bobbio N., "Freedom" in *Encyclopedia of the Twentieth Century*, Treccani.

Brand S., *For God's Sake, Margaret a conversation with Margaret Mead and Greg- ory Bateson*, in "CoEvolutionary Quarterly," June 10-21, 1976, pp. 32-44.

Brown F., *The Answer*, in *The World's Shortest Tales*, Fahrenheit 451, Rome, 1993.

Butler S., *Erewhon or Over the Range*, 1872.

Chalmers D., *What is consciousness?*, Castelvecchi, Rome, 2020.

Chomsky N., *Syntactic Structures*, Mouton & Company, 1957.

Christian B., *The Alignment Problem. How Can Artificial Intelligence Learn Hu- man Values*, Atlantic Books, London, 2021.

Collingridge D., *The Social Control of Technology*, Palgrave Macmillan, London, 1980.

Cutuli C., *Artificial intelligence & public administration. A guide to AI applications for the public sector*, ISSRF, Giarre (CT), 2024.

Cymek D.H., Truckenbrodt A., Onnasch L., *Lean back or lean in? Exploring social loafing in human-robot teams*, in Frontiers in Robotics and AI, 10 (2023) 1249252.

Diamond L., *The Spirit of Democracy*, Henry Holt and Co., New York, 2008.

Eco U., *Apocalyptic and integrated*, Bompiani, Milan, 1964.

Faggin F., *Irreducible. Consciousness, life, computers and our nature*, Mondadori, Milan, 2022.

Ford M., *Rise of the Robots: Technology and the Threat of a Jobless Future*, Basic Books, New York, 2015.

Gibson W., *Neuromancer*, Ace Books, New York, 1984.

Good I.J., *The Estimation of Probabilities*, MIT Press, Cambridge, MA, 1965.

Heidegger M., Fabris A., *Philosophy and cybernetics*, ETS, Pisa, 1988, pp. 34-35.

Hubinger E., Denison C., Mu J., et al, *Sleeper Agents: Training Deceptive LLMs that Persist Through Safety Training*, in "ArXiv," (2024) 2401.05566.

Hwang G.-J., Chen N.-S., *Exploring the Potential of Generative Artificial Intelligence in Education: Applications, Challenges, and Future Research Directions*, in "Educational Technology & Society," no. 2 (2023) 26.

Jordan M.J., *Serial Order: A Parallel Distributed Processing Approach*, in "ScienceDirect," vol. 121 (1997), pp. 471-495.

Kelly K., *The Inevitable: Understanding the 12 Technological Forces That Will Shape Our Future*, Penguin Book, New York, 2016.

Kidder R., *How Good People Make Tough Choices: Resolving the Dilemmas of Eth- ical Living*, Harper Perennial, New York, 2009.

Koenig G., *La fin de l'individu: Voyage d'un philosophe au pays de l'intelligence artificielle*, L'Observatoire, Paris, 2019.

Kurzweil R., *The Singularity Is Near: When Humans Transcend Biology*, 1st edition, Penguin Books, London, 2005.

Larson E.J., The Myth of Artificial Intelligence: Why Computers Can't Think the Way We Do, Belknap Pr, Cambridge, MA, 2021.

Lee E.A., The Coevolution: The Entwined Futures of Humans and Machines, MIT Press, Cambridge, MA, 2020.

Lee K.-F., *Super-Powers: China, Silicon Valley, and the New World Order*,

Houghton Mifflin Harcourt Publishing Company, New York, 2018.

Lehdonvirta V., *Cloud Empires*, Piccola Biblioteca Einaudi, Turin, 2023.

Levi P., *The versifier*, in *Storie naturali*, Einaudi, Turin, 1966.

MacAskill W., *What We Owe the Future*, Basic Books, New York, 2022.

McAfee A., Brynjolfsson E., *The new machine revolution. Work and pros- perity in the age of triumphant technology*, Feltrinelli, Milan, 2017.

Mead M., "Cybernetics of Cybernetics," in *Purposive Systems: Proceedings of the First Annual Symposium of the American Society for Cybernetics*, ed. in H. von Foerster *et al.*, Spartan Books, New York, 1968, pp. 4-5.

Nida-Rümelin J., Weidenfeld N., Digital Humanism: For a Humane Transfor- mation of Democracy, Economy and Culture in the Digital Age, Springer, Berlin, 2022.

Polt R., "A Heideggerian Critique of Cyberbeing," in *Horizons of Authenticity in Phenomenology, Existentialism, and Moral Psychology*, edited by H. Pedersen and
M. Altman, Springer, Dordrecht, 2015, p. 181.

Poppi S., Sarto S., Cucchiara R., et al, Multi-Class Explainable Unlearning for Image Classification via Weight Filtering, in "ArXiv," (2023) 2304.02049.

Prensky M., *Digital Natives, Digital Immigrants*, in "On the Horizon" 9(5), 2001, pp. 1-6.

Id., H. Sapiens Digital: From Digital Immigrants and Digital Natives to Digital Wisdom, in "Innovate" 5(3).

Ribble M., Digital Citizenship in Schools, ISTE, 2007.

Rivera J.-P., Mukobi G., Reuel A., et al, *Escalation Risks from Language Models in Military and Diplomatic Decision-Making*, in "ArXiv," (2024) 2401.03408.

Sarker I.H., Furhad M.H., Nowrozy R., *AI-Driven Cybersecurity: An Overview, Se- curity Intelligence Modeling and Research Directions*, in "SN Computer Sci- ence," 2021, 2.

Searle J.R., *Minds, brains, and programs*, in Behavioral and Brain Sciences, vol. 3, 1980.

Shannon C.E., *A Mathematical Theory of Communication*, in "The Bell System Technical Journal," 27 (1948) 3, pp. 379-423.

Shumailov I., Shumaylov Z., Zhao Y., *et al.*, Papernot N., Anderson R., *The Curse of Recursion: Training on Generated Data Makes Models Forget*, in "ArXiv," (2023) 2305.17493.

Sohl-Dickstein J., Weiss E.A., Maheswaranathan N., *et al*, *Deep Unsupervised*

Learning using Nonequilibrium Thermodynamics, in "ArXiv" (2015) 1503.03585.

Sousa J.P., *The Menace of Mechanical Music*, in "Appleton's Magazine," vol. 8 (1906), pp. 278-284.

Standing G., *The Precariat: The New Dangerous Class*, Bloomsbury, London, 2014.

Stephenson N., *Snow Crash*, Spectra, 1992.

Topol E., Deep Medicine: How Artificial Intelligence Can Make Healthcare Human Again, Basic Books, New York, 2019.

Tu T., Palepu A., Schaekermann M., Saab K., *et al, Towards Conversational Diagnostic AI*, in "ArXiv", (2024), 2401.05654.

Turing A.M., *Computing Machinery and Intelligence*, in "Mind," 59 (1950) 433-460.

Ulam S., *Tribute to John von Neumann*, in "Bulletin of the American Mathematical Society," 64, #3, part 2: 5, May 1958.

Weizenbaum J., Computer Power and Human Reason: From Judgement to Cal- culation, W.H. Freeman, San Francisco, 1976.

Wiener N., *Cybernetics*, MIT Press, Cambridge, MA, 1961.

Yehya N., Homo cyborg. The posthuman body between reality and science fiction, Eleu- thera, Milan, 2005, p. 15.

Zimbardo P., The Lucifer Effect: How Good People Turn Evil, Rider, 2008.

Zuboff S., The Age of Surveillance Capitalism: The Fight for a Human Future at the New Frontier of Power, Hachette Book Group, New York, 2019.

SITOGRAPHY

http://jmc.stanford.edu/articles/dartmouth/dartmouth.pdf

https://acadmin.ambrosetti.eu/dompdf/crea_wmark.php?doc=L2F0dGFjaG1lbnRzL3BkZi8yMDIzMTAxNi1hbWJyb3NldGRRpLXNhbGVzZm9yY2Utd2ViLTIwMjMxMDE2MTgucGRm&id=18983&muid=corporate

https://aicyberchallenge.com/

https://asana.com/work-innovation-lab/wp-content/uploads/2023/08/The-State-of-AI-at-Work.pdf

https://assets.publishing.service.gov.uk/media/656856b8cc1ec500138eef49/Gov.UK_Impact_of_AI_on_UK_Jobs_and_Training.pdf

https://assets.sophos.com/X24WTUEQ/at/h5pcccctzhzvxg35c8hp69/sophos-managed-detection-and-response-ds.pdf

https://c2pa.org/

https://caiml.org/dighum/

https://caiml.org/dighum/dighum-manifesto/

https://crfm.stanford.edu/fmti/

https://d1io3yog0oux5.cloudfront.net/_36101ec9e31212e78a57da0b7aece66f/veritone/db/2223/21101/pdf/VERI+1Q23+Investor+Presentation+%285-2-23%29+vf.pdf

https://data.consilium.europa.eu/doc/document/ST-5662-2024-INIT/en/pdf

https://dataandtrustalliance.org/

https://deepmind.google/technologies/synthid/

https://digital-strategy.ec.europa.eu/it/node/924

https://docdrop.org/static/drop-pdf/Vinge---Technological-Singularity-

Cyberhumanism

Tx5uZ.pdf

https://elias-ai.eu/

https://eur-lex.europa.eu/eli/reg/2019/881/oj

https://femtech.it/

https://futureoflife.org/open-letter/lethal-autonomous-weapons-pledge/

https://futuretech-site.s3.us-east-2.amazonaws.com/2024-01-18+Beyond_AI_Exposure.pdf

https://gizmodo.com/chatgpt-ai-anthropic-constitution-claude-openai-chatbot-1850416532

https://health.ec.europa.eu/ehealth-digital-health-and-care/european-health-data-space_en

https://horizoneurope.apre.it/chips-act-arriva-lapprovazione-finale-dal-council-European/

https://imagen.research.google/

https://issues.org/generative-ai-copyright-law-crawford-schultz/

https://newsroom.accenture.com/news/2016/artificial-intelligence-poised-to-double-annual-economic-growth-rate-in-12-developed-economies-and-boost-labor-productivity-by-up-to-40-percent-by-2035-according-to-new-research-by-accenture

https://nightshade.cs.uchicago.edu/whatis.html

https://nsuworks.nova.edu/cgi/viewcontent.cgi?referer=&httpsredir=1&article=1020&context=innovate

https://nvlpubs.nist.gov/nistpubs/ai/NIST.AI.100-2e2023.pdf

https://op.europa.eu/en/publication-detail/-/publication/d81a0d54-5348-11ed-92ed-01aa75ed71a1/language-en

https://openai.com/research/preparing-for-malicious-uses-of-ai

https://openreview.net/pdf?id=eyykI3UIHa

https://repubblicadigitale.innovazione.gov.it/it/

https://www.38north.org/2024/01/north-koreas-artificial-intelligence-research-trends-and-potential-civilian-and-military-applications/

https://www.brookings.edu/articles/detecting-ai-fingerprints-a-guide-to-watermarking-and-beyond/

https://www.cbsnews.com/news/china-announces-goal-of-leadership-in-artificial-intelligence-by-2030/

https://www.cedefop.europa.eu/en/tools/skills-intelligence/automation-risk-occupations#1

https://www.cepitalia.eu/fileadmin/user_upload/cep.eu/cepAdhoc_IA_conflictUkraine-IT.pdf

https://www.cnbc.com/2023/05/04/white-house-announces-ai-hub-investment.html#:~:text=TheWhiteHouseannouncedit,Microsoft%2CandOpenAIonThursday.

https://www.cybok.org/media/downloads/Security_Privacy_AI_KG_v1.0.0.pdf

https://www.darpa.mil/

https://www.dw.com/en/ai-how-far-is-china-behind-the-west/a-66293806

https://www.effectivealtruism.org/

https://www.fao.org/fileadmin/templates/wsfs/docs/expert_pafor/How_to_Feed_the_World_in_2050.pdf

https://www.ft.com/content/e0ba1b34-ddc9-4b42-941e-6f8114ba41c9

https://www.garanteprivacy.it/documents/10160/0/Regolamentation+EU+2016+679.+Enriched+with+references+to+the+Considerati on+Adjourned+to+the+rectifications+published+in+the+Official+Journal+of+the+European+Union+127+of+23+May+2018

https://www.gazzettaufficiale.it/eli/id/2023/08/14/23G00122/sg

https://www.gov.uk/government/publications/ai-safety-summit-2023-the-bletchley-declaration/the-bletchley-declaration-by-countries-attending-the-ai-safety-summit-1-2-november-2023

https://www.iiss.org/en/

https://www.interpol.int/en/News-and-Events/News/2024/Grooming-radicalization-and-cyber-attacks-INTERPOL-warns-of-Metacrime

https://www.iso.org/obp/ui/en/#iso:std:iso-iec:42001:ed-1:v1:en

https://www.itu.int/dms_pub/itu-s/opb/gen/S-GEN-UNACT-2022-PDF-E.pdf

https://www.marcprensky.com/writing/Prensky%20-%20Digital%20Natives,%20Digital%20Immigrants%20-%20Part1.pdf

Cyberhumanism

https://www.marketsandmarkets.com/Market-Reports/artificial-intelligence-ai-cyber-security-market-220634996.html

https://www.moralmachine.net/

https://www.newsguardtech.com/it/

https://www.nytimes.com/2023/06/08/nyregion/lawyer-chatgpt-sanctions.html

https://www.pwc.com/gx/en/issues/analytics/assets/pwc-ai-analysis-sizing-the-prize-report.pdf

https://www.pwc.com/it/it/Upskill/doc/pwc-upskilling-preparing-everyone-everywhere-for-a-digital-world_ITA.pdf

https://www.reuters.com/article/us-amazon-com-jobs-automation-insight/amazon-scraps-secret-ai-recruiting-tool-that-showed-bias-against-women-idUSKCN1MK08G

https://www.safe.ai/

https://www.safe.ai/statement-on-ai-risk

https://www.senato.it/documenti/repository/istituzione/costituzione.pdf

https://www.state.gov/political-declaration-on-responsible-military-use-of-artificial-intelligence-and-autonomy/

https://www.theedadvocate.org/vision-future-artificial-intelligence-education/

https://www.treccani.it/enciclopedia/liberta_%28Enciclopedia-del-Nove- one hundred%29/

https://www.unesco.it/wp-content/uploads/2023/11/RECOMMENDATION-ON-OPEN-SCIENCE-2021-Certified.pdf

https://www.unesco.org/en/articles/recommendation-ethics-artificial-intelligence

https://www3.weforum.org/docs/WEF_Future_of_Jobs_2023_News_Release_EN.pdf

INDEX OF NAMES

Allgrove B., 227
Altman S., 74, 188, 277
Amodei D., 74
Anderson B., 161
Anderson C., 10
Andreessen M., 264
Aristotle, 18
Artsrouni G., 66
Asimov I., 62, 92, 93, 263

Bakke C., 154
Barrat J., 229
Bateson G., 18
Baumhart R., 248
Benanti P., 9, 11, 203, 311
Bender E.M., 122
Bengio Y., 67, 194, 195
Berners-Lee T., 52, 280
Biden J., 189, 283, 285
Bobbio N., 18, 19
Brand S., 318
Branson R., 263
Brin S., 74
Brown F., 77
Brynjolfsson E., 91, 92
Buckminster Fuller R., 263
Butler S., 79
Butti A., 273

Cavallaro L., 220
Chomsky N., 47, 48, 66
Clarke A.C., 173
Clinton H., 187
Collingridge D., 294
Crawford K., 235
Cucchiara R., 144
Cutuli C., 98

Cymek D.H., 232
Da Vinci L., 28
Daniels S., 187
De Vivo M., 106, 107
Denison C., 214
Diamandis P., 263
Diamond L., 39
Dijkstra E., 77
Ducharme R., 318

Echo U., 193
Einstein A., 75, 263
Heron of Alexandria, 84

Fabris A., 15, 17
Faggin F., 80, 81
Fallon J., 89
Philo of Byzantium, 84 Francis, pope, 229, 248, 286

Gates B., 74, 263, 280
Gaynor G., 239
Gebru T., 122
Gibson W., 41
Good I.J., 76
Goodfellow I., 68
Guterres A., 294, 295

Haffner P., 67
Halamka J., 106
Hanson C., 156
Hassabis D., 74, 118
Heidegger M., 14, 15, 17
Herzberg E., 250
Hinton G., 74, 194, 195
Hoffman R., 74
Holz D., 89

Hubinger E., 214
Hwang G.-J., 122

Jenks A., 307
Jordan M.I., 67

Kant I., 19
Kelly K., 229
Kidder R., 259
Kindred D.P., 62
Kingma D., 68
Koenig G., 155, 156
Krizhevsky A., 67
Kubrick S., 61
Kurzweil R., 76, 263

Larson E., 76, 117, 118
LeCun Y., 67, 195, 237
Leibniz G.W., 77
Lessig L., 203, 204
Levi P., 62
Louis XIV, 88
Lynch M., 121

Mass S., 189
Matisse H., 239
McAfee A., 91, 92
McCarthy J., 271
McCulloch W., 18
McLuhan M., 263
McMillan-Major A. 122
Mead M., 16, 18
Mikolov T., 68
Milei J., 189
Minato V., 190
Minsky M., 271
Morelle J., 240
Mukobi G., 212
Musk E., 74, 89, 177, 186, 216, 230, 263,
280

Neumann J., von, 75
Ng A., 194
Nida-Rümelin J., 40

Page L., 74
Pearl. J., 67
Perry K., 239
Petrov S., 191, 192
Picasso P., 239
Prensky M., 11, 12, 13

Rembrandt, 238
Ribble M., 276, 277
Ricci A., 273
Ricoeur P., 22
Rilke R.M., 23
Rochester N., 271
Rolling Stones, 239
Rousseau J.-J., 19
Rutte M.,- 180

Sanders B., 263
Sarker I.H., 220
Schaake M., 295
Schultz J., 235
Schwartz S.,- 226, 227, 228
Scott R., 61
Searle J., 62, 63 ,64
Shannon C.E., 14, 271
Shumailov I., 179
Simecka M., 186
Skinner B., 271, 272
Sousa J.P., 233
Spielberg S., 61
Standing G., 92
Starmer K., 186
Stephenson N., 51
Studman A., 117
Sturgeon T., 62
Swift T., 240

Tesla N., 263
Thaler S., 241
Thiel P., 74
Topol E., 104
Townsend R., 267, 268
Toy M., 67
Trump D., 188

Index of Names

Turing A.M., 62, 63, 172, 173, 271

Ulam S., 75

Viénot V.-M., 299
Vinge V., 76

Watt J., 41
Weidenfeld N., 40
Weiwei A., 239
Weizenbaum J., 67, 202

Welling M., 68
Wichman G., 67
Wiener N., 14, 17, 41
Winograd T., 67

Yehya N., 10
Yudkowsky E., 62, 74

Zimbardo P., 211
Zuckerberg M.,

Printed in Poland
by Amazon Fulfillment
Poland Sp. z o.o., Wrocław
15 April 2024

b4b77a65-5f29-4e33-8986-1fbc741d00ebR01